ESSAYS ON
OPERA AND
ENGLISH MUSIC

Sir Jack Westrup

ESSAYS ON OPERA AND ENGLISH MUSIC

In honour of
Sir Jack Westrup

Edited by
F. W. Sternfeld
Nigel Fortune
Edward Olleson

OXFORD · BASIL BLACKWELL

0 631 15890 1

Printed in Great Britain by
The Camelot Press Ltd., Southampton

Contents

vi　　　　　　　　　　　*Contents*

List of Plates

Preface

Sir Jack Westrup died when this volume was in final proof, and what was to have been an offering to one of the most eminent musical scholars of our time has become a tribute to his memory. Sir Jack's career spanned fifty years, during which he amassed a corpus of work too voluminous and varied to be surveyed here. Some indication of its scope can be gleaned from Eric Walter White's 'Note' and Peter Ward Jones's bibliography. To capture this rich diversity within the covers of a book is difficult. Two areas, however, the history of opera and the history of English music, Sir Jack made peculiarly his own, and it seemed fitting that these should be the subjects of a volume in which his friends, colleagues and pupils have joined to honour him.

His professional life began with the edition of Monteverdi's *Orfeo* prepared for the inaugural production of the Oxford University Opera Club in 1925. In the following five decades he distinguished himself in the operatic field as editor, translator, conductor and scholar. Happily, he lived to witness the golden jubilee—appropriately celebrated with another performance of *Orfeo*—of the University Opera Club which owed so much to him.

In his quarter of a century as Heather Professor of Music at Oxford (1947–71) Sir Jack's duties became more and more demanding as the Music Faculty broadened and grew under his direction in response to an increasing number of students. At the same time, his love and real understanding of English music were known to those who served with him in the Royal Music Association, particularly in its sponsorship of *Musica Britannica*. Of his publications two volumes must be mentioned here: *Purcell* (1937) and the revision of Ernest Walker's *History of Music in England* (1952).

He shunned the tendency of our age towards a proliferation of books that are, in fact, inflated articles. He wrote *multum non multa* and brought his erudition and musicianship to bear on a wide variety of topics in concise and trenchant articles which, in spite of their modesty and urbanity, invariably broke new ground. The diversity in the contents of the present volume reflects something of the scope of his own work and indicates the international nature of his activities.

Habent sua fata libelli. Two of our contributors have died: Mme Solange Corbin in 1973 and Dr. Egon Wellesz in 1974; and on 21 April 1975 death overtook Sir Jack himself. In now offering the completed volume to the reader we record our gratitude for his life, confident that the man will live in his work.

F. W. S.

N. F.

E. O.

The Neumes of the Martianus Capella Manuscripts

SOLANGE CORBIN

Among the treasures of the Bodleian Library is a fine manuscript of Martianus Capella under the shelf-mark Laud Latin 118 (Madan catalogue 1597), whose French origin is confirmed by its use of Aquitanian (Provençal) neumes.[1] This notation can be related on the one hand to the manuscript tradition of Martianus and on the other to the musical tradition of the Classical poets—Virgil, Horace, Statius and Lucan— about which information is available.[2]

A description of the manuscript must give an account of its contents and place it in the context of the surviving sources of Martianus. The work is acknowledged as being difficult. The nine books under the title *De Nuptiis Philologiae et Mercurii* are written in an exaggeratedly complex prose interspersed with passages in verse.[3] They constitute a

[1] I am indebted to Dr. R. W. Hunt, Keeper of Western Manuscripts at the Bodleian Library, for drawing my attention to the Aquitanian notation.

[2] Thanks to the invaluable assistance of Mme D. Jourdan, the research in progress is well advanced, and the volume on Lucan is ready.

[3] Information on Martianus will be found in the usual encyclopaedias: there is a very clear article by M. Cappuyns in the *Dictionnaire d'histoire et de géographie ecclésiastiques*, xi (1949), art. 'Capella'; see also *Paulys Real-Encyclopädie der Altertumswissenschaft*, rev. Georg Wissowa *et al.*, xiv (1930), art. 'Martianus'. Another significant contribution is Pierre Courcelle, *Les Lettres grecques en Occident de Macrobe à Cassiodore* (Bibliothèque des écoles françaises d'Athènes et de Rome, clix), 2nd edn., Paris, 1948, pp. 198–204. Dating seems to raise no problem: see Courcelle, op. cit., p. 198, note 3. The definitive text is the Teubner edition, ed. Adolf Dick, Leipzig, 1925 (rev. with additions, ed. Jean-G. Préaux, 1969). It is this edition which is cited here, the first figures indicating page references and the italicized figures the number of the line. For a study of the manuscripts see Claudio Leonardi, *I codici di Marziano Capella*,

last defence of pagan civilization against Christianity, which was spreading rapidly at the time: the work was written between A.D. 410 and 439, in other words during the fall of Rome. The first two books recount the arrival of Philology—magically purged of her terrestrial elements—in the various regions of heaven, and the orations with which the characters of Olympus greet her. The seven books that follow comprise an encyclopaedia of the seven liberal arts—the *trivium* and the *quadrivium*—with one book devoted to each. The encyclopaedia is based on Varro's lost work *Novem Disciplinae*; the ninth book, *De musica*, however, is a commentary on Aristeides Quintilianos.[4] Throughout the nine books the interpolations in verse are frequent; it is among these alone that musical notation is found, never in the prose sections, and according to our present knowledge only in Books I, II and IX. Neumes occur most often in Book II, in which the nine Muses welcome Philology at the gates of heaven, each of them reciting a long passage in verse ending with the refrain:

> Scande caeli templa, virgo digna tanto foedere,
> Te socer subire celsa poscit astra Jupiter.

The refrain is found with musical notation in four manuscripts known to the writer, likewise two different interventions by the Muses, one of them in the Oxford manuscript.

The manuscript tradition calls for some discussion. Since the work in question is an encyclopaedia one might expect it to have been much copied and studied during the Middle Ages; and in fact, as has been mentioned, Leonardi has listed 243 manuscripts.[5] Losses and destruction must be taken into account; but in scanning the list one notices that many sources include only excerpts. Moreover, often only one or other of the books is drawn upon, depending on the requirements of a particular school—thus Book VIII, on Astonomy, is frequently found alone. Similarly the first two books often occur together without the others,

---

Padua, 1962 (originally published in three instalments in *Aevum*, xxxiii (1959), 443–89, and xxxiv (1960), 1–99 and 410–524). Leonardi lists 243 manuscripts and gives a detailed analysis of each and its contents. Other articles will be cited later; special mention should be made of William H. Stahl, 'To a Better Understanding of Martianus Capella', *Speculum*, xl (1965), 102–15. Stahl's subsequent study in collaboration with Richard Johnson and B. L. Burger, *Martianus Capella and the Seven Liberal Arts*, vol. 1: *The Quadrivium*, New York & London, 1971, appeared too late for consideration in the present article.

[4] Bibliography in Courcelle, op. cit., p. 200, notes 3–6; a study is in progress at the Ecole Pratique des Hautes Etudes in Paris.

[5] See above, note 3.

probably on account of their more lyrical character. Among all the manuscripts only thirty-two complete collections are known, a far smaller proportion than for the Classical authors whose work is preserved in its entirety. Martianus was considered a writer apart, certainly because of his decadent language and probably because of the mythological nature of his subject.

Nevertheless, a substantial number of collections must be consulted to assess the importance invested in any one of them. The difficulty is more apparent than real: experience of this kind of manuscript shows that it is fruitless to look for musical notation later than the twelfth century (and many twelfth-century manuscripts are already lacking the features of notated manuscripts). Nearly eighty manuscripts of Leonardi's list are thus too late for our purposes. A great deal of work has been done on the remainder.[6]

Later we shall have to consider the chances of finding musical notation in the sources which have yet to be examined. Research to date, however, has discovered neumes in only four of the Martianus manuscripts; we have had direct access to two of them (Laud 118 and Paris, Bibliothèque Nationale, Latin 8670), and the other two (Vatican, Regin. lat. 1987 and Leiden, B.P.L. 88) are known from the published work of other scholars.[7] In the case of the Vatican manuscript we have

[6] Mme Jourdan has checked the thirty or so collections surviving in Paris, and nearly forty are available on microfilm at the Institut de Recherche et d'Histoire des Textes. The examination has been conducted as a team effort by Mlle M. N. Pattyn, Mme Jourdan and myself; the sources studied to date are as follows: Bamberg, Staatliche Bibliothek, Class. 9 (HJ. IV. 19) and Class. 55 (HJ. IV. 22); Berne, Stadtbibliothek, 56 B, 92 A, 265 and 331; Cambridge, Corpus Christi College, 153 and 206, Fitzwilliam Museum, McClean 165, Trinity College, R. 15. 32; Cologne, Dombibliothek, CXCIII; Copenhagen, Kongelige Bibliotek, G. Kgl. S. 277 fol.; Florence, Biblioteca Riccardiana, 916; Leningrad, Publícnaya Bibliotéka, Class. lat. F. v. 10; London, British Museum, Cotton Tiber, C. I. Cotton Vitell. E. II, Harley 647, 2685 and 3826, Royal 7 A. III; Munich, Bayerische Staatsbibliothek, lat. 384; Prague, Narodní a Universitní Knihovna, VIII. H. 17; St. Gall, Stiftsbibliothek, 872; Trier, Dombibliothek/Bibl. des Priesterseminars, 100; Vatican, Barb. lat. 10, Regin. lat. 309 and 598, Vat. lat. 645; Venice, Biblioteca Marciana, lat. xiv, 203 (4337); Vienna, Österreichische Nationalbibliothek, 2269 and 2521.

In the provinces the examination has been carried out by the librarians of Avranches, Besançon and Orléans; at Montpellier, Mlle J. Mas helped us. Abroad, at Oxford we were assisted by Dr. A. C. de la Mare and by Dr. J. R. L. Highfield of Merton College, at Bamberg by the librarian, Dr. Thomann. To all of these we express our warmest thanks.

[7] The four manuscripts are cited by Jean-G. Préaux, 'Deux manuscrits gantois de Martianus Capella', *Scriptorium*, xiii (1959), 15–21; the two Ghent manuscripts in question are Vatican 1987 and Leiden 88, which are described

consulted the existing facsimile, and we are awaiting reproductions of the Leiden manuscript.

The known notated sections are as follows:

(*a*) in all four manuscripts the Muses' refrain ('Scande caeli . . . ') quoted above;

(*b*) Further, in Laud 118 the passage for Polyhymnia, 'Tandem laborie fructus . . . ', linked to the refrain (see Pl. Ia);

(*c*) in the Paris manuscript 8670:

BOOK I

f. 1 The exordium of the whole work: invocation to Venus, 'Tu quem psallentem thalamis . . . ', notated for a line and a half (Dick, 3, *5*)

f. 2 Phoebus's speech 'Anxia cum trepidis nutat sententia rebus . . .', notated for three lines (Dick, 15, *19*)

ff. 5ᵛ–6 The speech of Apollo to Juno, protector of Hymen: 'Possem minore ambigens fiducia . . . ', notated for five lines (Dick 20, *22*)

f. 10 Jupiter's speech to all Olympus: 'Ni nostra astrigeri nota benignitas . . . ', notated for four lines (Dick, 38, *13*)

BOOK II

f. 11ᵛ The exordium of this book: 'Sed purum astrificis celum scandebat habendis . . . ', notated for three lines (Dick, 42, *2*)

f. 14ᵛ The Muses' refrain ('Scande caeli') and the first four lines of Erato's tirade: 'Caput artibus, inclita virgo . . . ' (Dick, 51, *3*)

---

in greater detail. Laud 118 is similarly cited by H. M. Bannister, *Monumenti Vaticani di paleografia musicale Latina* (Codices e Vaticanis selecti, xii), Leipzig, 1913 (repr. Farnborough, 1969), p. 101, note 1; contrary to what Préaux suggests, Bannister does not indicate that British Museum, Arundel 375 contains neumes for the 'scrawled' refrain: the matter remains to be resolved by an examination of the manuscript. Préaux includes two plates of reproductions of the Vatican manuscript, from which the refrain is reproduced here (Fig. I). It seems unlikely that the Leiden manuscript will substantially change our conclusions.

BOOK IX

f. 109 The epithalamium sung by Hymen: 'Aurea flammigerum cum luna subgerit orbem / Rosis jugabo lilia . . . ' (Dick, 477, *14*)

Clearly many other passages from these nine books are in verse and therefore might have been notated. In particular it remains to be seen whether the Leiden and Vatican manuscripts contain neumes other than those for the refrain. But even at this early stage certain facts can be established.

In the first place one should note the infrequency of musical notation. Whereas in the case of the great Classical poems music is found in something like a sixth of the sources (covering the period between the ninth and the twelfth centuries),[8] only four notated sources of Martianus are known at present, all of them dating from before the twelfth century. They are thus older than the bulk of the neumed tradition of the Classics—or rather the Martianus tradition seems to have been of shorter duration: neumed manuscripts of the Classics survive from the twelfth century, but none of Martianus. There is, moreover, little likelihood of our discovering many more notated sources for Martianus: only about sixty manuscripts outside France remain to be examined. Of these at least fifteen contain no more than short fragments or brief quotations, and only about ten include the whole work. The others often contain Book VIII (Astronomy), in which no musical notation has been found up to now, or Books I and II, which are the favourite ones for neumes.

The nature of the notation itself should also be considered. The Laudian manuscript, with its Aquitanian notation, belongs to a region in which the *punctum* takes on an ornamental, elongated shape, instead of the classic square or lozenge form. Two regions adopted this form —Clermont-Ferrand and a less definable area (possibly Limoges–Angoulême) to the west of the Massif Central. The first of these is unlikely to be relevant, since its neumes show a close relationship to those of Lorraine.[9] The second provides a much more probable place of

[8] A point established by my research with Mme Jourdan.

[9] For a detailed study of this notation as the link between Aquitanian and Lorrainian notation, see Solange Corbin, *La Notation musicale neumatique, les quatre provinces Lyonnaises* (unpublished dissertation), Paris, 1957, pp. 477–8 and bibliography, p. 481. The most accessible facsimile, despite its date, is that in *Album de la Société des anciens textes français*, Paris, 1875, Pll. 3, 8 and 9; see also Pierre Aubry, *Les plus anciens monuments de la musique française*, Paris, 1900, Pl. 1.

origin. Notation of this kind is found in the Bibliothèque Nationale MS
Latin 1240.[10] But several manuscripts coming basically from St. Martial,
though certainly written for different churches in the region, could also
have served as models for such handwriting.[11] There is no mystery
about MS 8670: its notation establishes its provenance from Corbie.[12]
The Vatican and Leiden manuscripts share the same Lorrainian notation and were written for the monastery of St. Pierre at Ghent. Notation
of the same type is found throughout the domain of Lorrainian notation
and is not characteristic of a clearly defined *scriptorium*.[13]

The known passages of musical notation to the 'Scande caeli' refrain
may now be compared. As Fig. I demonstrates, the three available
versions of the refrain can be correlated only with some difficulty, since
they have few points of concordance.[14] The musical version was therefore neither standardized nor well known. In contrast, the musical
versions of the great Classical poems are almost identical with one
another; there are no problems of correlation between their neumes,
even where the versions are, geographically, far apart. Analysis of the
Martianus passages other than this refrain is not easy, since each survives in only one notated version, and the passages in question consist
of lines of differing metres. Therefore no working hypothesis is possible.
Attention may, however, be drawn to the fact that Polyhymnia's speech
(Laud 118, see Pl. Ia) reproduces exactly the same formulae for each
line, the sole difference being a *climacus* on the fifth syllable of every
third line and at the end. Apart from this group whose role is not clear,
the same pattern is applied to each line. We are not far from a cantillation formula. A similar point occurs in MS 8670: in the epithalamium
the formula extends over two lines and is repeated five times, since ten
lines are notated.

Another observation may be made. Although there is no regular
procedure, in many manuscripts we find that the verse sections are preceded by an announcement of their metre, which is variable; in MS 8670

[10] Facsimile in Ewald Jammers, *Tafeln zur Neumenschrift*, Tutzing, 1965,
Pl. 30 (almost illegible because of over-enlargement), and Gregorio Suñol,
Introduction à la paléographie musicale grégorienne, Paris, 1935, Pl. 66. The
bulk of the notation is fairly similar, except that the *virga* has a different *ductus*.

[11] A study is in progress by Mme Jourdan.

[12] A study of the *scriptorium* and neumes of Corbie by M. Denis Escudier
is in progress. We are much indebted to him for information on this manuscript (and on many others).

[13] Dom Hourlier, 'Le Domaine de la notation messine', *Revue Grégorienne*,
xxx (1951), 96–113 and 150–58, does not identify the local *scriptoria* but provides
documentation.

[14] Vatican version after Préaux, *Scriptorium*, xiii (1959).

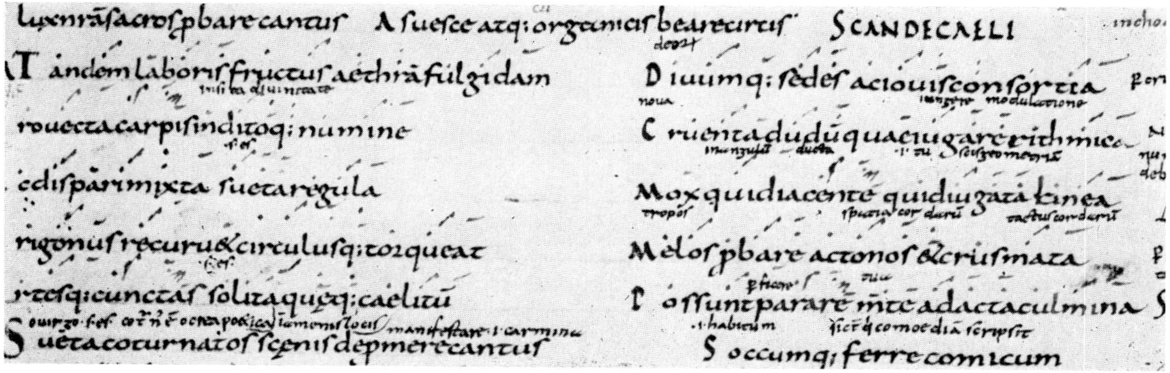

(a) f. 11v

i. Bodleian Library, Laud Lat. 118

(b) f. 12

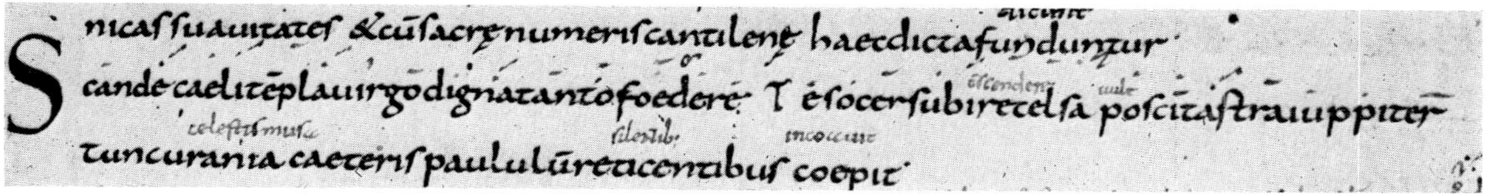

Vatic. 1987

Paris 8670

Oxf. L. 118

Scan - de cae - li tem - pla vir - go dig - na tan - to foe - de - re

Vatic. 1987

Paris 8670

Oxf. L. 118

te so - cer su - bi - re cel - sa pos - cit as - tra ju - pi - ter

this occurs once, before the epithalamium: 'heroicum conjunctum dimetro iambico'. This was probably done to suggest a cantillation model suitable for the metre in question. It is known, in fact, that similar procedures are still used in civilizations in which memory plays a dominant role in the transmission of knowledge. It follows that the metres and verbal rhythms would be recited to a suitable musical formula, which in turn would help to determine the succession of verbal elements.[15] It seems probable that the notated versions of the Odes of Horace are a case in point, while the hexameter settings are much closer to cantillation.

[15] This procedure was described in detail for the teaching of Arab versification by M. Boubakeur in a lecture at the Ecole Pratique des Hautes Etudes.

Instrumental Titles to the Sequentiae of the Winchester Tropers

ANDREAS HOLSCHNEIDER

In the medieval mass the Alleluia had a brilliant musical conclusion. Attached to the verse and introduced as a rule by a shortened reprise of the first Alleluia section, there rang out a wide-ranging, clearly constructed melody, the sequence. This could be executed in at least two ways: either as a melismatic *jubilus* to the vowel '-a', or paraphrased by a poetic text underlaid syllabically to the notes of the melisma.

The untexted sequence melodies (called *sequentiae* in West Frankish manuscripts) and the underlaid poetic texts (*prosae*) have always presented medieval scholarship with an abundance of complex problems of both a musical and a literary nature. The fundamental questions concern in particular the musical origin of the melodies and their performance. One point constantly recurs, namely the idea that the melodies might contain instrumental influences—indeed, might even to some extent have been minstrels' secular instrumental pieces. The invasion of church music by these pieces might possibly be explained thus: that here, in the freest section of the liturgy, where mankind joins the heavenly host to worship God with every kind of glorification, instrumental music too should be heard, as in response to the psalmist's call: 'Alleluia—Laudate Dominum in sono tubae, in psalterio et cithara, in tympano et choro, in chordis et organo, in cymbalis benesonantibus, in cymbalis iubilationis'.

The most substantial reason for suspecting instrumental influence in sequence melodies is the fact that a number of them are named after instruments; one melody actually bears the title *Tractus iocularis*. These titles have received some attention in an essay by Hans Spanke,[1]

[1] 'Aus der Vorgeschichte und Frühgeschichte der Sequenz', *Zeitschrift für deutsches Altertum*, lxxi (1934), 1–38.

and it is with them that the following investigation is concerned.

In general two types of sequence titles can be distinguished. In the first group the melody takes its name either from the Alleluia verse to which it is attached or from its *prosa* or one of its *prosae*. The initial word of the Alleluia verse or *prosa*, or even a key-word to their content, can determine the name of the melody: e.g. *Beatus vir*, derived from the beginning of the Alleluia verse 'Beatus vir qui timet Dominum'; *Fulgens praeclara*, derived from the start of the *prosa* 'Fulgens praeclara rutilat per orbem hodie dies'; *Captiva*, derived from the words 'captivam duxit captivitatem' in the Alleluia verse 'Dominus in Sina'. The second category comprises those sequences in which the title refers to the origin and musical character of the melody, to its geographical or social background: e.g. *Duo tres, Occidentana, Tractus iocularis*. With this group I should like to class all the titles that are clearly of vernacular origin, e.g. *Frigdola*, and further (with due caution) the Latin ones that have no apparent connection with any Alleluia verse or *prosa*—though one must of course allow for lacunae in the surviving sources, particularly with regard to the *prosae*.

The instrumental titles are divided between the two categories. Remarkably, they occur almost exclusively in West Frankish and English manuscripts. In East Frankish sources the only rubrics with possible instrumental associations are the ambiguous terms *Organa* and *Symphonia*, together with the titles *Nostra tuba* (derived from the *prosa* adopted from the West Frankish repertoire 'Nostra tuba regatur fortissima Dei dextra')[2] and *Fidicula* (to the *prosae* 'Gaude semper serena' and Waltram's 'Sollemnitatem huius devoti').[3] *Fidicula* is the one title in the East Frankish repertoire that is of instrumental derivation. *Fidicula* (small fidel) has no connection with the text of either of the *prosae*. *Nostra tuba*, on the other hand, corresponds exactly with the opening words of the *prosa* cited, and a plausible instrumental interpretation of this incipit is not easily found.[4] It is extremely doubtful whether *Organa* and *Symphonia* are to be understood as denoting instruments (*Organa* meaning instruments in general, the organ in particular, *Symphonia* meaning bagpipes, or alternatively a stringed instrument).[5]

[2] *Analecta hymnica medii aevi*, ed. G. M. Dreves in collaboration with Clemens Blume and H. M. Bannister, 55 vols., Leipzig, 1886–1922, liii.33.

[3] Ibid., liii.180 and l.184 respectively.

[4] It does not mean 'our trumpet'; much rather, in the figurative sense, 'may our praise be guided by God's almighty hand'; cf. v.4 and the beginning of 'Tuba nostrae vocis elevetur' (*Analecta hymnica*, liii.183).

[5] Charles Dufresne du Cange, *Glossarium ad scriptores mediae et infimae latinitatis*, ed. Léopold Favre, Niort, 1883–7, vii.687.

Notker's *prosae* for these melodies ('Laudes Deo / concinat orbis / ubique totus' for *Organa*, and 'Concentu parili / hic te Maria / veneratur populus / teque piis colit cordibus' for *Symphonia*) suggest a metaphorical interpretation of the titles: *Organa* as an all-embracing, timeless jubilation of the whole world, *Symphonia* (a translation of *concentu*) as the consonance of adoration, a harmony of hearts. The figurative meaning seems all the more legitimate, since Notker mentions instruments in none of his *prosae*; nor are there other musical allusions, such as to modes or polyphonic music. We do not know if Notker deliberately avoided musical imagery, or whether there are definite historical reasons for the lack of musical terms in Notker and in the East Frankish *prosa* repertoire as a whole.

Particularly problematical is the use of the title *Organa*, instead of the usual *Metensis maior*, in the Reichenau manuscript Bamberg, Staatliche Bibliothek, lit. 5 (for the *prosae* 'Nos Gordiani', 'Hodie laeti' and 'Dignis hodie').[6] Can we, like Blume and Bannister,[7] attribute any special significance to this use of the Notkerian title by the Reichenau school? In any case, the *prosae* in question contain no allusions that would justify any specific musical interpretation of the title *Organa*, whether as instruments or polyphony.

The West Frankish *prosa* poetry presents a different picture. Many West Frankish *prosae*, like the psalms, begin with a call for instrumental music and instrumental accompaniment. That such cases are intended not only as symbolic imagery but also to sustain a literal musical interpretation is shown by the often precise musical terminology (especially significant is the specific indication of the modes). Apart from that, the style of notation in the 'Winchester Troper' (Cambridge, Corpus Christi College 473) confirms that at Winchester at any rate the *prosae* were instrumentally accompanied. In a proportion of the *prosae* of this manuscript the neumatic notation is supplemented by 'Frankish' letter-notation. This system does not belong to the family of Boethian and Guidonian alphabetic notations, in whose scales semitones lie between the second and third and between the fifth and sixth degrees; rather it corresponds to our major scale, with semitones between the third and fourth and between the seventh and eighth degrees. This system is otherwise known only from writings on instrumental practice, including those of Hucbald, Notker Labeo and Bernelinus.[8] So far as I know, the 'Winchester Troper' is the sole musical manuscript to contain 'Frankish'

[6] *Analecta hymnica*, liii.153, xxxiv.38 and 39 respectively.

[7] Ibid., liii, foreword, p. xvi.

[8] The theoretical evidence is given in Hugo Riemann, *Studien zur Geschichte der Notenschrift*, Leipzig, 1878, appendix.

letter-notation; and there is substantial correspondence between these instances of letter-notation in the *prosae* of the Cambridge manuscript and the instrumental titles of the sequence melodies.

The following table lists all the English/West Frankish titles that are probably or certainly of instrumental derivation, as they appear in the sequentiaries of the Cambridge manuscript (*CC*) and of Oxford, Bodleian Library, Bodley 775 (*Bod*), which is likewise of Winchester provenance. The Cambridge reading of the titles is given first, followed by variant readings in the Bodleian sequentiary. Variants in the wording of the *prosa* and *organa* titles are indicated separately.[9]

CC	*Bod*	Title	Melody published
f. 81	f. 122	SEQUENTIA MUSA DE NATALE DOMINI *Bod* without title	Bannister-Hughes 36
f. 81ᵛ	f. 122ᵛ	CHORUS/CHORUS IN EPIPHANIA CHRISTI *CC* f. 153ᵛ (to organum): CHORUS SIVE BAVVERISCA	Bannister-Hughes 9
f. 82ᵛ	f. 123ᵛ	SEQUENTIA CITHARA/CITHARIS ORGANISQUE DEUM MODULEMUR OVANTER	Bannister-Hughes 11
f. 84ᵛ	f. 126	SEQUENTIA LIRA/LIRA PULCHRA	Bannister-Hughes 34
f. 87	f. 126ᵛ	SEQUENTIA TIMPANUM/TYMPANUM	—

[9] The complete list of sequence titles from *Bod* and *CC* with comparison of the corresponding *prosae* will be found in W. H. Frere, *The Winchester Troper*, London, 1894. Cf. the East Frankish titles of St. Gall 484 in Spanke, *Deutsche und französische Dichtung des Mittelalters*, Stuttgart, 1943, pp. 17 ff., also the index of melody titles in *Analecta hymnica*, liii.

As a published source of the English/West Frankish corpus of sequence melodies, Anselm Hughes, *Anglo-French Sequelae, edited from the Papers of the late Dr. Henry Marriott Bannister*, Plainsong and Mediaeval Music Society, 1934, is still indispensable. Unfortunately, in the Bannister–Hughes edition the particular sources on which the editions of the respective melodies are based are not given. Comparison of the sources reveals, however, that when possible Bannister and Hughes follow the two Winchester manuscripts and the prosary of British Museum, Cotton Caligula A.XIV. For another printed source of melodies see Anselm Schubiger, *Die Sängerschule St. Gallens vom 8. bis zum 12. Jahrhundert*, Einsiedeln, 1958.

By virtue of its 'Frankish' letter-notation *CC* offers in part the oldest established reading of the melodies altogether. *Bod* has no letter-notation, it is true, but the prosary contains several melodies in diastematic notation from the twelfth century. In the case of the bipartite Cotton Caligula A.XIV, the first part (tropes of the Proper) dates from the end of the eleventh century (still notated in staffless neumes), the second part (tropes of the Ordinary, prosary) from the end of the twelfth century (notation on four lines).

f. 83   f. 126ᵛ   SEQUENTIA IERONIMA/HIERONIMA   Schubiger 11
                                                    (*Frigdola*)
f. 86ᵛ   f. 127ᵛ   SEQUENTIA TUBA/TUBA VEL FISTULA   Bannister-Hughes
                                                    52
—   f. 128   BUCCA EXCELSA   —
                    CC f. 133 to *prosa* 'Laude pulchra';
                    Bod. f. 173 to *prosa* 'Ad te pulchra'
                    only BUCCA

NOTES ON THE INSTRUMENTAL TITLES

MUSA as a musical instrument (cf. the etymology of the late Latin 'musus' (mouth) in W. von Wartburg, *Französisches etymologisches Wörterbuch*): wind instrument, specifically (*a*) bagpipe; (*b*) organ pipe.

'Inflatile genus autem, quod spiritu vel vento impellitur, ut in tibiis, musis, fistulis, organis, et his similibus' (Regino Prumiensis, *Epistola de Harmonica Institutione*. Martin Gerbert, *Scriptores ecclesiastici de musica sacra potissimum*, St. Blasien, 1784, i. 236).

(*a*)'Musa, ut diximus instrumentum quoddam est omnia musicae super-excellens instrumenta, quippe quae omnium vim atque modum in se continet: humano siquidem inflatur spiritu ut tibia, manu temperatur ut phiala, folle excitatur ut organa' (Johannes Affligemensis, *De musica cum tonario*, ed. Joseph Smits van Waesberghe (Corpus scriptorum de musica, i), Rome, 1950, p. 54).

(*b*) 'Et rugiat pleno kapsa referta sinu,
    Sola quadringentas, quae sustinet ordine musas
    . . . . .
    Musarumque melos auditur ubique per urbem'
(Wulfstan Wintoniensis, *Epistola ad Elpheg*, lines 150–51 and 169; A. Holschneider, *Die Organa von Winchester*, Hildesheim, 1968, pp. 139–40). See Du Cange, *Glossarium*, v. 554; Frédéric Godefroy, *Dictionnaire de l'ancienne langue française*, Paris, 1881 ff., v.455a; Edward Buhle, *Die musikalischen Instrumente in den Miniaturen des frühen Mittelalters, i: Die Blasinstrumente*, Leipzig, 1903, p. 47.

The sequence title *Musa* occurs only in *CC*, the usual title for this widely known melody being *Mater*, probably from the key-words 'Felix mater' in the Christmas *prosae* 'Caelica resonant' (*Analecta hymnica*, liii.19) and 'Hodie puer natus est nobis' (ibid., liii.18), which were written to this melody. This melody should not be confused with *Mater sequentiarum* (Bannister-Hughes 37).

CHORUS as a musical instrument: (*a*) bagpipes (bladder-pipe); (*b*) plucked stringed instrument.
    Iconographical evidence for both meanings is afforded by the illustra-

tions to the apocryphal *Epistola ad Dardanum*, long ascribed to St. Jerome. See Reinhold Hammerstein, 'Instrumenta Hieronymi', *Archiv für Musikwissenschaft*, xvi (1959), 117–34, esp. pp. 131–2; text: Jacques Paul Migne, *Patrologiae cursus completus: Series Latina*, Paris, 1844–55, xxx.213–15; on the oriental sources of the Dardanus letter: Hanoch Avenary, 'Hieronymus' Epistel über die Musikinstrumente und ihre altöstlichen Quellen', *Anuario musical*, xvi (1961), 55–80.

(*a*) 'Chorus quoque pellis simplex est cum duabus cicutis aereis et per primam inspiratur, per secundam vocem emittit' (*Epistola ad Dardanum*; Hammerstein, op. cit., p. 131).

Evidence, albeit rather late, that the 'chorus' really was the bladder-pipe is the miniature *Unum genus chori* in the St. Blasien manuscript (?thirteenth-century, now lost; illustrations reproduced in Gerbert, *De cantu et musica sacra*, St. Blasien, 1774, ii, Pl. XXXIII), also Mantua, Biblioteca Comunale, MS C.III.20 (late twelfth-century psalter from the monastery S. Benedetto di Polirone). The latter has often been reproduced (e.g. in M. Salmi, *Italienische Buchmalerei*, Munich, 1956, Pl. IV); the wholepage miniature shows King David with a pillarless triangular harp (*Winkelharfe*), surrounded by four instrumentalists (fidel, bells, chorus, horn); the blowpipe, bladder and chanter of the 'chorus' can be distinguished, and the instrument answers exactly to that illustrated in Gerbert and the 'chorus' of the 'Instrumenta Hieronymi'. For further evidence of the bladder-pipe in the Middle Ages see Heinz Becker, *Zur Entwicklungsgeschichte der antiken und mittelalterlichen Rohrblattinstrumente*, Hamburg, 1966, pp. 167 ff.

(*b*) The *Epistola ad Dardanum* lacks a textual description of the stringed 'chorus', but in several sources a D-shaped instrument with four strings is depicted, as well as the bladder-pipe form (see Hammerstein, op. cit., p. 132; Georg Kinsky, *A History of Music in Pictures*, London, 1930, p. 38, Pl. II—a reproduction from British Museum, Cotton Tiberius C.VI). The pictorial representation of this type speaks for the actual existence of such an instrument, despite the lack of description in the text. Moreover, this is substantiated by English and Irish sources: see Francis W. Galpin, *Old English Instruments of Music*, 4th edn., rev. Thurston Dart, London, 1965, pp. 55 f.

On the etymology Curt Sachs (following Galpin, whose book first appeared in 1910) conjectures: 'On British soil the word [chorus] undergoes a change of meaning; here phonetic similarity results in its becoming associated with the Celtic crwth' (*Reallexikon der Musikinstrumente*, Berlin, 1913, p. 80). Hammerstein (op. cit., p. 132) offers another explanation: 'This change of meaning into a sort of cithara is perhaps the result of the allegory of "concordia", which is common to cithara and chorus since antiquity'.

'Alii chorum dixerunt a concordia, quae in caritate consistit' (St. Isidore, *Etymologiae*, vi.19).

'Omnes cordae vestrae vocales sint. Non potest esse cithara, si una corda defuerit' (St. Jerome. Migne, *Patrologia Latina*, xxvi.1120).

In this connection it is worth reflecting that the sequence melody *Chorus* is called *Concordia* in German sources. Could *Concordia* therefore be the allegorical title that was chosen in St. Gall in preference to the ·specifically musical title *Chorus*? Or did the path the title took lead in the opposite direction, from St. Gall to Winchester? Bruno Stäblein ('Die Sequenz-melodie "Concordia" und ihr geschichtlicher Hintergrund', *Festschrift Hans Engel*, Kassel, 1964, pp. 364 ff.) relates the title *Concordia* to the longing for political harmony after the disintegration of the Frankish kingdom, as expressed in the West Frankish *prosa* 'Gaude eia' (*Analecta hymnica*, ix.67) and Notker's Peter and Paul *prosa* 'Petre summe Christi pastor' (ibid., liii.210; see W. von den Steinen's edition of Notker, text-volume pp. 62 and 169, commentary-volume pp. 359 and 579). The con-clusion could be that the Notkerian title *Concordia*, misunderstood in Winchester in its Isidorian sense of musico-allegorical etymology, acquired a new meaning as the real *Chorus*. The title *Chorus* is encountered only in *Bod* and *CC*. In France and Italy the melody is called *Epiphaniam Domino* or *Ecce vicit* after the *prosae* to which it belongs (*Analecta hymnica*, liii.28 and liii.39 = vii.50).

BAVVERISCA. E. W. B. Nicholson (*Early Bodleian Music*, ed. John Stainer, London, 1901–13, iii, p. xliii) interprets the word thus: 'Bavver-isca, a word (etymologically identical with our "boorish") which clearly indicates a Germanic origin and rustic affinities'. Against this Spanke ('Aus der Vorgeschichte . . . der Sequenz', p. 11) argues: 'Bavverisca can have nothing to do with "boorish" [bäurisch], as Nicholson believes; it must mean "Bavarian" [bairisch]'. The precise linguistic explanation 'Bavarian' speaks for the South German provenance of the title in the sense advanced above: the Winchester title *Chorus* is a misinterpretation of the South German ('bairisch', *recte* Notker's) *Concordia*. *Bavverisca*, like *Occidentana*, *Metensis* and other titles, refers to the extraction. Never-theless, the geographical explanation alone is not satisfactory. The con-juction 'sive' points to an additional, instrumental interpretation of the term *Bavverisca*; 'sive' suggests that by *Chorus* and *Bavverisca* one and the same instrument is meant, though the question still remains as to whether this signified a bagpipe, e.g. 'Musa bavverisca', or a stringed instrument, e.g. 'Cithara bavverisca'. In the second case Bavverisca might subsequently have become associated with St. Isidore's *Cithara barbarica* (*Etymologiae*, iii.22).

CITHARA: in the Middle Ages a collective term for plucked stringed instruments: psalteries, harps and plucked lyres (crwth, rotta).

'Delectat me quoque cytharistam habere qui possit citharizare in cithara, quam nos appellamus rottam' (*Epistolae S. Bonifatii*, ed. M. Tangl (Monumenta Germaniae Historica, Epistolae selectae, i), Berlin, 1916, p. 251).

'Dunstanus sumpsit secum ex more cytharam suam, quam lingua paterna hearpam vocamus' (*Memorials of Saint Dunstan*, ed. William Stubbs (Rolls Series, lxiii), London, 1874, p. 21).

In old English psalter glosses one encounters only *hearpe* (or *hearpan, herpe, hearpansweʒe*) as a translation of *cithara*; see K. Wildhagen, *Der Cambridger Psalter*, Hamburg, 1910, and the variants noted there. In the Dardanus letter the cithara is illustrated in two forms: as a triangular instrument with 24 strings and also as an instrument in the shape of a capital D with seven strings. The allegorizing text of the letter concerns only the first form; see Hammerstein, op. cit., pp. 125 ff.

In East Frankish sources, but frequently also in West Frankish ones, the melody *Cithara* bears the title *Occidentana*. The paraphrase in *Bod*, 'Citharis organicisque deum modulemur ovanter', is not derived from a *prosa*: the melody rules out a hexametric underlay. In *Bod* and *CC* the text to this melody is the famous Ascension *prosa* 'Rex omnipotens' (*Analecta hymnica*, liii.66). In *CC* it is provided with instrumental letter-notation; besides this *CC* contains the text markings for the organum of this sequence melody (the part itself is not present). The letter-notation and the organum give the sequence title in *Bod* a concrete meaning.

LIRA: a counterpart to *cithara*, a collective term in the Middle Ages for plucked and bowed stringed instruments (fidel, vielle, rebec) and also bowed lyres (bowed rotta).

The title *Lira* is apparently deduced from the beginning of the *prosa* 'Lira pulchra' (*Analecta hymnica*, xl.52), known only from *Bod*. The melody's usual title is *Ecce pulchra*, from the *prosa* 'Ecce pulchra canorum resonat voce Alleluia' (ibid., liii.114 = vii.116), which survives in English, French and Italian sources. In German sources this melody, which is suggestive of instrumental music (hexachordal tonality with triadic progressions, sequential treatment of short phrases), does not appear.

TIMPANUM. Apart from meaning 'drum', both tuned and pitchless, *timpanum*, like *chorus*, had two meanings in the Middle Ages: (*a*) bagpipe; (*b*) plucked stringed instrument (Irish *timpán*).

(*a*) Proof of this first meaning is found only among the 'Instrumenta Hieronymi' of the Dardanus letter: 'Timpanum . . . est quasi tuba cum uno fistulo in capite angusto per quod inspiratur'; and 'tympanum pellis pilacis est inflata habens calamos duos [!] in labis et unum in collo'. Hammerstein (op. cit., p. 131) surmises: 'The connecting link between percussion and wind instrument is presumably the animal skin (*pellis*), which is present in both drum and bagpipe'.

(*b*) The *timpanum* as a stringed instrument is known from English and Irish sources.

'Iterum cum videret dominum regem saecularibus curis fatigatum, psallebat in tympano sive cithara sive alio quolibet musici generis instrumento' (*Memorials of Saint Dunstan*, ed. Stubbs, p. 79).

In old English psalter glosses *timpanum* is translated by *timpan* and *wifhearpan* (*wif*- harking back to Exodus, xv.20), thus as a stringed instrument and not as a wind or percussion instrument; the French word for dulcimer is still 'tympanon' today. See Galpin, op. cit., pp. 50 f., and Eugene O'Curry, *On the Manners and Customs of the Ancient Irish*, ed. W. K. O'Sullivan, Dublin, 1873, *passim*.

The melody title *Timpanum* exists only in *Bod* and *CC*. Apart from *Bod* and *CC* (*sequentia* and *prosa* 'Aule rutile' (*Analecta hymnica*, xl.152)) the melody occurs in the Cluny manuscript Paris, Bibliothèque Nationale, lat. 1087, under the name *Gemebunda* (also in unheighted neumes). According to Spanke (op. cit., p. 38) this title derives from the *prosa* 'Psallat mens nostra Domino gemebunda'; it comes down to us in three, albeit late, manuscripts from Rheims (*Analecta hymnica*, x.269).

HIERONIMA. This title too could be derived from a musical instrument, from the *Cithara Hieronima*, the psaltery. Cf. the psaltery among the 'Instrumenta Hieronymi' in the tenth-century St. Emmeram manuscript Munich, cl. 14523, f. 52 (reproduced in Kinsky, op. cit., p. 30, Pl. II), with the inscription 'Cythara ut hieronymus dicitur in modum deltae litterae cum XXIIII cordis' (see Hammerstein, op. cit., p. 126).

The melody title *Hieronima* is already present in the oldest neumed source of sequences, Autun, Bibliothèque Municipale, 28 S, which according to Jacques Handschin (*The New Oxford History of Music*, ii (London, 1954), 152) dates from as early as the ninth century; see Stäblein, 'Zur Frühgeschichte der Sequenz', *Archiv für Musikwissenschaft*, xviii (1961), 7 and Pl. I. An expanded version of this melody is found in East and West Frankish sources under the title *Frigdola*.

TUBA. The addition 'VEL FISTULA' in *Bod* suggests that by 'tuba' a more versatile instrument than the bull's horn or war horn is meant. FISTULA: flute, pipe and also (more commonly than *musa*) organ pipe (the evidence is presented in Buhle, op. cit., pp. 32 ff.). Indeed, the *Epistola ad Dardanum* describes as *fistula* an extremely complicated instrument comprising twelve pipes, to whose great loudness attention is particularly drawn. The emphasis on loudness allows comparison with the *tuba*, which in the Dardanus text signifies a curious instrument blown through three bronze fistulae: 'Tuba autem consuetudinis apud rerum peritissimos hoc modo intelligitur. Tribus fistulis aereis in capite angusto inspiratur. In capite lato per IIII vociductas aereas, quae per aerum fundamentum ceteras voces producunt. Mugitum nimium vehentissimumque proferit' (Hammerstein, op. cit., p. 122). The association of *Tuba* and *Fistula* could possibly have been caused by a misunderstanding of the Dardanus text.

The melody *Tuba vel Fistula* to the widely-known hexametric *prosa* 'Alma chorus domini' (*Analecta hymnica*, liii.87) is not the same as the melody cited above as *Nostra tuba*. In Winchester and other (West Frankish) manuscripts this is called *Dominus regnavit*.

BUCCA: from Latin *bucca* (cheek, mouth), or (?) in place of 'sambuca'. Sambuca: (*a*) flute, shawm (late Latin *sambucus*, elder bush); (*b*) plucked stringed instrument (Greek σαμβύκη, small harp).

(*a*) 'Sambuca in musicis species est symphoniarum. Est enim genus ligni fragilis, unde tibiae componuntur' (St. Isidore, op. cit., iii.20).

'Artificialis vero instrumentum est, quod non per naturam sed per artificium ad reddendum sonitum adaptatur. . . . Fistula namque illa, qua dicipiuntur aviculae vel etiam olla pergamento superducta, unde pueri ludere solent, indiscretum reddunt sonitum. At vero in sambuca, in fidibus, in cymbalis, atque in organis consonantiarum bene et distincte discernitur diversitas' (Johnnes Affligemensis, *De Musica*, ed. Smits van Waesberghe, p. 57).

(*b*) 'Sambuca genus citharae rusticae' (Papias Lombardus Grammaticus, *Glossar anno 1053*, after Du Cange, *Glossarium*, vii.296).

See also Godefroy, op. cit., vii.301; Buhle, op. cit., p. 36.

The allegorizing text of the Dardanus letter speaks of the sambuca as a wind instrument. The inscriptions to the illustrations (in the Angers and Boulogne-sur-Mer psalters) mix elements of various instruments; see the analysis in Hammerstein, op. cit., pp. 129 f.

The sequence title *Bucca* occurs only in *Bod* and *CC*, and the melody itself is also known only from those two sources, notated in staffless neumes: in *Bod*, *sequentia* and *prosa* 'Ad te pulchra' (*Analecta hymnica*, xl.41); in *CC*, *prosa* 'Lauda pulchra' (ibid., xl.42).

What, then, are we to make of the instrumental titles of the *Bod* and *CC sequentiae*, and what is their significance? The medieval terminology for instruments is inconsistent and indefinite. The combination of allegorical and concrete concepts, and the various etymological combinations, commonly result in the use of one and the same name for several instruments—indeed not only for different members of the same family but for quite different types of instrument. The instrumental titles of the sequence melodies are consequently ambiguous as well. Furthermore, one can hardly overlook the fact that the titles are influenced by the *Epistola ad Dardanum* (e.g. *Hieronima* and *Tuba vel Fistula*)—or, to put it another way, they reveal an awareness of the organological teaching of the time as it is found in psalter prefaces, which are themselves based on the Dardanus text.[10] This does not affect

[10] See Hammerstein, op. cit., pp. 118 f.

the case for supposing that the titles refer to actual instruments.

The titles *Musa*, *Chorus* (and *Chorus sive Bavverisca*), *Timpanum* and *Bucca*, and the comprehensive rubric 'Citharis organicisque deum modulemur ovanter' are encountered only in *Bod* and *CC*. The title *Tractus iocularis* (thus in *Bod*, in *CC* only *Tractus*) is of particular significance. The melody survives only in *Bod* and *CC* (as *sequentia* and to the *prosa* 'Consona caterva')[11] and cannot be transcribed. Are we to assume the existence of a separate instrumental tradition in Winchester? —or is it rather a question of a tradition which is known to us only in *Bod* and *CC* because of the loss of the corresponding French monastic sources from Fleury, Jumièges and especially Corbie, with which Winchester was closely associated? As mentioned in the introduction to this essay, some *prosae* in *CC* survive with 'Frankish' letter-notation, which is otherwise known only from instrumental treatises. This notation, however, points presumably to an accompaniment by the organ, on the claves of which the letters may have been written, as was the custom. The instrumental origin of the melodies cannot be deduced from the titles. But, with all critical distance, we may deduce that *sequentiae* were played on instruments—and obviously by musicians who did not belong to the church (*Tractus iocularis*).[12]

---

[11] *Analecta hymnica*, xxxvii.42.

[12] As supplement to this article see my book *Die Organa von Winchester*: on the dating of *CC* and *Bod*, pp. 19 f. and 24 ff.; on the palaeographic relationship between *Bod* and Cotton Tiberius C.VI, pp. 22 f.; on the links between Winchester and French monasteries, pp. 9 f. and 68 ff.; on the musical terminology of West Frankish *prosae* and particularly on the indication of mode, pp. 131 ff.; on the Winchester organ, pp. 139 ff.; on the 'Frankish' letter-symbols in the Prosary of *CC*, pp. 89 ff. and 143 ff.; and for discussion of the 'Organa super Sequentia', pp. 144 ff.

An English Broadside of the 1520s

A. HYATT KING

The sheet of music reproduced as Plate II may not, at first glance, seem a very promising subject for musicological enquiry. Even in its fragmentary state, however, it is of considerable importance, because it is a unique survival of printed popular music from the time of Henry VIII and is of a kind to which nothing comparable is known at present in any other country. Yet this sheet has attracted very little attention, partly because all printed fragments, and especially musical ones, are notoriously difficult to catalogue according to normal rules. The adoption of a short cut, however expedient, such as was applied to this piece, is always liable to cause a fragment to lapse into obscurity, especially in a large library.

This is indeed what happened when the British Museum acquired the sheet, in 1904. It was then decided—*erubui referens*—to catalogue it solely under the name of the printer, John Rastell. This was all the more extraordinary because his name does not appear on the sheet at all. (It bears only his initials, which form the centre of the device printed under the last stanza of the text. This device includes his motto, 'Justicia regat', the initial letters of which correspond to those of his name.) The entry was duly made in the general catalogue of printed books and repeated in the music catalogue (pressmark K.8.k.8). It is hard to see what possible justification there was for such obscurantism because, although Rastell was a versatile, remarkable man and connected with music indirectly, he was certainly no composer, and there is no evidence at all that he wrote the words of this song. A brief outline of his life may serve to introduce this account of the nature of the sheet and the music on it.

Born in about 1475, Rastell was trained in law and shortly before

1504 married the sister of Thomas More. He spent some seven years in Coventry, where he served as coroner and was active in business and litigation. Returning to London in about 1512, he began a career as printer which lasted for over twenty years. Besides serving in the French wars, he made a considerable reputation as a designer of pageants and a decorator of buildings erected for great occasions of state. In 1517 he launched an unsuccessful expedition to Newfoundland. He built the earliest known private theatre in England and wrote and printed a play, well known in the annals of early Tudor drama, *A New Interlude and a mery of the Nature of the iiij Elements*. He became a Member of Parliament in 1529 but fell foul of authority and died in prison in 1536.

The *Interlude* was printed, almost certainly, late in 1519 or early in 1520.[1] It has received some attention from musicologists because it contains a three-part song, 'Tyme to pas', which requires brief mention in the context of the broadside. Henry Davey pointed out[2] that Stafford Smith had printed this song in his *Musica Antiqua* (1812) on p. 45, with Henry VIII's three-part song 'Pastyme with good cumpanye' facing it on p. 44. Smith remarked in his preface that 'Tyme to pas' formed a 'satyrical counterpart' to the other song. In passing, one may wonder how Smith knew of the manuscript (since 1882 British Museum, Add. MS 31922), then in private hands. John Stevens, apparently unaware that Smith had printed 'Pastyme with good cumpanye', records[3] that the MS was 'not known to the eighteenth-century historians, nor to Chappell when he compiled his *Popular Music* (1853–59)'. Stevens has also discussed 'Tyme to pas'[4] and pointed out, what Smith failed to notice, that it is a parodic adaptation of 'Adeu madame et ma maitresse' in Add. MS 31922, and he prints both in his *Musica Britannica* volume. 'Tyme to pas' is also of great interest because it is

---

[1] John Stevens (*Music and Poetry in the early Tudor Court*, London, 1961, p. 456) gives *c*.1517, which is impossibly early. The [1539?] which Stevens gives on p. 102 of *Music at the Court of King Henry VIII* (Musica Britannica, xviii), 2nd edn., London, 1969, and which is found in other books too, comes from a misinterpretation of some bibliographical evidence first made by Robert Steele in *The Earliest English Music Printing*, London, 1903, pp. 5, 6, 93. My own dating is based on a study of textual, bibliographical and documentary evidence, which I have stated at length in 'The Significance of John Rastell in Early Music Printing', *The Library*, September 1971. Here I have also discussed the bibliographical aspects of the fragmentary broadside, its possible chronological relation to the *Interlude* and the implications of Rastell's use of single-impression music printing in its European context.

[2] *History of English Music*, 2nd edn., London, 1921, p. 93.

[3] *Music at the Court of King Henry VIII*, p. xxiii.

[4] *Music and Poetry*, p. 258.

the only complete piece of music, printed or manuscript, found in an English drama of the sixteenth century. One other noteworthy remark was made by Stafford Smith, who wrote at the head of the song: 'It is probably the first printed Score or Partition in this Kingdom'. The fact is that, up to the end of the fourth line of the text, the song is printed in quasi-score, barred by poetic lines and not by time, after which the parts run in sequence. (The reason for this change was that the printer wished to save space and end the music on the recto of the leaf, leaving its verso clear for the start of a new passage of text.)

Since this partsong and the fragmentary broadside constitute the whole of Rastell's extant music printing, it is important to realize that he used the same type for both. But while the partsong can be dated with fair certainty, the date of the broadside must, unfortunately, remain conjectural. It probably lies between 1519 and 1528, with some likelihood that it appeared in the earlier part of that period.[5] The sheet must have been part of Rastell's surplus stock, for it found its way into a bindery where some books were being bound for Westminster Abbey or perhaps for Westminster School. The binder trimmed the sheet heavily at the head and at the left hand side, and then pasted it with the recto (text-face) downwards on to the front board of a book. On the blank verso (Pl. III) several monks of Westminster attested their ownership within the next ten years or so, certainly before the dissolution of the monastery in 1539.

As so few notes have survived the binder's knife, it is important to try to reconstruct the size and layout of the untrimmed sheet, and so get some idea of how much music it originally bore. In this respect the watermark is important. It is a unicorn (which shows that the paper was made in France), situated close to the top edge and about one and a half inches in from the left. The position of watermarks in sixteenth-century broadsides is subject to some variation, but they were generally not far from the horizontal centre and rather more than half way up the vertical centre. The area of the present sheet lost by trimming was four to five inches in height. The original must therefore have been about 11 to 12 inches wide and 17 to 18 inches high. Such dimensions would correspond roughly to those of extant untrimmed sheets bearing proclamations and other documents of the period.

Let us now look at the surviving notes. Because the clef has been lost, we cannot be certain what the voice was. But in any case the notes hardly make sense as part of a solo melody at whatever pitch. Indeed,

---

[5] Stevens (*Music and Poetry*, p. 448) dates it *c.*1520.

solo song is virtually excluded, for two reasons. First, the untexted notes just visible at the end of the second stave and at the top right corner of the sheet must have been played by instruments, for the gaps seem too long to be explained as inexact underlay and there is no evidence of verbal repetition. Moreover it is most unlikely that a song would have been printed just for one voice and one instrument. Secondly, the spatial relation between text-syllables and notes shows that the type-width required for a whole stanza would have amounted to barely two and a half staves. The sheet would in that case have been of an impossibly squat size, quite incompatible with the position of the watermark which postulates such dimensions as I have given above.

But if it is assumed that the music was a partsong the content of the sheet becomes clearer. There are two possibilities. The surviving notes are either from the lower voice of a two-part song or from the middle voice of a three-part song. In either case, the parts were printed in sequence, as at the end of 'Tyme to pas'. For a two-part song, the stave space would all have been above the level of the first complete stanza and the typographical symmetry of the sheet would have been maintained by more stanzas, probably five, printed parallel to those extant. For a three-part song, symmetrical printing would have been achieved by printing the lowest voice in parallel with the extant stanzas. The two alternatives are shown in the tentative reconstruction in Fig. I. Which of the two is the more likely to represent the original it is hardly possible to say. It might be thought that a deciding factor lay in continuity of text. But the words surviving from the first stanza are really too few to determine whether or not its sense can lead directly into the ideas of the first complete stanza, without any lost intervening verses.

The head of the sheet would have carried two or three lines of printing, which probably included some information about the occasion for which the song was produced, the address of one of Rastell's shops and perhaps a date. As to the text of the song, nothing is known: it seems to be unique and has apparently been overlooked by students of the poetry of this period.

From so small a fragment it is difficult to draw any certain inference about the nature of the music. But the evidence of the untexted notes suggests that what Rastell printed was a song of a somewhat old-fashioned type which was still popular in England early in the sixteenth century. Such polyphonic songs are found in all the English manuscripts of the early Tudor period. Popularized by Newark, they were elaborated by Cornysh and Pygott in the next generation. As John

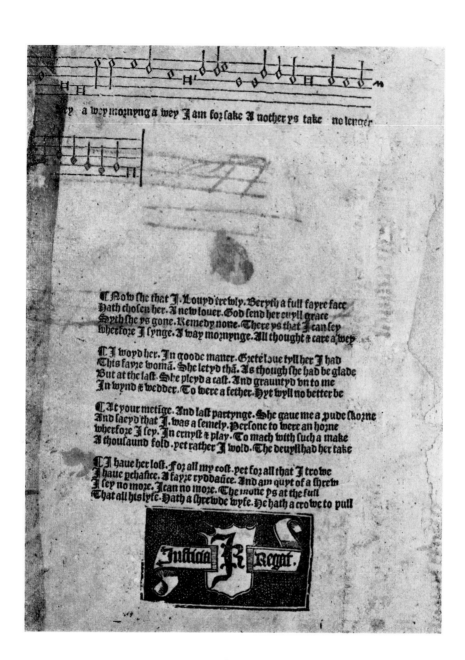

ii. Rastell's broadside, recto

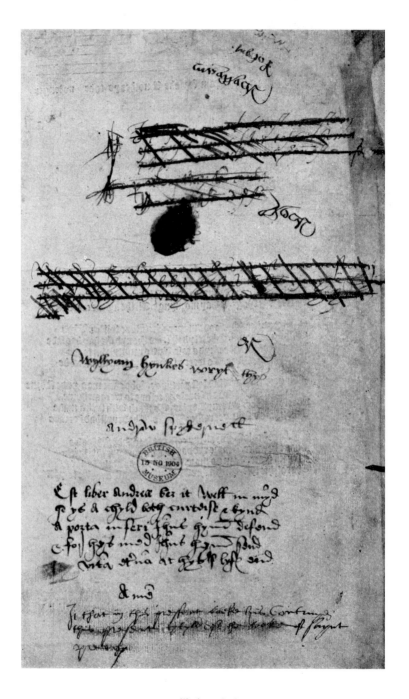

iii. Rastell's broadside, verso

TENTATIVE RECONSTRUCTION OF RASTELL'S BROADSIDE

As a Three-Part Song

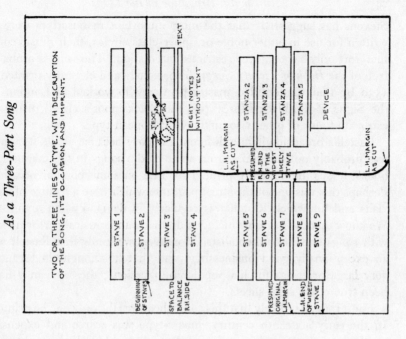

TWO OR THREE LINES OF TYPE, WITH DESCRIPTION OF THE SONG, ITS OCCASION, AND IMPRINT.

STAVE 1

STAVE 2 — BEGINNING OF STAVES

STAVE 3 — SPACE TO BALANCE R.H. SIDE

STAVE 4 — EIGHT NOTES WITHOUT TEXT

TEXT

L.H. MARGIN AS CUT

STAVE 5

STAVE 6 — PRESUMED ORIGINAL L.H.MARGIN

STAVE 7

STAVE 8 — L.H. END OF WIDEST STAVE

STAVE 9

STANZA 2

STANZA 3 — PRESUMED R.H. END OF THE WIDEST STAVE

STANZA 4 — LIKELY STAVE

STANZA 5

DEVICE

L.H. MARGIN AS CUT

As a Two-Part Song

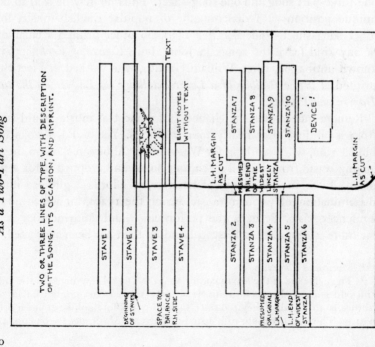

TWO OR THREE LINES OF TYPE, WITH DESCRIPTION OF THE SONG, ITS OCCASION, AND IMPRINT.

STAVE 1

STAVE 2 — BEGINNING OF STAVES

STAVE 3 — SPACE TO BALANCE R.H. SIDE

STAVE 4 — EIGHT NOTES WITHOUT TEXT

TEXT

L.H. MARGIN AS CUT

STANZA 2

STANZA 3 — PRESUMED R.H. END OF THE WIDEST STANZA

STANZA 4 — LIKELY STANZA

STANZA 5

STANZA 6

STANZA 7

STANZA 8

STANZA 9

STANZA 10

DEVICE !

PRESUMED ORIGINAL L.H.MARGIN

L.H. END OF WIDEST STANZA

L.H. MARGIN AS CUT

Stevens has suggested[6] that the most important manuscripts were all written for use in either noble or upper-class circles, their music could therefore only have enjoyed restricted circulation.[7] The same is probably true of the *Book of Twenty Songs* so spaciously and elegantly printed in 1530 by that unidentified master-printer who worked in London 'at the Signe of the black Morēs' (i.e. the Blackamoor's Head), using an exquisite fount of otherwise unknown European type.

Rastell's broadside is in a different category because, while its music was probably not dissimilar from some of the songs in the manuscript books, it was undoubtedly printed for sale on some popular occasion. Perhaps this was one of the street pageants which were a feature of state visits and for which Rastell was regularly in demand as an organizer. We know that the pageants included dramatic and musical performances with songs and instrumentalists. Moreover, we know that Rastell was an exceptionally good businessman and that he thought in terms of very large printings for his popular publications; the same may have been true of his song-sheets.

For it is most unlikely that this song-sheet was the only one he printed. In the early sixteenth century, music-type was scarce and expensive and had to be procured from abroad. Rastell would hardly have obtained this type and cherished it (he bequeathed it to his widow) just to print one three-part song and one song-sheet. Thus he may be said to hold a unique position as a disseminator of popular English music, for no other song-sheet—indeed, after 1530, no other printed secular music of any kind (save the songs in John Hall's *Courte of Vertu*, 1565)—is known until 1568, when William Griffith, who worked in Fleet Street, printed *A Newe Ballade of a Lover extollinge his Ladye. To the tune of Damon and Pithias*.

Remote indeed was the chance that a sheet of music would survive from a binding after nearly four centuries. Yet it did, thanks to the binder who, when working for Westminster Abbey, picked up the sheet among waste from Rastell's printing house and cropped it for a paste-down. Even in this fragmentary state, it affords a glimpse into the dissemination of popular music during the 1520s, for which no other evidence exists. Perhaps the performance and enjoyment of it were far more widespread, at least in London, than has been suspected.

---

[6] *Music and Poetry*, p. 5.

[7] The evidence of the leaves comprising the Drexel fragments in the Library and Museum of the Performing Arts, New York, is too limited for any conjecture as to whether they too once formed part of a book written for a noble patron. The fragments are fully listed in Stevens, *Music and Poetry*, pp. 426–8.

Old and New in Byrd's Cantiones Sacrae

JOSEPH KERMAN

The most ambitious composition written by William Byrd in his early years seems to have escaped recognition as such. It is a large motet for six voices in three *partes*, set to a long collect:

[PART 1] Tribue, Domine, ut donec in hoc fragili corpore positus sum
laudet te cor meum, laudet te lingua mea, et omnia ossa mea dicant: Domine, quis similis tui? Tu es Deus omnipotens, quem trinum in personis, et unum in substantia deitatis colimus et adoramus:
Patrem ingenitum, Filium de Patre unigenitum, Spiritum Sanctum de Utroque procedentem et in Utroque permanentem,
sanctam et individuam Trinitatem, unum Deum omnipotentem.

[PART 2] Te deprecor, supplico et rogo, auge fidem, auge spem, auge charitatem: Fac nos per ipsam gratiam tuam
semper in fide stabiles, et in opere efficaces,
ut per fidem rectam, et condigna fidei opera, ad vitam, te miserante, perveniamus aeternam.

[PART 3] Gloria Patri, qui creavit nos: Gloria Filio, qui redemit nos: Gloria Spiritui Sancto, qui sanctificavit nos:
Gloria summae et individuae Trinitati, cuius opera inseparabilia sunt, cuius imperium sine fine manet.
Te decet laus, Te decet hymnus, Tibi debetur omnis honor,
Tibi benedictio et claritas, Tibi gratiarum actio, Tibi honor, virtus, et fortitudo Deo nostro, in saecula saeculorum. Amen.

The three parts appeared separately, but consecutively, as Nos. 30–32 of the famous *Cantiones, quae ab argumento sacrae vocantur* published jointly by Tallis and Byrd in 1575, when Byrd was thirty-two. By this time he had apparently decided to split up the motet and present its components as three separate pieces. So far as I am able to tell, it has not been pointed out before that these three pieces go together.[1]

But go together they must. Reading through the text makes this seem likely, and reading through the music makes it certain when we hear so many links of one kind or another among the three ostensibly separate numbers. Parts 1 and 3, for example, have a passage in common: when the Trinitarian formula 'sanctam et individuam Trinitatem' comes back as 'summae et individuae Trinitati', it comes back with very similar music. Parts 2 and 3 must belong together because of the treatment of mode. All three parts have the same signature of two flats, but only Part 1 begins and ends in the same mode, Ionian transposed (B flat). Part 2, after beginning in B flat, changes to and ends in the Aeolian mode (G minor); Part 3 begins in G minor and ends in B flat. Such behaviour, which would certainly be aberrant for free-standing motets, makes sense only for interdependent parts of a larger composition.

Furthermore 'Tribue, Domine', 'Te deprecor' and 'Gloria Patri' all share certain details of musical treatment not found in any other compositions in the 1575 *Cantiones*. The initial phrase or phrases of the text are sung by a three-voiced semichoir or by several successive semichoirs before the full six voices enter with new words at a later point in the text. Part 1 begins with one such phrase, Part 2 with two, and Part 3—the doxology—with three.[2] In these initial three-voiced sections Byrd employs essentially the same formula to make the first cadence in each part of the motet—a formula that is as distinctive as it is, for Byrd, unusual (Ex. 1). The cadence in Part 1 comes on B flat, in Part 2 on C, and in Part 3 on D.

The six-voiced sections of the three parts have something in common too, something that will occupy us later in this essay. These sections include much matter composed in many different styles, ranging from block chords to fully-developed points of imitation. Five weighty imitative passages occur, each comprising either one long point or two shorter ones linked rhythmically and sometimes also melodically (that

[1] It was pointed out to me during a seminar meeting at the University of California by Philip Brett and Pierluigi Petrobelli, in concert. The motet is printed in *Tudor Church Music*, ix (London, 1928), 132–48, and in *The Collected Vocal Works of William Byrd*, ed. Edmund H. Fellowes, London, 1937, i. 245–74, transposed up a tone into C and with note values reduced by half. It is recorded in *Tallis–Byrd, Cantiones sacrae 1575*, by the Cantores in Ecclesia, director Michael Howard, 1969 (Oiseau-Lyre, SOL 311–13).

[2] There is some parallelism in the make-up of the semichoirs. Part 1 employs discantus (D), contratenor 1 (Ct 1), tenor (T); Part 2 D, Ct 1, T and superius (S), Ct 2, bassus (B); Part 3 D, Ct 1, Ct 2 and Ct 1, T, B and S, D, Ct 2.

Ex. 1

(a) PART. 1   (b) PART 2

fra - gi - li cor - po - re   po - si - tus sum   au - ge cha - ri - ta - - - - -

(c) PART 3

- tem: qui   cre - a - - - - - - vit   nos:

is, there is no sharp rhythmic break between the points, and their motives exhibit some melodic similarities). It is in these five passages that surprising parallels can be observed. In each the superius voice reaches its highest pitch, f'', shortly before the final cadence; and then, on the way to this cadence, the superius climax is echoed by a contratenor voice staking out its own climax on f', an octave lower. The cadences come out on different degrees, yet many of the climax zones are furnished with distinctly similar harmonic progressions (Ex. 2).[3]

If Byrd had a specific model in mind when he planned this singular composition it has not turned up in any of the likely places I have looked. His model in a general sense, however, is obvious. The text, the division into semichoir and full sections, the schematic elements in the structure, and those startlingly archaic cadences, all point back to the votive antiphon of the early sixteenth century. 'Tribue, Domine' is one of the last compositions to bear the strong imprint of this tenacious musical form (though not the very last, as we shall see). If we are right to discern a thin line connecting the votive antiphon with the later verse anthem, a form that Byrd pioneered, as Peter le Huray has made quite clear,[4] then 'Tribue, Domine' assumes extra interest. Around the same time that Byrd was first experimenting with the new verse style he also modelled an actual Latin motet on the form of the old votive antiphon.

This act of archaism is not altogether surprising, even though the antiphon is supposed to have been extinguished along with the Sarum rite by the Reformation. The youngest composers known to have written antiphons in the traditional large-scale form are John Sheppard ('Gaude Maria virgo'), William Mundy ('Gaude virgo mater Christi',

---

[3] Ex. 2 (overleaf) shows only the two parts in question and the bass.
[4] *Music and the Reformation in England, 1549–1660*, London, 1967, p. 224.

Ex. 2

(a) PART 1, *end*

(b) PART 2, *middle*

(c) PART 2, *end*

(d) PART 3, *middle*

(e) PART 3, *end*

'Maria virgo sanctissima' and 'Vox patris coelestis') and Robert Parsons ('O bone Jesu'). However, still older antiphons such as Taverner's 'Gaude plurimum', Robert Johnson's 'Ave Dei patris filia' and Tallis's 'Salve intemerata mater' retained their popularity late into the century, if not in their full (and very considerable) length, at least in the form of three- or four-voiced semichoir fragments truncated from the main

bodies of the compositions.[5] A fragment from the Tallis piece was included in the Mulliner Book. And while actual antiphons could not
have been written in Elizabethan times, the form of the antiphon
lingered on, for it had proved its utility as a medium for setting long
texts of various kinds—psalms mainly,[6] but also Lamentations (see
Robert White's setting for six voices) and prayers. Several prayers have
survived which are set in the fully fledged style of the votive antiphon:
'Domine Deus coelestis', 'Peccavimus' and 'Quaesumus, omnipotens
Domine' by Christopher Tye, who seems to have made a speciality of
such prayers, and 'Exurge, Domine' by a certain John Woode.[7]

By setting a collect in this form, then, Byrd was following a recog-
nizable tradition. In any case his collect devotes a suspicious amount
of energy to out-and-out adoration in the fashion of a votive antiphon.
Votive antiphons to the Trinity were not particularly common; but
they were required by Wolsey's statutes for Cardinal College, for
example.[8] Byrd's text was pieced together from a variety of liturgical
sources.[9] Since the text is of broad general applicability, there is not

---

[5] I have discussed the circulation of these fragments briefly in 'Byrd's
Motets: Chronology and Canon', *Journal of the American Musicological
Society*, xiv (1961), 373–4.

[6] See Joseph Kerman, 'The Elizabethan Motet: a Study of Texts for Music',
Studies in the Renaissance, ix (1962), 278–83, and Frank Ll. Harrison in *The
New Oxford History of Music*, iv (1968), 478–80.

[7] 'Domine Deus coelestis' appears in Bodleian MS Mus. Sch. e. 423, the
other three pieces in Christ Church 979–83, and 'Peccavimus' also in Tenbury
807–11. Semichoir fragments of 'Dominus Deus coelestis' and 'Exurge, Domine'
circulated separately too: see note 5 above.

Some phrases of Woode's text recall 'Tribue, Domine': 'ut per te . . . ad
veram vitam veniamus', 'fac nos a fide in fidem proficere'. This text appears in
the Henrician Primer of 1545, entitled 'Precatio pro concordia ecclesiae
Christi' (also in the Elizabethan Latin Primer of 1560—see W. K. Clay, *Private
Prayers during the Reign of Queen Elizabeth*, Cambridge, 1851, pp. 184–5—but
with a variant that does not show up in Woode's composition).

[8] Harrison, *Music in Medieval Britain*, London, 1958, pp. 168 and 332; but
see Hugh Benham, 'The Music of Taverner: a Liturgical Study', *The Music
Review*, xxxiii (1972), 261.

[9] The following Trinity texts can be compared with Parts 1 and 3 of Byrd's
motet: 'Te Deum Patrem ingenitum, te Filium unigenitum, te Spiritum
Sanctum Paraclitum, sanctam et individuam Trinitatem, toto corde et ore
confitemur, laudamus atque benedicamus . . . ' (*Magnificat* antiphon, second
vespers); 'Gloria tibi omnipotens Deus, / Trinus et unus magnus et excelsus; /
Te decet hymnus, honor, laus et decus, / Nunc et in aevum' (Sarum hymn
'O Pater sancte'); 'Benedictio, et claritas, et sapientia, et gratiarum actio,
honor, virtus, et fortitudo Deo nostro, in saecula saeculorum. Amen' (Revelation, vii.12—an All Saints chapter, echoed in the Trinity respond 'Tibi laus,
tibi gloria, tibi gratiarum actio in saecula sempiterna . . . '). Cf. also the Roman

much basis for guessing-games about a particular occasion (and a particular date) on which the music may have first been sung.

My own guess would be that 'Tribue, Domine' was prompted not by an occasion but by a 'friendly aemulation', to use Henry Peacham's pleasant term for one of Byrd's bouts of competitive composition. Tallis too included a setting of a collect in the *Cantiones sacrae* of 1575, 'Suscipe, quaeso, Domine'—his largest composition in the print, as well as one of his most modern in style. Byrd's largest composition might have been planned in reference to Tallis's; it would not be the only instance of collaborative planning in the *Cantiones*. But if this was the case, how strange it is that the form and scope of 'Tribue, Domine' should have been obscured by publication as three separate pieces. Perhaps some other factor intervened at a later stage. Perhaps Byrd even thought better of the competition once he saw Tallis's marvellous motet.[10]

Whatever happened, Byrd did not lose interest in motets modelled on the ancient antiphon form. The next of his publications to allow for any six-voiced motets, the *Liber secundus sacrarum cantionum* of 1591,[11] includes two more such compositions. Both have now abandoned the jubilant tone of 'Tribue, Domine' in favour of penitential sentiments

---

tract 'Te Deum' for the votive Mass to the Holy Trinity in Lent. In the Sarum rite the fifth Matins lesson ends with the words 'cuius opera inseparabilia sunt'.

With the help of Father Pfleiger's *Liturgicae orationis concordantia verbalia* one can also find various liturgical sources for the wording of Part 2 of Byrd's motet. Compare the following collects: 'ut (corda servorum) . . . in fide inveniantur stabiles, et in opere efficaces . . . ' (Wednesday in the second week of Lent); 'et concede . . . ut . . . ad vitam perveniamus aeternam' (Secret of the Mass, Ascension); 'Omnipotens sempiterne Deus, da nobis fidei, spei, et caritatis augmentum . . . ' (13th Sunday after Pentecost, Rome; 14th Sunday after Trinity, Sarum).

The two themes, adoration of the Trinity and the augmentation of faith, hope and charity, come together most clearly in the processional respond 'O beata Trinitas': ' . . . te adoramus; auge in nobis fidem, auge spem, auge charitatem, O beata Trinitas. Tibi laus, Tibi gloria, Tibi gratiarum actio in saecula sempiterna'. This respond appears in some but not all of the pre-Pian processionals etc. that I have been able to consult. It does not occur in Sarum books.

[10] See *Tudor Church Music*, vi (1928), 222–36. The two parts of the motet, marked 'Prima' and 'Secunda pars', are provided with separate numbers in the print, Nos. 27 and 28. This numbering tends to allay speculation that Byrd might have broken up 'Tribue, Domine' into three numbers as a way of swelling his tally of items in the print—perhaps in order to match Tallis in a grand total of seventeen. Tallis indicated the various parts of his collect as such while also giving them separate numbers; Byrd could have done the same.

[11] *Collected Vocal Works*, iii.

of the most abject kind. 'Cunctis diebus' is set to a relatively short text, made up of fragments from the Book of Job; one wonders why Byrd bothered to maintain the successive three-, six-, four- and six-voiced sections so stiffly—indeed, why he bothered at all, for the piece is dreary to listen to and must have been dreary to compose. 'Infelix ego' is quite another matter. This motet is set to a long text, a very striking one which Byrd appears to have taken from Lassus's *Sacrae cantiones vulgo motecta appellatae* of 1566:

PART 1 Infelix ego, omnium auxilio destitutis, qui coelum terramque offendi:
Quo ibo? quo me vertam? ad quem confugiam? quis mei miserebitur? Ad coelum levare oculos non audeo, quia ei graviter peccavi; in terra refugium non invenio, quia ei scandalum fui.

PART 2 Quid igitur faciam? desperabo?
Absit. Misericors est Deus, pius est Salvator meus.
Solus igitur Deus refugium meum; ipse non despiciet opus suum, non repellet imaginem suam.

PART 3 Ad te igitur, piissime[12] Deus, tristis ac moerens venio:
quoniam tu solus spes mea, tu solus refugium meum.
Quid autem dicam tibi, cum oculos levare non audeo? verba doloris effundam, misericordiam tuam implorabo, et dicam: Miserere mei, Deus, secundum magnam misericordiam tuam.

And between 'Infelix ego' and 'Tribue, Domine' there is a remarkable coincidence in general layout (see Fig. 1). The two motets employ the same transposed Ionian mode and exactly the same combination of clefs.[13] The dimensions are roughly similar and the sectionalization broadly analogous: 'Infelix ego' mirrors the opening three-voiced sections to new words in each part of 'Tribue, Domine' and also the five-voiced interlude in Part 2 (though not the semichoir sections in the middle of Parts 1 and 3; in Part 1 of 'Infelix ego' the two semichoir sections at 'in terra refugium non invenio' employ the same words—a rather different principle). Closer still are the large-scale harmonic parallels between the two motets, as marked by the main cadences. The cadences at the ends of the parts come on B flat, G minor and B flat. Important central cadences come on B flat, D (a half close in each

---

[12] The print and modern editions have 'ipsissime'; the word is correct in early manuscript copies.
[13] C clef on each of the five lines of the staff and F clef on the second line (bass clef). Byrd used an evenly balanced six-voiced choir of this sort in only one other composition—'Cunctis diebus'.

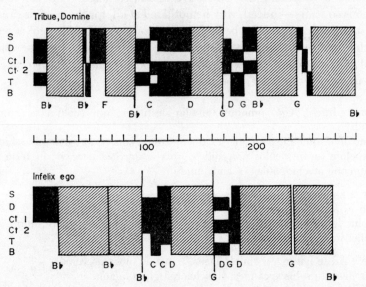

case) and G minor. Within the initial three-voiced sections, correspondence in the cadence degrees extends to the schematic feature illustrated in Ex. 1, the successive use of B flat, C and D cadences in the successive parts.

'A composer quite exceptionally impatient of repeating himself', says Oliver Neighbour of Byrd on the basis of a study of his instrumental music. Byrd 'rarely undertakes a composition without some special technical idea and aesthetic intention in mind, and writes two closely similar pieces only where he feels that he has not done justice to his conception at the first attempt'.[14] With the small technical reservation that 'Tribue, Domine' and 'Infelix ego' are closely similar only in some respects, not in all, Neighbour's observation seems to fit the case very well. 'Tribue, Domine' cannot be regarded as a great success; its three parts have never been favourites—of which there are few, anyhow, among Byrd's early motets—and the restitution of the parts into a single unit should not occasion any massive reassessment. 'Infelix ego' is much superior. It is easy to believe that some dissatisfaction with the

[14] 'New Keyboard Music by Byrd', *The Musical Times*, cxiii (1971), 657.

piece on Byrd's part was, first of all, at the bottom of the mix-up in the 1575 *Cantiones*, then also a decisive factor in the undertaking of 'Infelix ego'.[15]

If we can formulate the 'special technical idea' that interested Byrd in the writing of 'Tribue, Domine', even in quite general terms, this may help us to understand some of the difficulties he ran into. In most of the 1575 motets he seems to have been working over single stylistic ideas, one at a time, with the tenacity of a young bulldog: *cantus-firmus* treatment in 'Libera me, Domine, de morte aeterna', uninterrupted affective homophony in 'Emendemus in melius', rigid antiphony in 'O Lux, beata Trinitas', endless brisk imitations in 'Laudate, pueri, Dominum', continuous measured polyphony in 'Peccantem me quotidie' and 'Da mihi auxilium'. In 'Tribue, Domine' the idea was rather stylistic variety and contrast. Stylistic contrasts were easy to achieve—were indeed hard to avoid—when the unusual length of the text forced Byrd to write unusually concise periods; furthermore, stylistic contrasts served well the brilliant Trinitarian exclamations of this text. So Byrd worked with homophony, antiphony, semi-homophony, two-, three-, five- and six-part polyphony of various different sorts; presumably the votive antiphon form was chosen to impose a certain order on the proceedings. But it is scarcely enough of a 'form' to bring all the manifold contrasts under control. For this Byrd relied on large blocks of imitative polyphony placed at strategic junctures of the long motet. And whereas many phrases of the text are set very concisely, this is not true of those that generate these large blocks. Here the polyphony is spun out on a massive and leisurely scale, just as it is in other Byrd motets of the same period.

Imitative polyphony is of course at the heart of Byrd's style and that of every other major sixteenth-century composer. Although careful studies have been made of local contrapuntal practice in the work of Palestrina and Byrd, the way these composers used polyphony in the large, to construct phrases, periods and total pieces, is not well understood. Tovey remarked in another connection that 'the grammatical

---

[15] It has also occurred to me that possibly 'Cunctis diebus' and 'Infelix ego' were both commissioned from Byrd by a patron advanced in years and still loyal to the musical fashions of his youth. The texts, particularly that of 'Cunctis diebus', would certainly seem more appropriate to an old man occupied with thoughts of death than to a rather young one launching his career in London. On the text of 'Infelix ego', which was also set in whole or in part by Willaert, Clemens, Rore and Vicentino, see Edward E. Lowinsky, *Secret Chromatic Art in the Netherlands Motet*, New York, 1946, p. 116. On Byrd's importation of foreign motet texts, see my essay cited in note 6 above.

exercise nowadays called counterpoint contributes nothing beyond brick-making towards the architecture of a fugue'. Everybody knows that Byrd made pretty rough bricks in his early years. What was his architecture like?

In 'Tribue, Domine' this question is put in relief by Byrd's evident desire for variety, even among his large polyphonic sections. He tries different types of organization for polyphonic periods with different functions in the total form. There is also the unifying device that was mentioned above, the similar external handling of the melodic climax in each of the five main imitative passages. This certainly shows us a composer with a special idea—a special self-consciousness, we might even say. In cases like this it is always interesting and often revealing to compare and contrast, to gauge the different effects obtained by similar devices, and to estimate how far intentions seem to have been realized.

Examination of the imitative passages in 'Tribue, Domine' shows first of all that those that come in the middle of the parts are constructed differently from those that end the parts and make the weightiest cadences. The passages in the middle of Parts 2 and 3 ('et in opere efficaces', 'cuius opera inseparabilia sunt') are constructed around ostinatos of one kind or another. In Part 2 this has the effect of stabilizing the most important change of mode in the motet, the move towards G-Aeolian or G minor (with an admixture of D-Phrygian and C-Dorian) which is then maintained until after the beginning of Part 3. In Part 3 the ostinato appears to have the complementary effect of restoring and stabilizing the B flat-Ionian mode; but after this has been accomplished G minor returns for a considerable time prior to the final B flat cadence. Indeed, this final cadence emerges relatively suddenly from the G minor area. Perhaps Byrd thought this a brilliant effect, and perhaps he thought it was prepared and justified by the earlier return to B flat, which had been stabilized by the ostinato. And perhaps it is significant that in 'Infelix ego' an early return to B flat[16] followed by a G minor digression does not happen. This is one feature of 'Tribue, Domine' that was not taken over.

In Part 2 the ostinato comes in the second of two linked points, 'et in opera efficaces'. The pitch D sounds in all but one of the 29 *tactus* of this point, either as a member of the main harmony or (occasionally) as

---

[16] There is a return to B flat at a later point, still prior to the final cadential section, but it is not brought out by a B flat cadence (at the point 'misericordiam tuam implorabo').

a suspended note resolving to C or C♯. D almost always comes at the beginning of the motive or on the key word 'efficaces'. Ending the point is a plagal cadence in D-Phrygian, which we tend to interpret as a half-close in G minor. This is stabilization with a vengeance; even Beethoven would not have hammered away at a dominant more stubbornly. There is really no call for organization around a melodic climax in a passage of this kind. Since the soprano climax on high f'' emerges from d'' (see Ex. 2b) it comes about naturally enough and sounds like an attempt to escape from the ostinato. But the attempt is frustrated, and the climax is bound to sound fitful because it has not been broadly prepared and because it is denied any real influence on the cadence. The effect of climax is perhaps also undercut by the prominence of the same pitch, f'', in the superius voice during the first point of this linked pair, 'semper in fide stabiles'. A closely knit stretto on an unusually forceful motive, this point surges up to f'' at the beginning and at the end, in a nearly symmetrical fashion.

In Part 3 the ostinato comes in the first of two linked points, 'cuius opera inseparabilia sunt'. The motive is made up essentially of descending scale fragments; such motives are so easy to work in stretto that they can overwhelm a composer with possibilities, especially if the style he is working in happens to be permissive towards parallel sixth-chords. Byrd's style certainly was, and the first nine bars of 'cuius opera inseparabilia sunt' consist of long scales down to B♭ in the bass (or other lowest-sounding voice) with strettos making thirds and sixths above all the scale notes. Thus the cheerful, dense, enthusiastic chiming of the scale strettos is organized over a loose bass ostinato. Afterwards the strettos organize themselves into a quicker and stricter ostinato on the descending fifth F–B♭. The skeleton score below (Ex. 3) shows how Byrd used this curious ostinato to link in to the new point, 'cuius imperium sine fine manet'.

It is after taking this neat junction in its stride that the music seems to lose its way. As the harmony swings away from B flat the counterpoint grows amorphous, and the reappearance (in two voices only) of the striking 'sprung' version of the motive, hingeing on the leap of a minor seventh, does not sound like a strong return and provides no focus for the activity. The superius climax on f'', which coincides with the second appearance of the sprung motive (Ex. 2d), absent-mindedly comes and goes without making any particular impression.

A different type of organization is used for the points that conclude Parts 1 and 3 of the motet ('unum Deum omipotentem' and 'in saecula saeculorum. Amen'). They both start away from the Ionian mode and

Ex. 3

move towards it with considerable vehemence; they are concerned less with solidity than with brilliance. They do not employ ostinatos but a method of construction based on short phrases and contrasts in texture, a method I shall call 'cell construction'. The composer starts with a clearly defined, rather light phrase or 'cell' for semichoir. Clear definition comes about because the cell is usually short and usually ends with a crisp little cadence; a typical texture involves three voices in stretto imitation. Overlapping this cadence, another semichoir sings a free repetition of the first cell, words and music; the music is perhaps presented in contrapuntal inversion, or transposed, or treated to some other modification. There may be more of these cells, but before long one of them will turn out to be the longest, the densest and the last—densest because it engages the entire choir in a full-scale stretto. Supported and prepared by the earlier phrases, this last phrase provides a natural climax in terms of texture, phrase length and contrapuntal intensity.

The concluding point of 'Tribue, Domine', Part 3, 'in saecula saeculorum. Amen', is a clear example. The opening cell (S, D, Ct 2) is a loose stretto reaching a neat cadence after only six semibreves. In the next cell, which overlaps the first cadence, the other three voices sing the identical music (save only for the first note in each voice) in inversion at the octave. As the overlapping becomes more complex, the third cell (Ct 2, S, D, T) uses slightly different music so as to cadence on B flat after five semibreves. The fourth cell (Ct 1, T, D, B) cadences on B flat again after seven. The superius voice leads off the next cell much in the style of the earlier ones, but now all the other five voices crowd in at once. Their well-contrived stretto on the crotchet figure for 'saeculorum' builds up sufficient intensity to run this final phrase for eighteen semibreves, without counting six more of plagal cadence to conclude the total motet.

The concluding point of Part 1 of 'Tribue, Domine' is also, I believe, an example of cell construction, though it cannot be said to be a clear example. In the point 'unum Deum omnipotentem' neither the cadences nor the textures are lucid at all. Nonetheless, I find that this passage can be heard best—that is, most coherently—as a fourfold presentation of the same basic cell, a two-voiced cell involving the Phrygian stretto A–Bb / D–Eb in one form or another (Ex. 4). The final cell abandons A–Bb and goes on to higher things (see Ex. 2a).

Ex. 4

Byrd makes much use of cell construction in his two books of *Cantiones sacrae* of 1589 and 1591. One can count over two dozen phrases composed with this technique or something very much like it; an example is the doxology of the motet 'O quam gloriosum', which makes a most interesting comparison with 'Tribue, Domine'. Among the phrases in the 1575 *Cantiones*, however, only a handful employ cell construction. In 'Tribue, Domine' it seems to have been so new to Byrd that he had not yet grasped its actual implications. For although the technique is perfectly suited to the organization of periods around a strong climax, and although Byrd had a prearranged melodic climax ready for use, somehow he failed to bring things together in a convincing way. The melodic climax does not fit in smoothly with the climax provided by texture, phrase length and contrapuntal intensity. In the point 'in saecula saeculorum. Amen' the peaks in the superius and first contratenor flicker up and down in a hasty, preoccupied way as though the composer were quite busy enough with the brilliant strettos on 'saeculorum' and the big plagal cadence. In linear terms the climax is trivial; as a result the total effect of the motet's ending is not strong, merely strenuous (Ex. 2e). The point 'unum Deum omnipotentem' (Exx. 4 and 2a) suffers from the reverse trouble. After preparing the soprano climax $d''-c''-f''$ carefully (indeed, even laboriously) by sounding prior patterns of $d''-e''\flat$, $d'-b\flat-e'\flat$, and so forth, Byrd holds to the plateau too inflexibly, keeps the bass fixed and reduces the upper voices to simple triad patterns. The unsubtle harmonic approach to the climax—juxtaposed D minor and B flat triads: a sudden switch from the Phrygian to the Ionian mode—sets up high tension that Byrd makes no effort to discharge. If the melodic climax in 'in saecula saeculorum. Amen' is underplayed, in 'unum Deum omnipotentem' it is overdone.

In 1575 cell construction counts as a modern technique for Byrd. Ostinato counts as an old-fashioned one, whose roots can probably be traced back to the medieval British composers' liking for rotas and similar devices. Almost all the 1575 motets contain ostinatos, except those in which some single-minded technical preoccupation can be seen to preclude them. Thereafter the technique is used much more rarely and selectively. A famous example occurs in 'Civitas sancti tui' ('Bow thine ear') in the 1589 set. What was perhaps new about Byrd's treatment of ostinato in 'Tribue, Domine' was his determination to graft on to it a melodic climax. An examination of Tallis's portion of the *Cantiones* shows that it was by no means taken for granted in English mid-century polyphony that periods should display clear organization in terms of a climax; Byrd's interest in such organization is one sign of his more modern position. In 'Tribue, Domine' he resolved to provide every one of his large imitative passages with a melodic climax, even the ostinato points. In these the technique did not require it, and, as we have seen, Byrd was not able to come up with convincing results.

Are we left, then, with the awkward conclusion that Byrd had a 'special technical idea' in planning his polyphony that was persistently unsuccessful in the realization? No, because there is another long polyphonic passage in the motet—perhaps the most unassuming of them all, at first hearing—in which the climax is properly conceived and admirably controlled. In the following pages I append a short analysis of this fine passage. Despite the use of a few rough bricks, it shows a mastery of architecture that is the more remarkable in the context of the abutting musical structures. It can provide some insight into Byrd's artistic methods in the motets and other music of his mature period.

The polyphonic passage ending Part 2 of the motet is another double period consisting of linked points with related motives: 'ad vitam, te miserante' and 'perveniamus aeternam' (Ex. 5). They are not built around ostinatos or according to the principles of cell construction. The organization can be described as linear: that is, the entire complex of some twenty bars can be heard as a rich, large-scale expansion of a relatively simple melodic progression in the superius voice. Besides melodic features, harmonic and contrapuntal ones contribute to the central melodic organization. If not all details, all salient details can be heard in this way. As a result, Byrd's inevitable climax on f''—a quintessentially melodic feature—does not feel like an addition, an addition that is either too weak or too strong but in any case arbitrary. It feels like the inevitable outcome of an organic growth process. Or to look at it the other way around, and to change the metaphor, the potential of the climax seems to have extended over and electrified the entire period.

For purposes of analysis, it may indeed be most convenient to look at it this way around. The climax phrase, which occurs in the second half of the period ('perveniamus aeternam'), has the superius melody arching up from c'' to high f'' and down again $(c''-\hat{f}''-c'':$ bars 13–15).[17] This phrase is preceded and followed, in the superius voice, by roughly sequential phrases pitched lower:

'perveniamus aeternam'	$a'-\hat{d}''-b'\flat$	$c''-\hat{f}''-c''$	$g'-\hat{e}''\flat-b'\natural$
	10–13	13–15	16–18

[17] The total range of 'Tribue, Domine' is three octaves from F to f''. The circumflex (e.g. $\hat{f}''$) depicts a melodic peak.

Ex. 5

The preceding phrase prepares the climax. The following final phrase mirrors it and reduces its tension at leisure—a function that is lacking in the other imitative points of 'Tribue, Domine'. The final phrase is lower, but receives new life of its own on account of modifications of the melodic pattern: the expansion of the opening step into a fourth and the introduction of the dotted rhythm (bar 16). These changes point up the minor sixth $g'-e''\flat$, which is expressive in itself and well calculated to guide in the final cadence.

Although the dotted rhythm has been heard occasionally before, this was only in the inner voices, and its appearance at this juncture in the superius has the effect of stressing the latent similarity in motive between the present point, 'perveniamus aeternam', and the previous one, 'ad vitam, te miserante'. The latter motive is circular rather than arch-shaped. In the superius it first circles the note c'', spanning the fifth $g'-d''$ (bars 3–6), then moves up in free sequence to circle d'', spanning the same sixth $g'-e''\flat$ (bars 7–10). Similarity between these two points makes a certain sense, since their text fragments form a grammatical unit. Beyond this the similarity also makes one hear the free sequence in 'ad vitam, te miserante' as a preparation for the free sequence in 'perveniamus aeternam'. The entire melodic structure in the superius may be set out as follows:

'ad vitam, te miserante' $c''-g'-\overset{\frown}{d}''-c''$ $d''-g'-\overset{\frown}{e}''\flat-d''$
                                            3–6   7–10

'perveniamus aeternam' $a'-\overset{\frown}{d}''-b'\flat$ $c''-f''-c''$ $g'-\overset{\frown}{e}''\flat-b'\natural$
                                            10–13   13–15   16–18

To this diagram may now be added an indication of the main entries other than those in the superius—one in each point, both imitating the superius at the lower octave: in 'perveniamus aeternam', the first contratenor entry (c'–$\hat{f}'$–c': bars 14–16) echoing the climax, which we have spoken of before, and in 'ad vitam, te miserante', a second contratenor entry (c'–g–$\hat{d}'$–g: bars 6–8) filling the large gap between the two superius statements. The diagram should also show the cadence degrees at the end of the various phrases (parentheses denote weak or deceptive cadences):

'ad vitam, te miserante'

$$c''\text{–}g'\text{–}\hat{d}''\text{–}c'' \qquad\qquad\qquad d''\text{–}g'\text{–}\hat{e}''\flat\text{–}d''$$

$$\Big| \qquad c'\text{–}g\text{–}\hat{d}'\text{–}g' \qquad\qquad \searrow$$

$$f \qquad\qquad (g) \qquad\qquad\quad G$$

'perveniamus aeternam'

$$a'\text{–}\hat{d}''\text{–}b'\flat \qquad c''\text{–}\hat{f}''\text{–}c'' \qquad g'\text{–}\hat{e}''\flat\text{–}b'\natural$$

$$\qquad\qquad c'\text{–}\hat{f}'\text{–}c'$$

$$\searrow \qquad\qquad\qquad\qquad \Big|$$

$$f \qquad\qquad\qquad\qquad\qquad G$$

The careful melodic parallelism between the two points is supported by an equally careful harmonic parallelism. We hear a twofold progression from a weak cadence on f to a strong one on G (a seventh lower); and we hear this in conjunction with the melodic climax on f''. The first F cadence (bar 6), a masculine half close, is certainly very unstable; the second F cadence (bar 13), with its very elegant quavers, is feminine and somewhat stronger. There is no true cadence, not even a weak one, for the climax phrase itself; the stepwise bass movement between bars 14 and 15, weak at best, comes too early as the soprano melody waits before trailing off to its curious, yet curiously expressive conclusion. Another thing that weakens cadential feeling here is, of course, the first contratenor pushing in with its strong stretto entry (as also happens with the soprano and the second cadence in 'ad vitam, te miserante', bar 8).

The presence or absence of cadences contributes to a cardinal feature of this passage, its subtle and paradoxical emphasis on B flat. Bars 11–16 are all shadowed by B flat-Ionian harmonies. The point is, I think, that even without a B flat cadence in bar 15, so lengthy a passage in B flat would ordinarily wreak havoc on a passage heading towards G minor. If not for the firm, carefully prepared double period, with its melodic and harmonic parallelism, the cadential goal would have been vitiated. On the other hand, having the parallelism Byrd was able to achieve a remarkable sense of solidity and relief when, in bar 17, D and F♯ reappear for the first time since the end of 'ad vitam, te miserante'. Notice also that the bass, for all its sly glances towards B flat, is tracing a line of classical Aeolian profile.[18]

Counterpoint works along with melody and harmony to create the total effect, as one can see by examining the network of secondary imitations. In 'ad vitam, te miserante' the counterpoint in the first few bars seems to serve as a sort of warm-up for action to come; this is often the case with Byrd's interior points. The previous cadence was on C. Quick stretto entries starting g–g, g'–g', g–c' and f'–f' (in T, D, Ct 2 and Ct 1) prepare for the superius entry on c'', which begins like a tonal answer. Once the top voice has taken command Byrd makes the stretto imitations regular in time interval, following the three main entries after a breve and then after a semibreve in each case. But the harmonic implications of these strettos differ greatly. The first soprano phrase—the one circling c''—is answered by strettos starting on $e♭$ and $b'♭$; these add nothing by way of harmonic stability but instead prepare the unstable half close on f. The immediately following second-contratenor phrase, again circling the pitch c', is answered by strettos starting on d' and d'', which move decisively, though still unstably, towards G minor. The second of these strettos becomes the third main phrase, the soprano phrase circling d''. When this is answered by strettos on g and c, they provide full solidity at last for the central G minor cadence in bar 11.

As for the point 'perveniamus aeternam', this begins with an entry in the first contratenor prefiguring the climactic f'—jammed into the prior G minor cadence, $f♯$ and all, as though to stress vertically the horizontal function of F in this total passage as support for the G-Aeolian mode (bars 10–11). In bars 11–13 a free octave stretto (discantus and bass) neatly guides in the feminine cadence on f. Then, in bars 13–14, strettos at the fifth ($b♭$–$ê'♭$, f'–$b'♭'$, c''–f'') lift up the climax phrase splendidly; there is even a try, in the T and Ct 2, at an echo of this whole contrapuntal complex as support for the following Ct 1 echo (bars 14–15). Again, strettos at the fifth (f'–$b'♭$, $B♭$–f, g–$ê'$) prepare the last soprano phrase, which this time floats a tenth above the final supporting entry (the diminution g–$ê'$ in Ct 1, bar 16).

[18] But the B♮ in bar 12 is an Ionian touch. Byrd could easily have written D here, preserving the Aeolian line—and making a more exact imitation.

Most effective, at the end of 'perveniamus aeternam', is the treatment of the very last entry, the second-contratenor entry *f–b♭* in bars 16–17. (The motive, by the way, suits the word 'perveniamus' very well indeed.) Entries covering these particular pitches in one octave or another are by far the most frequent; there are five in all, marked with small arrows in Ex. 5. They help create that shadowy, non-cadential emphasis on B flat that was mentioned a moment ago, and they even begin to create a faint ostinato feeling. After the peak note B♭ has arrived twice on a B flat triad and then twice on a G minor triad, it comes at last on a six-four chord on *d*. Now the insistent B♭ finally explains itself, by resolving down through A to the new final or tonic, G: an explanation that is echoed and amplified directly afterwards by the tenor. Even the stereotyped cadence formula here has been given a quiet supporting role in the total conception.

Whether the kind of writing we see in the passage 'ad vitam, te miserante, perveniamus aeternam' is really new in Byrd's motets of 1575 would indeed be hard to substantiate. A firm answer, as opposed to a guess, would have to rest on a comprehensive analytical study of English music in the first three quarters of the sixteenth century. At the basis of the passage there is no set procedure that can easily be isolated, such as ostinato or cell construction, but a broad compositional principle—really an attitude, a way of thinking about music and hearing its various elements. Perhaps the principle that melody, harmony, texture and everything else should work together to shape a phrase or period is neither old nor new but a timeless warrant of good music. This would also be hard to substantiate. Suffice it to say that our instinctive response to Byrd's music is, in my opinion, guided to a large extent by his application of this broad principle. It can be observed again and again in his mature compositions; it provides a key to the understanding of his powerful and justly admired musical rhetoric.

Two Studies of Purcell's Sacred Music

(*a*) The Stylistic Origins of the Early Church Music

PETER DENNISON

In the first generation after the restoration of Charles II the English Baroque style can be said to have come of age in the hands of Pelham Humfrey, John Blow and Matthew Locke. Following the largely cautious experiments with the newer styles by English composers before 1660, these three, Humfrey in his church, court and theatre music, Blow in his church music and Locke in his string-consort, theatre and church music, consolidated the new style with works that are inventive and accomplished. Furthermore, each was closely associated with the young Purcell and left his particular imprint on the latter's style. Purcell was brought up as a church musician, and most of his early works, to about 1680, lie in the field of sacred music. Thus it is here that the clearest picture of the origins of his style emerges.

Turning first to the early anthems, our study is well served by Purcell's autograph volume now at the Fitzwilliam Museum, Cambridge, as MS 88. The first section dates almost certainly from 1677, that is three years before the autographs of the domestic sacred pieces and the fantasias, and it contains twelve extensive verse anthems with instruments by Humfrey, Blow and Locke.[1] No less influential are the smaller anthems by Blow and Locke, together with anthems from the Renaissance polyphonic period, all of which were copied into the reverse end

---

[1] See Nigel Fortune and Franklin B. Zimmerman, 'Purcell's Autographs', *Henry Purcell, 1659–1695: Essays on his Music*, ed. Imogen Holst, London, 1959, pp. 108–10. The anonymous four-part instrumental fragment in this section on f. 26ᵛ is the first fourteen bars of Humfrey's symphony to the Club Anthem, 'I will always give thanks'. On the domestic sacred pieces, see the next essay in the present volume.

of the volume at some time before 1682 (the date appearing on a fly-leaf). These are the very pieces that Purcell copied to study at a time when his own style was at its most formative. Therefore it is to them that we ought to look first for the immediate stylistic origins of his early anthems.

The young Purcell was a chorister of the Chapel Royal under Humfrey until about Michaelmas 1673, and the importance that he still attached to the work of his old master three years after the latter's death is verified by the inclusion of no fewer than five anthems and a fragment by Humfrey in the front section of this score. Blow, who is represented by three anthems in the front section and seven in the reverse, is known to have taught Purcell, and this tuition began probably after the death of Humfrey in 1674. Blow stepped down as organist of Westminster Abbey in Purcell's favour in 1679, and three years later the younger man joined the older as one of the three organists of the Chapel Royal. Although evidence of the relationship with Locke is slender, Purcell did succeed him as a composer for the violins in 1677, and in writing an elegy on Locke's death referred to him as 'his Worthy Friend'. Locke's influence is to be seen at its most pervasive on every page of Purcell's string fantasias; but Locke's four large anthems copied into the front of the autograph volume about 1677, and the two smaller anthems copied into the reverse section a little later, played their part in shaping the style of Purcell's church music.

Any chronology of Purcell's early church music can only be approximate, as none of his anthems of these years can be dated. Several, however, can be confidently assigned to the period before 1680, and twelve were copied into the reverse section of Fitzwilliam MS 88, thus establishing 1682 as a *terminus ante quem*. Examples of each of the four types of anthem in use at the time, while illustrating the progressive consolidation of Purcell's own style, also reflect the decisive influence of Humfrey, Blow and Locke on his formative years.

The most extensive type of anthem of the period is the verse anthem with instruments. This is divided into sections, with primary importance assigned to solo voices both alone and in ensemble. A body of strings with the occasional addition of wind instruments provides symphonies and ritornellos and sometimes accompanies verses and choruses. In their original state these instrumental anthems would have been performed only in the Chapel Royal. A second category is the verse anthem that differs from the first only by the omission of instrumental movements and by its customarily shorter length. Again solo voices predominate, and the function of the chorus is secondary and often derived from the soloists' music. In the third category the chorus plays a more dominant role, and verses are introduced as inner sections to contrast with, and to separate, the choruses. Finally there is the full anthem for chorus alone, which has close affinity with the choral sections of the previous category. Seldom does either of the last two types have an independent continuo line.

The Restoration verse anthem with strings was largely the creation of Pelham Humfrey. From the fragmentary and disjointed type of Henry Cooke he evolved an extensive design based on a contrast of textures and tonality, yet integrated by means of structural symmetry and recurring thematic patterns. In a short composing life, covering little more than ten years if his juvenilia are included, he wrote sixteen verse anthems with strings, joined in the composition of the Club Anthem, and, of anthems without strings, composed only one and revised another. He grafted into the anthem instrumental movements derived from French models, but he enriched them with more active inner parts and more expressive harmony than may be found in their French counterparts.

Humfrey's most subtle strength lay in his feeling for words, their emotional content and accentuations, and in his acute sensitivity to the power of chromatic harmony. Much of his finest melody moves conjunctly. A particularly idiosyncratic type is the sinuously chromatic line where sharp and flat inflections of the same note are juxtaposed in lines which trace and retrace their steps in conjunct movement. This is aptly illustrated in the second verse of 'O Lord my God' (Ex. 1).[2]

Ex. 1

[2] Fitzwilliam MS 88, f. 4, and *Pelham Humfrey: Complete Church Music: ii*, ed. Peter Dennison (Musica Britannica, xxxv), London, 1972, p. 20.

Humfrey's lines are rich in chromatic inflections, which usually enliven significant words or ideas in the text. They include the sharpened sixth, a harmonic instance of which is found in the second bar of Ex. 1, and a variety of warmly expressive cross-relations. The last verse of the second version of 'Have mercy upon me, O God'[3] contains inflections producing a chord of the augmented fifth adjacent to the chord with a major third and a minor sixth that became so widely used in this period (Ex. 2). In common with most composers of the day Humfrey

Ex. 2

made frequent use of falling diminished fourths, fifths and sevenths and minor sixths to express the tender and the pathetic, for which his nature seems to have had a particular sympathy. He used triadic patterns in his melody rather less than most of his contemporaries; he reserved them for the directly declamatory or for expressions of praise and grandeur.

Although his harmony is bound up inextricably with his melody, Humfrey conceived his music in more intrinsically harmonic terms than either Blow or Locke. Never does his chromatic harmony result from the contrapuntal interaction of a large number of angular lines. A harmonic device particularly characteristic of Humfrey's language is the cadential pattern where, more commonly, a minor third over the subdominant becomes major before the bass moves to the dominant, and, less commonly, where a major third over the subdominant leads to a perfect fourth before the bass moves to the dominant. In both instances a seventh is usually present in the second chord of the progression. An example of the less common variety, in which the harmony

[3] *Pelham Humfrey: Complete Church Music: i*, ed. Dennison (Musica Britannica, xxxiv), London, 1972, p. 44.

is further enriched by a minor third sounded with the perfect fourth and the seventh in the second chord, is found at the last cadence in the third symphony of 'O Lord my God' (Ex. 3). The dialogue between the Babylonians and the Jews in 'By the waters of Babylon' provides an excellent example of Humfrey's language at its most dramatic.[4]

Ex. 3

The most expressive writing for solo voice is found in the ariosos, derived ultimately from Italians of Carissimi's generation. Here the flexibility of both melodic organization, with anacruses and rests, and harmonic rhythm allowed Humfrey the greatest opportunities to mould his music to the subtle fluctuations of the text. His verse ensembles are most often in two or three parts, and their textures extend from the homophonic (usually in triple time) to various types of dialogue between voices. The latter range from writing in which the voices maintain considerable linear independence to passages of prolonged imitation. Humfrey was not a natural contrapuntist, and the few contrapuntal textures in more than three parts are short-lived. Both his choral and string textures are almost invariably in four parts. His principal contributions to Restoration music were first to play a major role in the creation of the verse anthem with strings, and then to use it as a vehicle for expressing the affecting emotions so characteristic of the period.

Blow, unlike Humfrey, did not confine himself mainly to the verse anthem with strings, and in Fitzwilliam MS 88 alone he is represented by all three types of verse anthem. Blow tended to set texts expressing the tender and the pathetic as smaller anthems without strings and to reserve the larger type to express joy and praise. His language differs from Humfrey's in a number of significant respects. Blow was a more natural contrapuntist, and his distinctive species of chromatic harmony results to a considerable extent from the contrapuntal interaction of a large number of angular lines. There is not Humfrey's regular use of metrical contrast within and between sections in the anthems, although

[4] *Musica Britannica*, xxxiv. 6. Also quoted in Edmund H. Fellowes, *English Cathedral Music*, rev. J. A. Westrup, London, 1969, pp. 137–8.

cadential hemiola patterns in triple time are a distinctive mark of his style. Solo vocal writing is not as common as in Humfrey's work, but ensembles in as many as eight parts are handled with expressive skill.

Despite these differences Humfrey's verse anthems with strings provided Blow with a basic texture that he went on to extend and develop. His string movements reflect the influence of Humfrey in the vigorous activity of all four parts, but his symphonies show a greater structural resourcefulness than Humfrey's prototype, which is homophonic and in two main sections, respectively in duple and triple time. Blow sometimes accompanies a solo verse with a violin obbligato but more often includes violin obbligatos in ensemble verses and choruses, suggesting the influence of Locke.

Blow's most assured and inventive work on a smaller scale in the period up to about 1680 lies in the five verse anthems with more prominent choruses. The three choruses of 'O God, wherefore art thou absent from us'[5] (composed by 1676) are accomplished polyphonic movements in five parts with expressively angular intervals and chromatic harmony, and both choruses in 'God is our hope and strength'[6] (also composed by 1676) are extended fugal movements in eight parts. The verses are often more harmonically activated, and those in these two anthems add further contrast by antiphonally offsetting an upper and a lower trio in the Italian manner.

During the first fifteen years after the Restoration, when Francophilia was at its height, the most defiant champion of the Anglo-Italian manner was Matthew Locke. Locke wrote anthems in all verse categories, but his style was formed before 1660 and contains a greater variety of vocal and instrumental textures than those of either Humfrey or Blow. His symphonies, particularly those sections in triple time, show practically no affinity with the Lullian type and often anticipate thematic material in the first verse. 'Sing unto the Lord, O ye saints of his'[7] adds two oboes and later two flutes to the band of strings. Locke was an even more spontaneous contrapuntist than Blow. There is often prolonged thematic integration between voice and continuo in solo textures, and a number of solo verses are accompanied by four contrapuntally integrated string parts in the style of the older polyphonic viol anthem. There are two Italianate mannerisms in the first verse of 'The Lord hear thee' (Ex. 4)[8] that are distinctive features of Locke's style:

---

[5] Fitzwilliam MS 88, f. 138; ed. John E. West, London, n.d.

[6] Fitzwilliam MS 88, f. 141; ed. Heathcote D. Statham, Oxford, 1925.

[7] Fitzwilliam MS 88, f. 31.

[8] Ibid., f. 38ᵛ.

sounding of the note of resolution against the suspended dissonance
between inner parts in bar 4; and the figure between bars 4 and 5 where
the tenor leaps up a major third from an anticipatory dissonance to a
consonance. The first of these is to be found constantly in Purcell's
multi-part textures. Locke's melodic lines could be more relentlessly
disjunct than those of his English contemporaries. There is a suggestion
of this in the extract, but it is more forcefully illustrated in the first ten
bars of the anthem 'Lord, let me know my end'.[9]

Ex. 4

Locke's ensemble verses are customarily in four parts, although six-
part writing is not uncommon. Textures, particularly those in duple
time, are thoroughly contrapuntal, and independent instrumental lines
are found frequently in both ensemble verses and choruses. Verses and
choruses can be smoothly integrated, whereas Humfrey and Blow
usually kept them separate; the final 'Alleluia' of 'When the Son of
Man'[10] alternates verse and chorus accompanied by independent instruments in a manner that was to be extended by Purcell. Locke's harmonic
idiom is conceived in long fluent lines, and the acute chromatic in-
tensification of Humfrey and Blow is comparatively rare in his church

⁹ Ibid., f. 133ᵛ. Quoted in Fellowes, op. cit., pp. 126–7.
¹⁰ Fitzwilliam MS 88, f. 36ᵛ.

music. The tortuous chromaticism of the first two choruses of 'Turn thy face from my sins'[11] is exceptional.

Purcell's two earliest verse anthems with strings date from about 1680. Perhaps the most striking characteristic of 'Behold now, praise the Lord'[12] is the continuous experiment with chromatic inflections, often for more purely musical than illustrative reasons. They pervade the work from the symphony, where they preclude any internal repose, to the final ten-part paragraph for verse, chorus and instruments, where they contribute pungency to the dense harmonic texture. The technique derives from Humfrey and produces, for example, his pattern of a major third followed by a perfect fourth over subdominant-like degrees, in both the symphony and the second verse.[13] Other inflections found throughout this anthem include the augmented fifth and the sinuous juxtaposition of major and minor thirds and sevenths. The work concludes with a so-called English cadence juxtaposing minor and major thirds over the dominant such as was used commonly by Blow and Locke but never by Humfrey.[14]

The symphony falls into Humfrey's duple-triple homophonic mould; its first section has his unsettled tonality, and the second is dominated by his characteristic phrase structure of 2 + 2 + 4 bars. Each of the two ritornellos develops material from the previous verse, and each of the two ATB verses is predominantly homophonic, both suggesting the practice of Humfrey. Most interesting, however, is the final 'Gloria' for ATB verse, four-part chorus and independent strings, which culminates in a melismatic 'Amen' suggesting a later Italianate style. Its language and texture, in which the groups are offset antiphonally and finally united, are almost identical to the final sections of Locke's 'Sing unto the Lord, O ye saints of his' and 'When the Son of Man'.

The second early anthem in this category, 'My beloved spake', exists in two slightly different versions,[15] the first of which may well date from as early as 1679, the second from no later than 1683. It is a long work, which is unified by recurring sections and ritornellos that develop material from the preceding verse; the predominant influence is that of Humfrey. The symphony is in the latter's homophonic triple-time pattern, and the opening of its second version is dominated by the

[11] Ibid., f. 131; ed. Anthony Greening, London, 1968.

[12] Purcell Society, xiiia (London, 1921), 49.

[13] Ibid., p. 49, bar 5, and p. 54, bar 13, respectively.

[14] For a very similar instance in the work of Locke, see the end of the second chorus of his 'When the Son of Man', Fitzwilliam MS 88, f. 37v.

[15] The first version is found in Purcell Society, xiiia.24.

rhythm ♩♩.♪ | ♩.♪♩, which was grafted by Humfrey from French models into many of his own symphonies (Ex. 5).[16] All but one of the verses are ATBB ensembles; a number are in two sections, often with the change of metre introducing a significant change of texture in the

Ex. 5

manner of Humfrey. The second verse, 'For lo the winter is past', and its ritornello change the key to the tonic minor. This type of tonal contrast, which recurs in Purcell's later anthems, is unknown in Humfrey's mature work, but it is a feature of the first four sections of Blow's 'Sing we merrily'.[17] Perhaps the strongest single imprint of Humfrey's language is found in the homophonic verse 'And the voice of the turtle is heard in our land', where in the second bar the alto falls a diminished fifth to a major third over the subdominant and moves to a perfect fourth before the bass proceeds to the dominant (Ex. 6).

Ex. 6

[16] Fitzwilliam MS 117, p. 409.   [17] Fitzwilliam MS 88, f. 15ᵛ.

The verse that follows the central repetition of the symphony is a solo song in two sections for tenor with a violin obbligato. The combination of solo voice and obbligato violin is encountered in Humfrey's 'By the waters of Babylon', 'Hear my crying, O God' and 'O give thanks unto the Lord', but the instance in the second verse of 'Cry aloud and spare not'[18] is rare in Blow's work at this period. The opening of Purcell's verse provides an excellent example of the extent to which his chromatic harmony can result from the dictates of linear contour even in a small number of parts (Ex. 7). In this instance it differs from

Ex. 7

Humfrey's harmony, which is more often vertically conceived. The principal factor is the violin's imitation of the voice; the chromatic inflection on 'green', itself a technique derived from Humfrey, affects the interval of a sixth with the bass in bar 2, whereas in bar 3 it affects a third, and the same melodic phrase thus occasions in close proximity two quite different harmonic progressions. An innovation by Purcell is the use of the time-signature 𝄴 in the penultimate section, an 'Allelulia',[19] implying a brisk speed twice as fast as the section marked 𝄵.[20] There is no instance of its use in the church music of Humfrey or Locke, or of Blow as early as this, although both Humfrey and Locke used it in their secular music.

Purcell, like Blow, tended to reserve the verse anthem with strings for festive and paean-like texts and to use a more intimate medium for penitential settings. There are many of these among the smaller verse anthems without strings, the category in which most of Purcell's earliest church music is to be found. The four or five examples written probably by 1680 provide a clear picture of Purcell's most derivative and formative years. Furthermore, the technical insecurity, uncritical experimentation and awkward word-setting found in a number of them suggest that he had to labour over the medium for a number of years

[18] Ibid., f. 28v.   [19] Purcell Society, xiiia.44.
[20] John Playford, *An Introduction to the Skill of Musick*, London, 1674, p. 34.

before achieving the mastery of the early 1680s; the most uneven of these early anthems is 'O Lord our governor'.[21] 'Lord, who can tell'[22] probably dates from no later than 1678[23] and in both structure and language strongly reflects the style of Humfrey. It consists of three ensemble verses for TTB and a chorus setting of the 'Gloria'. The first two verses closely follow two structural patterns regularly employed by Humfrey. Both verses begin with a subject–answer dialogue in which the first voice sings the subject and each of the remaining voices in turn repeats a modified version. This culminates in a largely homophonic ensemble which can be related to the original subject.[24] The first verse is in duple time, and its subject is arioso-like; the second is in triple time, and its subject is more lyrical. At the central modulation of the binary structure of both verses, new thematic material is introduced. Purcell's continuo line is usually independent of the bass voice, and, like Humfrey's and unlike Locke's, it provides a comparatively slow-moving harmonic foundation thematically independent of the upper lines. In the third verse the third syllable of 'acceptable' falls awkwardly on the first beat of bar 69, but only seven bars later the word 'strength' is firmly placed at the height of a phrase on the chord with a major third and a minor sixth.

On the grounds of its highly derivative style and uneven quality, 'Turn thou us, O good Lord'[25] strongly suggests a date before 1678 and may well be Purcell's earliest extant anthem. Its single source is in an early eighteenth-century hand and provides no clue to the date of composition. Again the influence of Humfrey predominates. The work is made up of three solo verses for tenor and a central ATB verse and chorus which are repeated at the end. The solos are all passages of arioso with short phrases and frequent cadences, and the word-setting ranges from a cumbersome first phrase to the sensitive handling of 'thou sparest' at bar 20 with the rhythm | ♩ ♩.♪ |, and the repetition of 'look' on weak beats, separated by rests on strong beats, in bar 69. There are continual reminders of Humfrey's species of sinuous chromaticism (Ex. 8). The flat inflection in the second bar is preceded by a momentary augmented fifth which is symptomatic of the harmonic

---

[21] Purcell Society, xxix.152.   [22] Ibid., xxix.28.

[23] Watkins Shaw, 'A Contemporary Source of English Music of the Purcellian Period', *Acta Musicologica*, xxxi (1959), 40.

[24] Examples of the subject-answer dialogue are found at the openings of Humfrey's anthems 'Like as the hart', 'Lord, teach us to number our days' and 'The King shall rejoice' (*Musica Britannica*, xxxiv.107 and 118 and xxxv.54 respectively).

[25] Purcell Society, xxxii.111.

Ex. 8

who turn to thee in weep-ing, fast - - - ing and pray - - ing.

concentration of the device. The ATB verse is harmonically propelled, with one voice continually pitted against the other two paired ones, and the end of the verse illustrates the cadential pattern of the minor third followed by the major third over the subdominant (Ex. 9a). That these

Ex. 9

(a)

- on, be brought to con - fu - si - on,

- on, be brought, be brought to con - fu - si - on,

- on, be brought to con - fu - si - on,

(b)

as scar - let, they ——————shall be as wool.

crim-son, like crim-son, they shall' be as wool.

crim-son, like crim-son, they shall be as wool.

details, textural and harmonic, are derived from Humfrey is clearly demonstrated by the end of the second verse of his 'Hear, O heav'ns' (Ex. 9b).[26] The consecutive sevenths between the upper parts at the cadence in the Purcell example—what Morley would have termed exasperating the cadence—were an Italianate mannerism common in Humfrey, Blow and Locke.

Another early Purcell anthem on which the strongest influence is still the work of Humfrey is 'Who hath believed our report',[27] dating probably from about 1679. Its long passages of solo arioso in both ATTB dialogues and solo sections are particularly reminiscent of

[26] *Musica Britannica*, xxxiv.87.   [27] Purcell Society, xiiia.11.

EEO

Humfrey's 'Hear, O heav'ns'. The melodic lines are permeated with chromatic intervals in the pathetic style, and the continuo ine is principally harmonic rather than being at all thematically integrated. Word-setting is handled more expressively than in the earlier anthems; it makes liberal use of anacruses, rests, and repetition of significant words. The last verse is a solo song for tenor, the first of its two sections an arioso in duple time, the second a more lyrical aria-like texture in triple time. This pattern is found regularly in Humfrey's work,[28] but he would mark the division between the sections with a modulation to a related key, whereas here and elsewhere Purcell remains firmly in the tonic. The short homophonic chorus, placed at the centre and repeated at the end of the anthem, is based largely on the ATTB verse which precedes its first appearance.

The most accomplished of these early anthems, and that showing the strongest signs of Purcell's emerging individuality, is 'Out of the deep',[29] which must date from about 1680. Humfrey's influence is still strong, but there are also demonstrable debts to Blow and Locke. Without any of the madrigalian illustrativeness of Morley's or Tomkins's settings, it opens with a subject-answer dialogue for TrAB in which the second and third entries are compressed, and the writing is more thoroughly contrapuntal than when Humfrey uses this pattern. A passage from the first verse, in which a succession of cross-relations results from the sharpened inflections in the top part (Ex. 10a), bears a remarkable similarity to a progression at the end of the first verse of Humfrey's 'O be joyful' (Ex. 10b).[30] In the second verse, from bar 16, Purcell subjects a declamatory parlando phrase, 'O let thine ears consider well', to imitation in a manner similar to Humfrey's treatment of 'My heart also in the midst of my body' from bar 64 of 'O Lord my God' (Humfrey's subject and answer can be seen in Ex. 1 above). The second half of the verse is a triple-time ensemble propelled by a striding bass, and it concludes with two chords in which the minor third of the first falls to an open octave in the second. Both techniques are distinctive features of Humfrey's language and became grafted on to Purcell's style, the second nowhere more poignantly than at the final cadence of 'Hear my prayer, O Lord'.[31]

The first verse after the central chorus (derived from the preceding

---

[28] See for example the tenor verse 'Now when I think thereupon' in 'Like as the hart' (Fitzwilliam MS 88, f. 7, and *Musica Britannica*, xxxiv.113).

[29] Purcell Society, xxxii.8.

[30] *Musica Britannica*, xxxiv.130.

[31] Fitzwilliam MS 88, f. 83ᵛ, and Purcell Society, xxviii.138.

Ex. 10

(a)

(b)

verse) is an aria in duple time for the bass, built over a two-bar ground. This is the earliest of the mere five instances of a ground in Purcell's church music, and its use could well have been influenced by Blow's slightly earlier anthem 'O give thanks unto the Lord and call upon his name',[32] whose symphony and first verse are built on a ground bass. Blow's influence is suggested also by the change to the tonic major from the beginning of the last verse. Locke is recalled by the rising-third mannerism to which attention was drawn in Ex. 4 above; it is found here at bar 20 in the treble.

With the third and fourth categories of anthem we move to a slightly later date and into the realms of some of Purcell's sacred masterpieces. Without being in any way derivative, his anthems in the chorus–verse–chorus category show a particular affinity with the five fine examples of this type by Blow referred to above. 'Lord, how long wilt thou be angry',[33] dating probably from about 1680–82, is made up of two five-part choruses separated by an ATB verse. The first chorus builds an intricate polyphonic and chromatic texture on a point whose principal

[32] Oxford, Christ Church MS 628, p. 96.
[33] Fitzwilliam MS 88, f. 87v, and Purcell Society, xxix.19.

characteristic is the affecting fall of a diminished fourth. This has an affinity with the point which opens Blow's earlier 'O God, wherefore art thou absent from us', and like Blow's it is answered in stretto. The second chorus of Blow's anthem (Ex. 11) illustrates how in his work traditional five-part contrapuntal textures can be permeated with expressive falling intervals and chromatic inflections in a manner whose influence on Purcell is readily apparent in anthems such as 'Lord, how long wilt thou be angry'. Like Blow's second chorus, Purcell's begins

Ex. 11

with massed homophony before breaking into angular counterpoint. Purcell's chorus, however, concludes with a triple-time section which opens in the relative major, and it has a remarkably clear sense of gathering momentum.

The short ATB verse which separates the two choruses is more harmonically activated. Its harmonic texture suggests the influence of

Ex. 12

writing such as the beginning of the verse following the first chorus in Blow's 'Save me, O God' (Ex. 12),[34] which was composed by 1676, though Purcell's voices have more melodic independence. By way of contrast, the single internal verse in Locke's 'Turn thy face from my sins'[35] is a contrapuntal dialogue between alto, tenor and bass voices.

For the sustained wealth of its invention and technique (Burney's strictures notwithstanding), the eight-part 'O Lord God of hosts',[36] dating from the same period, deserves a place among Purcell's finest works. It falls into five sections alternating choruses with a six-part and a five-part verse. Its choruses are almost devoid of falling pathetic intervals, and with long lines whose chromatic notes amount to little more than third- and seventh-like degrees of the scale, they accumulate a rich polyphonic web which suggests a direct descent from such a movement as the first part of Gibbons's 'O clap your hands together'.

The first verse begins with ten bars more pathetic in style for ATB, which are answered by another ten for TrTrA. This same antiphonal contrast between an upper and a lower trio in a similar harmonic style infects the last chorus at bars 109–20 and also characterizes the first verses of Blow's 'God is our hope and strength' and 'O God, wherefore art thou absent from us'. Blow is again recalled by the change of tonality in the second verse to the tonic minor. This contains perhaps the most exquisite moment in the whole anthem: at bar 81 the phrase 'Turn us again, O God' is repeated and developed at a higher pitch in a passage of penetrating harmonic insight.

The full anthem was the least common species at this period; neither Humfrey nor Locke left any examples, and there is only one by Blow written before 1683, the four-part 'The Lord hear thee'. The texture of Purcell's five-part 'Remember not, Lord, our offences',[37] probably

[34] Fitzwilliam MS 88, f. 134ᵛ; ed. West, London, n.d.
[35] See p. 51, note 11.
[36] Fitzwilliam MS 88, f. 92, and Purcell Society, xxix.130.
[37] Fitzwilliam MS 88, f. 99, and Purcell Society, xxxii.19.

dating from the early 1680s, is similar to that of the choruses of the anthems in the previous category. In its smooth integration of polyphony and homophony it reflects the influence of the anthems of the earlier polyphonic period while being an unmistakable product of its more harmonically conscious age. Purcell's mastery of the older style, and its renewal with the most advanced melodic and harmonic language of the day, is seen at its most expressive in another work from the same period, the unfinished eight-part 'Hear my prayer, O Lord'.[38] In its mere thirty-four bars, this noble torso illustrates both the diversity of his formative influences and the extent to which his genius outstripped all his contemporaries in its technical and emotional breadth. The anthem is constructed from a diatonic subject and a chromatic countersubject whose sinuous contours, both *rectus* and *inversus*, point clearly to the influence of Humfrey (Exx. 13a and 13b).[39] Unlike Humfrey,

Ex. 13

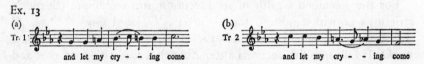

(a)
Tr. 1   and let my cry - - ing come

(b)
Tr 2   and let my cry - - ing come

however, Purcell builds a rich texture of wonderfully expressive chromatic harmony by means of an intricate contrapuntal interaction of just these three phrases in eight parts. By this time he had the experience of the string fantasias behind him, and 'Hear my prayer, O Lord' stands as a masterpiece of economy and compression among Purcell's very greatest works.

In examining the stylistic origins of Purcell's church music one is continually confronted with the pervasive influence of Pelham Humfrey. Purcell shared Humfrey's innate sensitivity to the expressive power of chromatic harmony, and the skill of the master undeniably fired the genius of the pupil. Furthermore, Purcell at length developed Humfrey's assured handling of the accentuations of language. From Blow he inherited both the compact anthem with substantial choruses separated by shorter verses, and a greater length and textural diversity in the verse anthem with strings. From Locke he learned the art of writing prolonged contrapuntal textures as Blow had done before him. It must have been the example of Locke that prompted Purcell to include in some of his verse anthems with strings sections in a large number of parts, in which verse, chorus and instruments are offset antiphonally and then integrated, with rich harmonic results. But the nature of Purcell's genius was such that he could appropriate and

[38] See p. 56, note 31.   [39] See above, p. 46, and Ex. 1.

develop those very diverse characteristics that defined the individuality of these three composers. Their influence on him played a decisive part in fashioning a style that was to produce an output second to none in the Europe of his day.

(*b*) The Domestic Sacred Music
NIGEL FORTUNE

In the first of these two studies the principal evidence is drawn from the music, both his own and others', that Purcell copied into the first of his three big autograph volumes, Fitzwilliam Museum, Cambridge, MS 88. The music in the second one, British Museum Add. MS 30930, is entirely his own: sacred vocal music at the front, string chamber music at the back.[1] He must have begun this volume about three years after the first, that is in 1680: this date appears at the front, and most of the four-part fantasias at the back bear precise dates in June and August of that year.

Of the sixteen vocal works one is the opening verse of an anthem, 'Hear me, O Lord, and that soon', found complete in a slightly different form in Fitzwilliam MS 88, and four are settings of Latin texts, which suggests that they may have been commissioned for private use; the remaining eleven belong to the category of English domestic ensemble music. The tradition of private devotional music stretches back through the seventeenth century. Much of it is for one or two voices, and Purcell's sacred songs and duets therefore belong more obviously to it. Among composers who, like Purcell here, wrote for three or more voices his most distinguished forerunner is probably George Jeffreys,[2] but he is unlikely to have known his music, which was written in the country well away from London.

Twelve such pieces by Purcell survive:[3]

[1] See Nigel Fortune and Franklin B. Zimmerman, 'Purcell's Autographs', *Henry Purcell, 1659–1695: Essays on his Music*, ed. Imogen Holst, London, 1959, pp. 110–12.

[2] See Peter Aston, 'Tradition and Experiment in the Devotional Music of George Jeffreys', *Proceedings of the Royal Musical Association*, xcix (1972–3), 105–15.

[3] They are published in Purcell Society, xxx (London, 1965), 109–201. Separate reprints of all but the first, fifth and eleventh of the pieces listed here have been issued, Purcell Society Reprints, viii–xvi, London, 1966.

Opening words	Voices (all plus continuo)	Text
Ah! few and full of sorrow (*unfinished*)	SATB	George Sandys: from Job, xvi
Early, O Lord, my fainting soul	SSAB	John Patrick: Psalm 63
Hear me, O Lord, the great support	ATB	Patrick: Psalm 4
Lord, I can suffer	SSAB	Patrick: Psalm 6, first version
Lord, not to us (*unfinished*)	ATB	Patrick: Psalm 115, second version
O all ye people, clap your hands	SSTB	Patrick: Psalm 47
O happy man (*unfinished*)	SSAB	Patrick: Psalm 112, second version
O, I'm sick of life	ATB	Sandys: from Job, x
O Lord our governor	SSAB	Patrick: Psalm 8
Plung'd in the confines of despair	TTB	Patrick: Psalm 130
Since God so tender a regard	TTB	Patrick: Psalm 116, first version
When on my sick bed I languish	TTB	Thomas Flatman

The one piece in this list that Purcell did not include in his autograph collection is 'O happy man', which is found in MS Mus.c.28 of the Bodleian Library, Oxford, and MS 518 (Vol. 1) of the Royal College of Music, London; these are sources of the later eighteenth century, but since they contain most of the companion pieces this twenty-one-bar fragment can be presumed to be by Purcell too. For all but one of the authenticated pieces British Museum Add. MS 30930, ff. 3 ff., is the only source that need be seriously considered; the exception is 'Plung'd in the confines of despair', of which there is, in Barber Institute, University of Birmingham, MS 5001, p. 328, an additional autograph copy, of a slightly different, apparently earlier, version; since it comes first in Add. MS 30930 this may have been the first of these pieces to be written, though following rebinding in 1896 the leaves of the volume may not be in their original order.

As can be seen, the words of nine of these works are adaptations of psalms. It was in 1679 that there was published in London John Patrick's *A Century of Select Psalms, and Portions of the Psalms of David, Especially those of praise. Turned into Meter, and fitted to the usual Tunes in Parish Churches. For the use of the Charter-House*; further editions appeared in 1684, 1689 and up to 1742, and in 1694 Patrick brought out a version of the complete psalter, *The Psalms of*

David in Meter, some of whose versions, including 'O Lord our governor' and 'Plung'd in the confines of despair', differ from his earlier ones. Patrick (1632–95), younger brother of Simon Patrick, Bishop of Ely, was 'Preacher at the Charter-House' from 1671 until his death and according to the *Dictionary of National Biography* was held in 'high repute among many dissenting congregations'.

Since the only copies of three of Purcell's pieces are unfinished, it is possible that he did not complete composing them. If therefore these pieces were not performed, conceivably the completed pieces were not performed either but were written as exercises. But the contrary possibility may be entertained that in his earliest years as a composer Purcell enjoyed a professional relationship with the Charterhouse—a foundation for some 180 men and boys established by Thomas Sutton in 1611—and that Patrick himself, in order to provide a change from 'the usual Tunes', asked him to compose settings of his texts (and even those of the other two poets as well). Certainly Patrick seems to have had some responsibility for music there: 'the Master and Preacher shall have Superintendancy over the Chappel Clerk, Organist, and Sexton, to see if each of them carefully perform the Duties of his place . . . the second, in teaching the poor Scholars to Sing, and playing on the Organs at set times of Divine Service . . . ' .[4] Other tentative evidence for Purcell's connections with the Charterhouse can be adduced. 'Who can tell how oft he offendeth' is from 'a preparatory prayer before the Sacrament' there.[5] Even though its text is not very similar, his anthem 'Lord, who can tell' could have been commissioned for, or at least sung in, a service in association with this prayer. If it is objected that this is unlikely because one source in which it appears is a set of part-books from the Chapel Royal it could in turn be countered that the repertory there was not necessarily an exclusive one. Indeed this work is also found in a set from St. Paul's Cathedral, and since it must therefore have been performed, and may even have originated, there, performance at the Charterhouse is likewise not impossible. It was written 'probably not later than 1678',[6] and although it is Purcell's one anthem whose verse sections are for TTB a quarter of the domestic sacred pieces are scored for this combination; these facts may not be unconnected. Finally, firmer evidence of Purcell's connections with the Charterhouse

[4] Samuel Herne, *Domus Carthusiana; or, An Account of the most Noble Foundation of the Charter-House near Smithfield in London*, London, 1677 p. 124.

[5] Ibid., p. 270.

[6] Watkins Shaw, 'A Contemporary Source of English Music of the Purcellian Period', *Acta Musicologica*, xxvi (1959), 40.

at a later date, 1688 or thereabouts, is afforded by his 'Blessed is the man', the best source of which describes it as a 'Psalm Anthem for ye Charterhouse sung upon ye Founders day . . . ' .[7] It may also be added that in the Birmingham University manuscript mentioned above 'Plung'd in the confines of despair' appears alongside music which is all known to have been composed for the court. This piece (and possibly some of its fellows) may also have been heard at court, but it is unlikely to have been commissioned for performance there.[8]

Like other such verses, Patrick's metrical psalms are generally commonplace in diction and pedestrian in rhythm. But one can readily see his appeal for a composer, especially one such as Purcell, who already at twenty-one knew how to invest even prosaic texts with music of the rarest poetry; occasionally, however, Patrick himself rises to subtler heights, as in the words quoted in Ex. 7 or as at the beginning of Psalm 4, which illustrates the rhyme scheme of all his texts set by Purcell except 'Plung'd in the confines':

> Hear me, O Lord, the great support
> Of my integrity;
> Thou hast my former troubles eas'd,
> Now to my pray'rs draw nigh.

> Fond men! that would my glory stain,
> My government despise;
> How long will you pursue vain hopes
> And please yourselves with lies?

Since in addition Flatman's text does nothing to disturb A. K. Holland's view of him as 'appropriately named', this leaves the two passages paraphrased by Sandys from the Book of Job as certainly the most distinguished words in this group of pieces. Not only are the texts of these two poets concerned with death, but, notwithstanding Patrick's claim that his psalms are 'Especially those of praise', more than half of Purcell's selection from them, like William Lawes's from Sandys in his *Choice Psalmes* of 1648, concentrates on the intimate, supplicating, penitential or gloomy ones. Despite a festive piece such as 'O all ye people', the overriding mood of these dozen works is dark and intro-

[7] See Zimmerman, 'Anthems of Purcell and Contemporaries in a newly rediscovered "Gostling Manuscript"', *Acta Musicologica*, xli (1969), 67. For information on the Charterhouse I am indebted to Mr John W. Wilson, lately Director of Music at the school that still bears this name.

[8] See Shaw, 'A Collection of Musical Manuscripts in the Autographs of Henry Purcell and other English Composers, *c*.1665–86', *The Library*, xiv (1959), 126.

verted, like so much else that Purcell was writing about 1680—anthems such as 'Out of the deep', the first settings of the funeral sentences, 'Jehova, quam multi sunt hostes' (one of the Latin pieces in Add. MS 30930) or the slow sections of the fantasias. This intensity is also no doubt a factor in his scoring: tenor and bass voices predominate, and the alto parts frequently lie so low as to be comfortably singable now only by a tenor.

All these pieces are of course to be sung by one voice to a part: they are certainly not choral music. Almost throughout it is Purcell's practice to alternate sections for the full complement of voices with sections for a single voice. Though naturally he ends with his complete ensemble it seems immaterial whether he starts with a full section or with a solo. In the settings of Patrick's texts, which because of their rhyme scheme are best seen as consisting of four-line stanzas, the changes of texture usually occur between stanzas. The two consecutive solos in 'Ah! few and full' and the setting as a duet (AB) of the fifth verse of 'Lord I can suffer' are exceptional. No singer has more than one solo. It is also rare for the same type of voice to be heard in two successive solos: the TTB 'O, I'm sick' is exceptional in having two tenor solos but none for bass. Except that the fifth verse is divided between two textures, the disposition of voices in the seven-verse ATB 'Hear me, O Lord' is typical: ATB–ATB–T–ATB–B/ATB–A–ATB. But one of the most remarkable features of these pieces is their endless textural variety, the complete assurance with which the young composer proclaims his imaginative response to the texts and spurns a stereotyped form. In 'Plung'd in the confines', for example, the bass solo for verse 2 spills over, across a change of time-signature from duple to triple, into the first two lines of verse 3, which are then repeated to new music continuing as a complete TTB ensemble to the end of the verse: the structure and tonality—touched on below—of the setting of these verses (bars 22–48) may derive from Pelham Humfrey,[9] but the imagination expressed through the choice of form and the quality of invention is wholly Purcellian.

'Since God so tender' affords one of the half-dozen instances in Purcell's sacred music of a ground bass. It is a simple one, four bars long. He establishes it as accommodating the setting of two lines of text, but later on he shows his early mastery of this type of structure in the subtlety with which he contradicts expectation by expanding or contracting this textual disposition. Even so, the overall textural scheme for the six verses is quite schematic: T1–TTB–B–TTB–T2–TTB,

[9] See the previous essay for references to bipartite structures by Humfrey.

the first two with the time-signature 𝄴 (²⁄₂), the next two with 𝄵 (⁶⁄₄), the last two with 𝄴 (⁴⁄₄). All but one of the verses are basically in F major. The exception is the second, and not the least skilful feature of the piece is the way in which, responding to a sharp emotional change in the text, Purcell set it in F minor while retaining the major ground (Ex. 1).

Ex. 1

This work is typical in being in one basic tonality. Purcell always, of course, varies his central key with transitory modulations, sometimes prompted by the text: one such occurs at the already mentioned third verse of 'Plung'd in the confines', when not only the triple time but also a change to the relative major, F, underlines the new sentiment in the text, 'But thou forgiveness dost proclaim'. Some of his short-lived modulations are to remote tonal areas: striking examples include the progress through distant sharp keys in the penultimate verse of 'O Lord our governor', which is in B flat, and, still more telling, because it comes within a few bars of the beginning and is more closely motivated by the text, the exploration of remote flat keys in the E minor 'Ah! few and full of sorrow' (Ex. 2). These passages are analogous to those found in other works by Purcell at this time in which he appears to delight in remote modulations for their own sake: certainly there is nothing in the text of the 'Gloria patri' to prompt the exploration of A minor in his

Ex. 2

C minor setting of this text,[10] and there are comparable 'neutral' examples in the fantasias. All, executed with breathtaking skill, serve to underline his precocious mastery. More settled changes are normally changes of mode, as in the case of 'Since God so tender' discussed above; in the adoption of C major instead of the prevailing C minor for the sixth verse of 'Hear me, O Lord' (whose structure is outlined above); and in the comparable G major close of 'Lord, I can suffer': 'The Lord hath heard my pray'r', runs the text, and the sense of relief after five verses of G minor supplication is heightened by a change from duple to triple time and prolonged by a thirteen-bar 'Alleluia', reverting to duple time but still in the major.

The texture found in Ex. 2 is highly characteristic of Purcell's ensemble writing for four or more voices in his early sacred music, especially in opening sections. A loosely imitative fabric, producing a good deal of passing dissonance, builds up through a busier network of contrasting note-values to more homophonic cadential bars. There are lines of text, as in Ex. 2, that demand two contrasting musical figures; their imitative treatment makes the texture denser still, as at the conflicting movement between the parts in the last two bars of this example. In the anthems an example of a comparable texture is the first section of 'Let mine eyes run down with tears', also an early work.[11] The technique is particularly close to Humfrey in the first section of 'Early, O Lord'. This clearly stems from the 'subject-answer dialogue' that Peter Dennison has found widely in Humfrey[12] in which the voices separately sing versions of a phrase before coming together in a loosely imitative and then more homophonic texture: the three stages are clearly seen in bars 1–9, 9–14 and 14–21 of 'Early, O Lord'.

Such textures are also found in the three-part ensembles in Purcell's domestic pieces. In these thinner textures separate entries are less common than more regular overlapping imitation as found at the start of 'Plung'd in the confines' (Ex. 9) and 'When on my sick bed'. Later in the second of these pieces at the text 'Methinks I hear some gentle spirit say: / "Be not fearful, come away!" ' Purcell hints at the instinctive dramatic composer he later proved himself: the second tenor, in the guise of 'some gentle spirit', is already singing the second line (soon echoed by the first tenor) before the bass enters with the first

---

[10] British Museum, Add. MS 30930, f. 7ᵛ, and Purcell Society, xxxii, rev. edn., London, 1967, p. 163.

[11] Purcell Society, xxix, rev. edn., London, 1965, p. 1.

[12] See above, p. 54, and idem, *The Life and Work of Pelham Humfrey* (unpublished dissertation), University of Oxford, 1970, pp. 123 and 201.

line. But the second verse of 'Hear me, O Lord' contains as forthright a passage of this kind as any in Purcell (Ex. 3); the major tonality also enters here with bold effect after fifteen bars of minor and helps to underline the change to more sharply etched melodic contours.

Ex. 3

The same piece shows another influence from Humfrey: the momentum engendered in arioso writing by the distribution of the text among all the voices. The extract shown in Ex. 4a may be compared with Ex. 4b from Humfrey's anthem 'Hear, O heav'ns'.[13]

One of Purcell's favourite ways of organizing a three-part texture also derives from earlier music. One voice, usually the highest, is pitted against the other two. Dennison illustrates this above[14] from Purcell's early anthem 'Turn thou us, O good Lord'. As he says, Purcell may have learned this device from Humfrey, who probably inherited it in turn from older composers: it is found, for instance, between bars 6 and 9 of Matthew Locke's 'In the beginning, O Lord', between bars 5 and 11

[13] *Humfrey: Complete Church Music: i,* ed. Dennison (Musica Britannica, xxxiv), London, 1972, p. 86.
[14] See Ex. 9a, p. 55.

Ex. 4

of his 'O give thanks unto the Lord' and at the words 'The Lord is the strength of my light' in William Lawes's 'The Lord is my light.[15] One of the clearest examples in Purcell's domestic music again occurs in 'Hear me, O Lord'. This begins with the alto and tenor singing the first two lines of text in thirds over the instrumental bass; then, when the bass voice enters in bar 4, the tenor, acting as a pivot, joins it in thirds, while the alto, now on its own, imitates them a third higher at the half bar. There is a striking variant of this principle, for dramatic ends, in the closing bars of the scena 'In guilty night', which could well date from the same period.[16] Soprano (the Witch of Endor) and bass (the ghost of Samuel) sing 'Farewell' together to doomed Saul (alto), who in counterpoint with them can reply only with repeated cries of 'Oh!'. 'O, I'm sick of life' (Ex. 5) begins with the bass voice set against the other two, between which, moreover, the intervals are less rigid than in 'Hear me, O Lord', then the succeeding bars show another texture that Purcell employs in this music—a sort of supple harmonic chanting, possibly deriving from psalm-singing or ultimately from Italian madrigals, at least one of which, Monteverdi's 'Cruda Amarilli', Purcell copied.[17] Such a texture contrasts sharply with imitative writing and heightens the impact of the words, especially in a long clause and especially when just previously, as in the present case, a short verbal phrase has been emphasized by repetition and imitation; other instances may be found in 'Hear me, O Lord' (bars 39–41) and more briefly in bars 14 and 17–18 of 'Early, O Lord'. The few bars shown in Ex. 5 afford a masterly demonstration of emotional intensity enhanced by the instinctively right timing of textural and metrical contrasts; and they tell us a lot too about Purcell's plastic handling of rhythm. The end of the same piece, on the other hand, offers one of the few examples of strict contrapuntal writing in Purcell's sacred music outside the canons. It is characteristic of him that the idea of 'confusion' in the words 'A land where death, confusion, endless night / And horror reign . . . ' should be fostered by movement in alternating voices

[15] The anthems by Locke ed. Hubert W. Hunt and John E. West respectively, London, n.d., the Lawes quoted in Peter le Huray, *Music and the Reformation in England, 1549–1660*, London, 1967, p. 348.

[16] Purcell Society, xxxii.136. The work appears in St. Michael's College, Tenbury, MS 1175, along with copies of the domestic sacred pieces apparently taken from Purcell's autograph volume; the lost autograph of 'In guilty night' may have been associated with that volume or even at some time been removed from it.

[17] See Zimmerman, 'Purcell and Monteverdi', *The Musical Times*, xcix 1958), 368.

Ex. 5

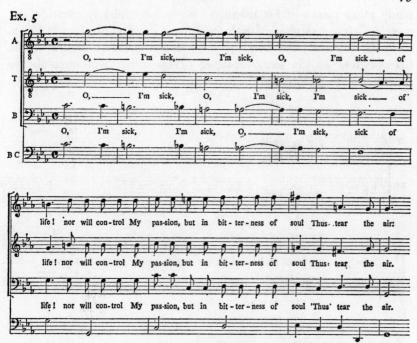

on each quaver beat and yet be underpinned by the discipline of a canon at a crotchet's distance, downward in the alto and tenor, by inversion in the bass (the directions are reversed when the text is repeated).

The solo writing in this music consists mainly of quite short ariosos, often shading into the succeeding ensemble sections. But one or two passages are aria-like, a type of movement also found in ensemble writing, as in the already mentioned third verse of 'Plung'd in the confines' or in the fifth verse (bars 46–64) of 'Hear me, O Lord'. This is true of the first two solos in 'Since God so tender', the first of which is very like a hymn tune. It is even truer of the soprano solo setting of verse 2 of 'Early, O Lord' and the alto solo setting of the penultimate verse of 'Hear me, O Lord', each isolated by a change of time. The latter, which brings a change of mode too, is disappointingly jogtrot; for once Purcell seems to have let a rigid metrical plan prevail over sensitive word-setting, especially in the last two lines. His ariosos are quite a different matter. Time and again the young composer, profiting perhaps from the example of Humfrey's meticulously lively word-setting in the ariosos of his sacred songs, shows the expressive response to English words that we know so well from the sacred songs and many other pieces of his maturity; he will completely override any metrical stresses conflicting with sense, as in the first two bars of Ex. 6, from 'O, I'm sick', and heighten key words by a more expansive line ('remorseless' in the same example) or by some vivid interval (the falling seventh at 'confound').

Ex. 6

Given the tortured pathos of so many of the texts of these pieces it is no surprise to find Purcell indulging frequently in a wide range of affective intervals in his melodic lines, in both solos and ensembles. The first few bars of Exx. 1 and 5 illustrate a common response to despairing words—an imitative chromatic descent. They are paralleled with almost neurotic obsessiveness in the second verse of 'Lord, I can suffer', one of the most intense passages in all Purcell (Ex. 7); possibly the continual crisp consonants were an added stimulus to him. He responds, moreover, with the same kind of supple madrigalian chanting as is found in Ex. 5. The same figure continues for a further five bars before yielding to a suaver one for the seven-bar setting of the last half of the verse. This section illustrates another common feature of Purcell's lines in this kind of music—their angularity. The remarkable contour of Ex. 8 is especially typical of bass parts, though by no means confined to them; it would not, however, be found in an imitative figure. As here, the jaggedness often stems from octave displacement,

Ex. 7

Ex. 8

While crush'd by thy hea — vy hand, O let' thy gent — ler touch - es heal.

and it is no surprise to find Purcell himself giving an *ossia*. This setting
was no doubt prompted by the words and is enhanced by the 'gentler'
continuation; at bar 53 in the alto part of 'Ah! few and full of sorrow'
a leap of an eleventh is associated with 'death'; and 'darkness' at the end
of 'O, I'm sick' is splendidly evoked in the first tenor by a major seventh
plunging down as from light into dark and reinforced on immediately
succeeding crotchet beats by plunging octaves in the other two voices.
Such passages can be paralleled in Purcell's other early works: for
example, in the harmonically rather immature progression at bar 89 of

the anthem 'Let God arise' and in the *ossia* at bar 149 of 'Man that is born of a woman'.[18]

Diminished intervals, invariably underlining an emotive text, are frequent. There is a striking one at the end of Ex. 6, another, to enhance 'despair', in the arresting opening of 'Plung'd in the confines of despair' (Ex. 9), another instance of a falling chromatic figure used

Ex. 9

imitatively and also including in the bass another diminished, because 'displaced', octave. Finally mention should be made of the many chromatically inflected melodies which Purcell possibly learned how to handle from Humfrey:[19] examples similar to those found in Humfrey and in Purcell's early anthems include the illustration of 'sighs and groans' at bar 35 of 'Lord, I can suffer', the second tenor line in the fourth bar of Ex. 1, and the setting of the words 'O, since I have so short a time to live' given to the alto in bars 40–41 (and again in bars 44–45) of 'O, I'm sick of life' (Ex. 10), which, like the instance referred to in

[18] Purcell Society, xxviii, rev. edn., London, 1967, p. 181, and xxix.50, respectively.
[19] See the previous essay, *passim*.

Ex.1, is very like the phrase suiting equally imploring words in the anthem 'Hear my prayer, O Lord' that Dennison quotes in the previous essay.[20]

Ex. 10

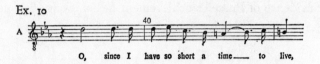

O, since I have so short a time___ to live,

It remains to say something more specific about Purcell's harmony in these domestic pieces. The textures and angular lines that we have seen give rise to incidental harmonic asperities and to the false relations that form part of his English inheritance: the foregoing examples include several instances, such as the simultaneous B♭ and B♮ in the last complete bar of Ex. 7. The same example and also Ex. 5 illustrate the harmony arising from imitative chromatic lines widely found in Purcell's early music, including, to mention just one instance, the opening section of 'In guilty night'. Such harmony makes emotive use of the augmented triad. In Exx. 5 and 7 this chord is associated with languishing or despairing texts, as it is by Blow in his anthem 'Save me, O God' (1676), quoted by Dennison as his Ex. 12. It was also used to intensify joy, perhaps in acute perception of the pain underlying true joy: Humfrey does this in 'Have mercy upon me, O God' (also quoted in the previous essay, in Ex. 2), and Purcell does too at the climactic point, bar 64, of his setting of the line 'No other joys can equal this' in 'Early, O Lord'. In this essay I have concentrated on the more introverted pieces, but even in his more straightforward, extrovert music Purcell uses harmonic change for emotive ends. For instance, the sudden intrusion of momentarily disturbed harmony at the very end of 'O all ye people, clap your hands', at the idea of God's judgement of the world, is all the more effective for coming after so much predominantly diatonic harmony.

Since they are a homogeneous group to which there is no exact parallel elsewhere in his career and because they were probably composed over a short period of time, the pieces discussed here afford important evidence of Purcell's imagination and technical assurance at a precise point in his career. That this should be the point when he reached his majority, not only as a man but as a composer, adds to their fascination. They are a contemporary counterpart to another self-sufficient group of pieces, the string fantasias: that Purcell copied these

[20] See Ex. 13a, p. 60.

two kinds of piece at either end of the same book emphasizes that as private chamber music for voices and instruments respectively they are complementary to each other. Only a very few other works, one or two of them anthems considered in the previous essay, offer comparably specific evidence of Purcell's achievement in his twenty-first year.

Some Notes on Editing Handel's 'Semele'

ANTHONY LEWIS

A composer's corrections, second thoughts and later versions are as much part of his workshop material as his sketchbooks and are equally fascinating: they give so many clues to the nature and habits of his creative thought. Handel did not leave much in the way of sketch material and one doubts if much ever existed. It would not have been typical of him or his age had it done so; the final structure was in most cases the justification of the initial idea, so what one finds are—rather than fragments—fully scored movements wholly or substantially completed and then set aside. In a sense Handel's works themselves are his sketchbooks; in them he can be seen shaping and modifying a theme or pattern over a long period of years with the care and persistence of Beethoven. Virtually any work of his one chooses, therefore, is likely to yield evidence of some aspect of his creative process, and *Semele*, of which a new edition appeared recently,[1] is no exception.

The various main changes that the musical text of *Semele* underwent have been admirably summarized by Winton Dean.[2] The chief casualties during the work's development were three arias, all delightful and two of them particularly striking. But Handel could be utterly ruthless with himself and nowhere more so—though this may surprise some—than in the number, order and length of his arias.

The first aria to be eliminated was one for Athamas in the first act. An E flat C Larghetto, it has two violin parts as well as continuo and explores some interesting chromatic ground. Of the two lines of text set in the first part:

---

[1] Ed. Anthony Lewis and Charles Mackerras, London, 1971.
[2] *Handel's Dramatic Oratorios amd Masques*, London, 1959, pp. 375 ff.

> See, she blushing turns her eyes;
> See, with sighs her bosom panting!

it is the second, with its reference to 'sighs', that has determined the character of the music (Ex. 1). Handel pursues this gently lyrical vein most expressively, just stopping to jolt his audience out of any complacency at the final cadence, with a disjunct pair of false relations of Purcellian audacity (Ex. 2). However, in his final scheme for the act this aria was clearly redundant, and it was replaced by a recitative. The only surviving trace of the aria is the melodic phrase opening the second part, which is transferred to the equivalent point in the recitative.

Another aria to be omitted belonged to the third act, at the stage in the libretto where Juno is flattering Semele and luring her to her doom. By means of a false mirror she persuades Semele (rather too easily, perhaps) that her face is of god-like beauty. This aria is unusual in construction; of the four lines of text, Handel separates the first from the remaining three:

> Behold in this mirror, whence comes my surprise;
> Such lustre and terror unite in your eyes,
> That mine cannot fix on a radiance so bright,
> 'Tis unsafe for the sense and too slipp'ry for sight.

There are two main balanced musical paragraphs, each representing both these verbal components, and a coda based on the second only. The key is E minor, and the first paragraph ends in G, the second in the dominant, giving an unusual and satisfying scheme. The setting (an Allegro in **C**—really $\frac{12}{8}$) is for full string orchestra supporting the voice, and apart from its formal interest does not appear on paper (how necessary that qualification is with Handel!) to be strongly characterized. It was replaced by a passage of recitative, which incorporates its first vocal phrase. Handel, now dividing the text evenly, set the first pair of lines as *secco* recitative, but he evidently felt that the second pair should be specially prominent and needed some lyrical element, so he turned them into three bars of measured arioso.

So far the new edition of *Semele* has concurred with Handel's final decision and has placed these arias in an appendix. But in a third case the editors have, no doubt presumptuously, decided to restore the aria to its original position. This is the aria for Cupid (the only music for the character) with which formerly the second scene of the second act opened. As the libretto describes it, 'She [Semele] is sleeping; Loves and Zephyrs waiting'. Cupid tells the Zephyrs to fan Semele with their 'silky wings' while he fills her dreams with pleasure and inspires 'new desire'. The music is ravishingly delicate; the strings are muted throughout, with no double basses or continuo and with the cellos doubling the violas—a truly ethereal texture. The 'larghetto' $\frac{3}{8}$ marking at the beginning changes to 'allegro' $\frac{6}{8}$ in the second part (in the minor), adding a further distinctive touch. Apart from the great attractiveness of the aria, its placing is both dramatically and musically relevant. Semele's 'Sleep' aria, which follows immediately, gains fuller meaning from Cupid's words that have preceded it, and the highly imaginative contrast of texture must surely have been deliberately contrived. Cupid, the airy deity, is supported only by upper-register string tone; Semele, the mortal, is accompanied by lower strings (marked 'Bassi', though usually played as cello solo) and continuo. The key relationship—G to E—is also very happy. It is difficult to understand why Handel banished such a delightful piece; perhaps he considered it not absolutely essential and in danger of unduly holding up the action at this point, or perhaps he simply could not find an adequate singer for such a finely poised aria. Certainly today it seems to add much to the effectiveness of the second act.

Later, Handel not only omitted complete arias but also made cuts and curtailments in other arias and recitatives in *Semele*. These are too many to enumerate here, but one is of special interest since it occurs in one of the best-known of all his arias, 'Where'er you walk'. The final, universally accepted version of this aria has a second part seven bars long leading to a cadence in C minor—the supertonic minor of B flat. There are two curious things about that relationship, one totally exceptional, the other unusual. First, one cannot call to mind any other aria in the whole of Handel in which the second part starts in the relative minor and ends in the supertonic minor. To an early eighteenth-century composer this would tend to create an awkward situation giving rise to the second curious feature of this tonal plan, namely the rather crudely exposed parallel fifths and octaves involved in the side-shift down to the tonic in the da capo. Both of these points are so untypical of Handel (though there is actually a very discreet pair of fifths in the course of the aria) that one is not surprised to find that his first thoughts were much more consistent with his usual practice. In the original version there were six additional bars culminating in a D minor cadence (Ex. 3). There is much to regret in the loss of these

Ex. 3

last six days—not least in the harmonic treatment of the first two of them—and the more satisfactory cadence. But Handel's acute sense of balance may well have been disturbed by two aspects of this original second part. He may have considered the last three bars too closely repetitive of what had gone before, and (possibly more important to him) the relative lengths of first and second parts were not in keeping with his preferred proportions. The first part is only nineteen bars long, and a second part of thirteen bars would have been longer than normal for him. His readiness to jettison such a beguiling continuation is further evidence of his self-critical attitude in all matters of structure and design.

Finally one must mention a passage in the libretto that did not achieve a setting at all, though Handel wrote out the words below staves as if he intended to set them. If formal considerations induced him to leave these four lines of Semele's without music, then it was a pity, since they have a bearing on that warm-hearted lady's motives. When at the crisis in the third act Jupiter swears to grant what she requires, Semele says:

> Then cast off this human shape which you wear,
> And Love since you are, like Love appear!

and then adds (without Handel's concurrence):

> When next you desire I should charm ye,
> As when Juno you bless,
> So you me must caress,
> And with all your omnipotence arm ye.

She was evidently resolved not to be a second-class wife and was prepared to risk incineration to prove it.

Anticipations of Dramatic Monody in the Late Works of Lassus

WOLFGANG BOETTICHER

My topic may seem unusual with regard to a composer who by 1585–90 had passed the prime of his life and who, like Palestrina, was regarded by the succeeding generation as a representative of a *stilus antiquus*, a *stilus gravis*. Hitherto Lassus has been classed as a conservative, a proponent of a *stilus ecclesiasticus* that has been contrasted with the *stilus theatralis* in the same way that the Palestrina tradition has been contrasted with the modern school of the time.[1] This clear-cut distinction between the old and new styles is still taken for granted even now, but its validity is doubtful. It is of course true that the achievements of the *prima* and *seconda prattica* were the work of different generations; but the most outstanding protagonist of this radical change of style grew up, after all, in the motet tradition, and only gradually evolved the declamatory technique of arioso and recitative that established his characteristic idiom,[2] an essentially modern style which was immediately dubbed 'dramatic'. Monteverdi's early works certainly came to Lassus's attention, and any attempt at a clear-cut distinction

[1] For a discussion of the issues in question, see H. H. Eggebrecht, 'Arten des Generalbasses', *Archiv für Musikwissenschaft*, xiv (1957), 62 ff. The subject of Lassus's reputation with his older and younger contemporaries, and the related terminology, are discussed in the author's article 'O. di Lasso als Demonstrationsobjekt in der Kompositionslehre des 16. und 17. Jahrhunderts', *Kongressbericht Bamberg 1953*, Kassel & Basel, 1954, pp. 385 ff.

[2] See J. A. Westrup, 'The Originality of Monteverde', *Proceedings of the Royal Musical Association*, lx (1933–4), 1 ff.; also H. F. Redlich, *Das Problem des Stilwandels in Claudio Monteverdis Madrigalwerk* (unpublished dissertation), University of Frankfurt, 1931, published in expanded form as *Claudio Monteverdi, i: Das Madrigalwerk*, Berlin, 1932, pp. 34 ff.

would be a mistake. For Lassus has never belonged happily within the concept of a *stilus ecclesiasticus* in the sense that the Palestrina style came to be regarded by the conservatives as a timeless ideal, in contrast to a style of the times, the *nuove musiche*.

Living away from the centres of musical culture in southern Germany, Lassus tended to move away from a linear style, based on intervallic relationships, towards one in which vertical sonority played a fundamental part. But Lassus also stands apart from early German Protestant counterpoint, whose formal rhetoric and strict adherence to a *cantus firmus* interested him little; he sought motives that were both flexible and suggestive, frequently with psychological overtones. In this respect it could even be said that his destiny was to anticipate the monodic reform and to contribute towards the decline of counterpoint as a structural principle.[3] In evaluating such stylistic ingredients in Lassus's early and late works a distinction must be made between internal and external influences. The following pages are devoted to an examination of the latter, for the most part on the basis of material that is not available in modern editions.

The stylistic factors based on external influences—those, that is, whose origins lie in a foreign repertoire that impinged on Lassus—involve the dance-like, chordal style which immediately after Lassus's death became the driving force of the early Baroque. The villanesche of his early twenties, with their dance-like regularity of metre, represent a framework that developed out of the slightly earlier models of composers like Fontana and Nola, mostly by the addition of an extra part.[4] A little later, in the early motets, pieces occur whose regularity of metre consciously harks back to Classical models. At about the same time we find a growing number of motet arrangements, both published and in manuscript, sharing these same stylistic characteristics, their distinguishing features being the soloistic nature of the highly embellished top part and the block chordal function of the accompanying lower parts in tablatures for keyboard and plucked instruments.[5] As the quantity of surviving material shows, this type of motet enjoyed great popularity. Two such pieces are 'Credidi propter' and 'Sidus ex claro', which become all the more significant in the light of their use by Lassus

[3] See E. Apfel, 'Zur Entstehungsgeschichte des Palestrinasatzes', *Archiv für Musikwissenschaft*, xiv (1957), 30 ff.

[4] See W. Boetticher, *Orlando di Lasso und seine Zeit*, Kassel & Basel, 1959, pp. 40–70.

[5] A bibliographical survey and stylistic breakdown will be found in W. Boetticher, 'Les Oeuvres de Roland de Lassus mises en tablature de luth' *Le Luth et sa musique*, ed. Jean Jacquot, Paris, 1957, pp. 143 ff.

as models for parody Masses. It can of course be said that these instrumental transcriptions, which have something in common with the contemporary lute air, did not provide the real impulse for the *nuove musiche*, but represent a pseudo-monodic style[6] brought about by the process of simplification for domestic performance, irrespective of the historical stylistic development. But the point remains nonetheless valid, for instances of the same style occur in the motet repertoire proper. As a result of the corrupt substitute texts of the posthumous *Magnum opus musicum* (1604), which served as a model for the old Lassus *Gesamtausgabe* (1894 ff.), these are insufficiently known as yet. In publications it is in the company of chansons that these middle-period pieces by Lassus are found. 'Pronuba Juno' and 'Praesidium Sara' survive in the now fragmentary Xeme *Livre de chansons* of Le Roy dating from about 1570,[7] an earlier impression of which had probably appeared some five years before.[8] This fusion of genres to the point that one can almost talk of a 'Latin chanson' in homorhythmic style is no less noteworthy than Lassus's essays in the foundation of a 'Latin madrigal'.[9] Not long afterwards came the short-lived period of *vers mesurés à l'antique* from the French literary circle led by Baïf, whose unrhymed verse matched long syllables with stressed positions, short syllables with unstressed.[10] Lassus paid homage to this principle in several of his later chansons, for example in the chordal 'Une puce j'ai dedans l'oreille' (designated 'Air' in the printed editions). It is noteworthy that this lowly Song of the Flea should have provided new impetus towards a

[6] This point has already been discussed by Alfred Einstein: see 'Der "stile nuovo" auf dem Gebiet der profanen Kammermusik', in G. Adler (ed.), *Handbuch der Musikgeschichte*, 2nd edn., Berlin, 1930, i.430 ff.; also A. Schering, 'Zur Geschichte des begleiteten Sologesangs im 16. Jahrhundert', *Zeitschrift der internationalen Musikgesellschaft*, xiii (1911–12), 190 ff.; for a more recent discussion of the concept, see Claude V. Palisca, 'Vincenzo Galilei and Some Links between "Pseudo-Monody" and Monody', *The Musical Quarterly*, xlvi (1960), 344 ff.

[7] Published by the author in *Gesamt-Ausgabe O. di Lasso, Neue Folge*, Kassel & Basel, 1956 ff., i, Nos. 1 and 2. 'Pronuba Juno' is a wedding piece with extended exclamations of 'hymen, hymenoee' in the refrain.

[8] Boetticher, *Lasso und seine Zeit*, p. 204.

[9] I.e. his early hexametric secular motets, the Virgil settings in which he anticipates the new style in the use of broad chordal writing (*Lasso und seine Zeit*, pp. 130 ff.).

[10] See D. P. Walker, *Vers et musique mesurés à l'antique* (unpublished dissertation), University of Oxford, 1940, and, by the same author, 'Musical Humanism in the 16th and Early 17th Centuries', *The Music Review*, ii (1941), 1 ff., 111 ff., 220 ff., 288 ff.; iii (1942), 55 ff.; German tr. *Der musikalischer Humanismus im 16. und frühen 17. Jahrhundert*, Kassel & Basel, 1949.

monodic style, for the same subject is found in the genre of the Latin secular motet, in the recently discovered 'Bestia curvafia pulices', one of Lassus's ballet-style pieces.[11]

Alongside this *stilus mixtus*, combining Latin words with the homophonic dance-style chanson, the hitherto quite unknown settings of the *Quatrains* of Guy de Pibrac (d. 1583) provide a further, very late group of chansons in which Lassus followed Baïf's principles. These villanella-like four-part pieces, on texts that are of an edifying nature or offer homespun philosophy, have a predominant top part which scrupulously follows the word-accent, and the four-in-a-bar metre is maintained with complete regularity. The loss of the altus precludes for the time being a modern edition of this group of nine chansons, Lassus's last—though it is probable that the missing voice was the least melodically independent part.[12] Nevertheless, an assessment can now be made of the work as a whole, and it can be recognized as important evidence of a simple homophonic, almost hymn-like style quite unlike the usual conception of Lassus's chansons.

The motets dating from the threshold of the late period show similar fluctuations. After the already discussed wedding songs of about 1570 come works commissioned for political festivities, in the case of one of which the nature of the occasion is known and a contemporary illustrated description survives.[13] This is the motet with allegorical characters (*Gallia, Pax, Prosperitas*) written to commemorate the coronation of the Polish king (later Henri III) in Paris in 1573. Here Lassus of course draws on the repertoire of stock devices traditionally used in this sort of motet: concluding sections in pronounced march rhythm, repeated use of triadic motives, scale figuration and splendid dialogues between *cori spezzati* in praise of princely virtures.[14] The fact that such motets were suitable for performance in a balletic manner is a remarkable symptom of the progression towards monody. It is also striking how Lassus has moved away from the intimacy of the dedicatory motet, which still occupied an important position in his Antwerp motet book of 1556, and now anticipates many features of the later festive Venetian

[11] *Lasso Gesamt-Ausgabe*, n.s., i, No. 13.

[12] The only source is Le Roy's *XXIIme Livre de chansons* of 1583, another impression of which, dating from 1585, is now also known (*Lasso und seine Zeit*, pp. 594 ff.).

[13] See *Lasso und seine Zeit*, pp. 384 f. Supplementary information is given on the allegorical groups of dancers and on the stage settings: see W. Boetticher, *Aus O. di Lassos Wirkungskreis*, Kassel & Basel, 1963, Pl. IV, figs. 4–6 (after J. Dorat, *Magnificentissimi spectaculi . . .* , Paris, 1573).

[14] *Lasso und seine Zeit*, pp. 364 ff.

motet. This implies that several works of Lassus's middle period could be put to festal use, if necessary with new words underlaid for the occasion.

A further tendency towards a monodic style is shown by the 'villanella crisis' of about 1575–9 that affected Lassus's compositions to German words.[15] In contrast to the massive sonority of the festal motets, this involved a move in the direction of J. Regnart's *Welsche Villanellen* (1576), from which Lassus actually quoted a phrase.[16] Here one finds a simple four-part texture and regular phrase structure, reminiscent of the modern canzonetta. The German tradition, prevalent since Senfl, of writing against a *cantus firmus* in an inner part, was here challenged for the first time. It is noteworthy that in these pieces Lassus followed the latest fashions, rather than pursuing further the older villanesca. The latter, deriving from the *commedia dell'arte*, was still claiming his attention for the occasion of court festivities around the period 1568–75. Lassus himself gives details of representations, processions and comic dialogues performed in costume and with scenery;[17] long before Orazio Vecchi's madrigal comedies we must reckon with Lassus using the villanesca in performances involving scenery and dancing. But it seems that the grotesque rustic style of the villanesca, incorporating foreign folklore in its *moresca* features, was quickly superseded by the greater refinement of the more modern canzonetta.

Adolf Sandberger's fundamental studies[18] failed to produce any evidence of this in Lassus's output. But now that all the part-books are accessible it has been possible to uncover an authentic five-part canzonetta by Lassus, 'La non vol esser più mia' (1584).[19] Significantly, an early Baroque score, probably intended for instrumental use, exists of this piece, with its strophic form, patter style and dominant top part.[20] To it may be added a further canzonet, in three parts, 'Quand' han più'; the superius survives only in the anthology *Giardinetto de*

---

[15] Ibid., pp. 511–15.   [16] Ibid., p. 514.

[17] Boetticher, *Aus Lassos Wirkungskreis*, pp. 49 f. It can be gathered from the surviving correspondence that *il magnifico*, *la francescina* and 'the Zanni' took part, under the direction of the Italian comedian Venturino. The fact that Lassus gives detailed accounts of these performances seems to prove conclusively that his own villanesche were involved; a later edition of further pieces (1581) confirms this supposition.

[18] 'O. di Lassos Beziehungen zur italienischen Literatur', *Altbayerische Monatsschrift*, i (1899), 65 ff.; reprinted in *Sammelbände der internationalen Musikgesellschaft*, v (1903–4), 402 ff., and in Sandberger's *Gesammelte Aufsätze zur Musikgeschichte*, i (Munich, 1921).

[19] *Lasso Gesamt-Ausgabe*, n.s., i. 152 ff. (No. 29); see the discussion of sources in that edition, and *Lasso und seine Zeit*, pp. 577 ff.

[20] Vienna, Österreichische Nationalbibliothek, Codex 10110, f. 54.

madrigali (Venice, 1588), and a bassus part has recently been discovered.[21] In this work too one may assume that the chordal progressions were of a simple nature.

Such evidence seems to contradict our picture of a 'Netherlandish composer, and further confirmation is provided by an elusive work of which we only know the title: *Musica nuova, dove si contengono madrigali, sonetti, villanelle . . . d'Orlando di Lasso, a 3 voci novamente da esso composte* (Munich, 1594 or 1595)[22]—though the wording varies in detail, one source giving 'composte questo anno'.[23] This surely demonstrates that at the close of his career Lassus was still contributing to the most modern type of composition of the time. This should cause no surprise when one considers that right to the end Lassus kept up with the most recent style of madrigal: the courtly pictorial manner of around 1565–8, whose chief examples still await publication in modern editions,[24] and the curious complexity of the mystical type of about 1575–85, now once more available for performance as a result of the rediscovery of missing material from the part-books.[25] Thus the existence of a third type around 1592, anticipating a monodic approach, would be quite consistent with the pattern of Lassus's development.

In respect of internal influences we have the evidence of recent discoveries, but we are also faced with sad gaps in the surviving material. In the case of external influences the material is more uniformly preserved, but there is as yet a total lack of modern editions of the relevant sections of Lassus's output. The following discussion is directed to the late settings of the *Magnificat*[26] and *Nunc dimittis*,[27] since these show

---

[21] *Lasso und seine Zeit*, p. 797; on the piece itself, ibid., p. 582.

[22] W. Boetticher, 'Zur Chronologie des Schaffens von O. di Lasso', *Kongressbericht Lüneburg 1950*, Kassel & Basel, 1951, pp. 82 ff.

[23] This title is confirmed by Draudius (*Bibliotheca exotica*, 1626), Clessius (1602) and several book-fair catalogues (A. Göhler, *Messkataloge*, Leipzig, 1902, No. 506), though 'sonetti', 'villanelle' and 'stanze' appear as alternatives.

[24] The pieces in question are the five-part madrigals 'Al dolce suon', 'Spent'è d'amor' and its *secunda pars* 'Ma che morta', and 'Ben convenne' and its *secunda pars* 'Solo n'andrò', together with the four-part 'Ove d'altra montagna'. See the account of the sources in my article, 'Aus Orlando di Lassos Madrigal- und Motettenkomposition (1567–1569)', *Archiv für Musikwissenschaft*, xxii (1965), 12–42. Plans for the publication of these madrigals are under way.

[25] Published in *Lasso Gesamt-Ausgabe*, n.s., i.131 ff. It is remarkable what proportion of these pieces are on Petrarchan texts dealing not with this life but with the beyond.

[26] See *Lasso und seine Zeit*, pp. 255 ff., 417 ff., 516 ff., 618 ff., 681 ff., 963 ff. The *Magnificat* settings are here referred to according to the enumeration on pp. 963 ff. of that work.

[27] Ibid., pp. 688 ff.

not only the application of parody technique but also the intrusion of other elements that anticipate monody.[28] The most productive period of Lassus's *Magnificat* settings as far as Italian models are concerned, from 1582 to 1585, does not of course exclude the older courtly madrigal style of composers like Arcadelt, Berchem, Rore and Verdelot.[29] Alongside these, however, are found astonishing instances of borrowings from the most recent repertoire.[30] Giovanni Maria Nanino's 'Erano i capei d'oro' served as the model for the *Magnificat* M.76, surviving only in the posthumous edition of 1619,[31] where it appears as No. LIII. Nanino's piece was published in his first book of five-part madrigals (Venice, 1579),[32] which went through several subsequent editions. Lassus probably knew the work from Phalèse's anthology *Musica divina* (Antwerp, 1583),[33] which also contained pieces by Lassus himself.[34] Nanino (*c*.1545–1607), to be sure, had grown up in the Palestrina tradition (in 1604, after a long period of service as a singer, he became

[28] For a survey listing the *Magnificat* settings and their models, whether Lassus's own or by other composers, see *Lasso und seine Zeit*, p. 625; also the unpublished dissertations of J. Erb (University of California, 1969), F. E. Dempster (Iowa State University, 1961), A. K. Dayritt (Ohio State University, 1960), F. M. Green (University of Southern California, 1968) and G. Gruber, *Beiträge zur Geschichte der Kompositionstechnik der Parodie-magnificat in der 2. Hälfte des 16. Jahrhunderts* (University of Graz, 1964), partly published in *Kirchenmusikalisches Jahrbuch*, li (1967), 33 ff.; further G. Reese, 'The Polyphonic Magnificat of the Renaissance as a Design in Tonal Centers', *Journal of the American Musicological Society*, xiii (1960), 68 ff. Lassus's *Magnificat* settings, ed. Erb, are to appear in the new collected edition.

I must express my renewed gratitude to the music department of the Bayerische Staatsbibliothek in Munich for allowing me access to the manuscripts and published sources cited below.

[29] To give but a few examples, the following are used as models: 'Vergine bella', 'S'io credessi', 'O s'io potessi', 'Ultimi miei sospiri', 'De le belle contrade', 'Quanto in mill'anni', 'Anchor che col partire', 'Quanto io lieta', 'Amor ecco colei' (*Magnificat* M.9, 33, 16, 26, 62, 28, 44, 46, 81).

[30] W. Boetticher, 'O. di Lassos Magnificat-Komposition', *Kongressbericht Hamburg 1956*, Kassel & Basel, 1957, pp. 131 ff., and *Lasso und seine Zeit*, pp. 625 ff. A substantial handicap in the identification of models is the continued lack of a master-index of Italian madrigal texts. Only the English repertoire is indexed by first lines, in E. H. Fellowes, *English Madrigal Verse*, 3rd edn., ed. F. W. Sternfeld and D. Greer, Oxford, 1967.

[31] *Jubilus Beata Virginis hoc est Magnificat ab O. de Lasso*, Munich, 1619. The sole surviving complete exemplar, formerly in the Bavarian monastery of Tegernsee, is referred to in *Lasso und seine Zeit*, p. 813.

[32] Sole surviving complete exemplar Munich, Bayerische Staatsbibliothek, Mus. pract. 4° 189/9.

[33] Munich, Bayerische Staatsbibliothek, Mus. pract. 4° 185/1 (from the music collection of the old court chapel).

[34] *Lasso und seine Zeit*, p. 787.

maestro pro tempore of the Sistine Chapel). But at the same time he was
one of the founders of the canzonetta. His first, three-part, book devoted to the genre (1593, second edition 1599),[35] which includes another
setting of 'Erano', designated *sonetto*, is completely modern in its
dance-like melodic style. The expressive dominant opening of Nanino's
five-part model (Ex. 1a), and the bass line that is characteristically

Ex. 1

harmonic in function rather than thematic, are faithfully followed in
Lassus's *Magnificat* (Ex. 1b), which, though still unknown, is an important work of his late period. The premature entry of the quinta
vox, certainly, is Lassus's own device, and the accentuation is displaced:
the 'quotation' begins a minim later in the other parts, and agreement

[35] Modern edition, ed. A. Schinelli and B. Somma (Polifonia Sacra e Profana
ii), Rome, 1941.

is only reached in the second bar. Also the conjunct rising figure in the lower parts at the approach to cadences (bars 3 and 6) is an addition by Lassus, as is the slower speed of the word-setting; but the overall picture is unmistakably that of the canzonetta.

Also instructive is the use of the six-part 'Ecco ch'io lasso' (Ex. 2a), by an anonymous composer from Giovanni Ferretti's circle, which again will have been known to Lassus from the Phalèse anthology of 1583.[36] The six-part *Magnificat* M.29 (Ex. 2b) was first published in 1587,[37] and on the evidence of Munich, Bayerische Staatsbibliothek, Codex 21, can be dated late summer 1585.[38] The altus of the model, $g-d'-c'-e'\natural-d'$, was of decisive influence, as was the melodic shape of the opening phrase, decorating the focal g' with the notes on either side of it; again there is a noticeable slowing down towards the cadence (bar 3). The germinal motive was the rising fifth $g-d'$ in the model, which spread through the whole texture. One may surmise that the anonymous composer was a pupil of Ferretti (b. *c.*1540), an artist who devoted himself exclusively to *canzoni alla napolitana*.[39] 'Ecco ch'io lasso' is also significant in the history of the English madrigal; it was included in Yonge's *Musica transalpina* (1588) and is found in English manuscript sources.

This model, however, provided Lassus with another feature that anticipates monody, namely the descending scale spanning up to an octave in range. The passage in question (Ex. 3a) is repeated sequentially one note lower in the model and is used by Lassus principally in the upper parts in the doxology (Ex. 3b). Motives such as these no longer involve simply the filling in of octave leaps, but are abstract scale patterns in their own right, whose sequential treatment demands a slow rate of harmonic change. Another typical case of the repeated use of this figure shows Lassus drawing on the most recent repertoire when he borrows Orazio Vecchi's 'O che vezzosa aurora' (Ex. 4a) as the model for *Magnificat* M.27 (Ex. 4b).[40] Vecchi's piece too appears in Phalèse's *Musica divina* of 1583 and was probably first published in the same

---

[36] First published in G. Ferretti's *II. libro delle canzoni a 6 voci*, Venice, 1575 (exemplar from the music collection of the old court chapel, Munich, Bayerische Staatsbibliothek, Mus. pract. 4° 31/8).

[37] *Lasso und seine Zeit*, pp. 618 f. In the 1619 edition it appears as No. LXXII.

[38] Ibid., pp. 619, 625.

[39] Books I and II, in six parts, 1573 and 1575; also five-part pieces.

[40] Copied into Munich, Bayerische Staatsbibliothek, Codex 48 in about 1582–5 (*Lasso und seine Zeit*, p. 622). The only known printed source is the 1619 edition, where it is found as No. LXX.

Ex. 2

year (in Vecchi's first book of six-part madrigals). Vecchi was another composer who turned from the classical madrigal to the *canzonetta alla napolitana*, which soon after Lassus's death gave rise to dance-style pieces in Germany; his first two books of four-part pieces appeared in 1580, by 1590 he had reached his fourth book, and these were reprinted by Gerlach and Kaufmann in Nuremberg. Clearly Vecchi's madrigal

Ex. 4

comedies, whose role in the foundation of opera is not undisputed, were not the only harbingers of the change of style. Of more fundamental importance for Lassus was this scale motive, embodying both faithfulness to the expression of the text (the *affetti delle parole*) and dance-like character, which so well conveys the burlesque style of Vecchi, whose motto was 'dilettare con ridicolo'.[41] The central portion ('Fecit potentiam') of the same *Magnificat* also uses a canzonetta motive from Vecchi's model (Ex. 5).

ch'u-na più bel-,l'Au-ro· - ra

There is another contact with the young precursors of monody in the person of Giuseppe Caimo, who was associated with Duke Wilhelm of Bavaria and visited Landshut.[42] This composer, who died as early as 1584, provided the model for Lassus's *Magnificat* M.93 (Ex. 6).[43]

Here the homophonic principle, with its strongly harmonic bass line and song-like regularity of phrase structure, is taken over completely. This 'aria'-type is also found in the remarkable *Magnificat* M.94 *super Aria di un' sonetto* (No. LX in the 1619 edition, the only surviving source). Here the model and Lassus's *Magnificat* have a very similar melodic curve in the dominant top part, $b'-d''-c''-a'-b'-d''-e''-a'$, which apart from the approach to the cadence on a' is almost identical with the Caimo piece mentioned above (Ex. 7). It is striking that the older hexachordal motivic style is abandoned in favour of lines having

[41] *Die Musik in Geschichte und Gegenwart*, art. 'Orazio Vecchi' (O. Mischiati).

[42] *Aus Lassos Wirkungskreis*, pp. 130 ff. (correspondence of the Bavarian emissary to Milan, Prosper Visconti; Caimo is mentioned in association with the theorist Nicola Vicentino, and is praised as 'raro virtuoso con la mano assai gagliarda e velocissima').

[43] Only known in the 1619 edition, as No. LIX. The model is found in the anthology *Fiamma ardente* of 1586 (surviving complete only in the Biblioteca Estense in Modena), but its first publication may antedate this if it was included in one of the three lost madrigal books by Caimo, before 1584 (*Lasso und seine Zeit*, p. 634, note 39).

Ex. 7

an early monodic character, with prominent melodic fifths and marked
dance rhythm. Alessandro Striggio, one of the earliest composers of
intermedi, contributed to this process. His madrigal 'D'ogni gratia
d'amor' (Ex. 8)[44] provided the model for Lassus's *Magnificat* M.80
(No. LXXXVI in the 1619 edition).[45] In this case Lassus went so far

Ex. 8

as to change the successive polyphonic entries into block harmonies,
and an important contribution to the monodic tendencies is the use of
repeated chords. It is no accident that at the words 'Fecit potentiam'
Lassus employs emphatic repeated notes based on Striggio's model
(there to the words 'bel sembiante'):

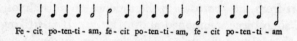

When one takes an overall view of the stylistic influences that impinged on Lassus's late *Magnificat* settings, it is clear that more is involved than mere borrowing or quotation. How appropriately he dealt

[44] From the second book of six-part madrigals, which Lassus probably knew
from the 1582 impression (Munich, Bayerische Staatsbibliothek, Mus. pract.
4° 45/8).
[45] The date of its being copied in Munich, Bayerische Staatsbibliothek,
Codex 56 can be set at early 1585.

with the transfer of material can be observed in his two final *Magnificat* settings, of 1592, M.13 and M.100, on his own motets 'Memor esto' and 'Aurora lucis rutilat'.[46] Lassus's aim was a direct transfer of affection;[47] despite differences in the prosodic scheme, in putting the structural and sonorous elements to new use he was at pains to preserve propriety of the *affetto*—witness a similar procedure in his parody Masses, where for example the word 'tace' of the motet 'Certa fortiter' becomes 'pax' in the *Gloria* of the Mass based on it, and so on.

A similar technique forms the basis of Lassus's still unpublished *Nunc dimittis* settings.[48] In the one based on Cipriano de Rore's madrigal 'Come havran fin' Lassus draws on a model of considerable age. His deeply serious setting retains the arch-shaped phrase spanning the hexachord that opens Rore's madrigal (Ex. 9), a typical example of the

Ex. 9

older ideal of balance. But in the second versicle he introduces a deliberately modern touch by extending the range to the octave and abandoning the imitative treatment of the subject. At this point the top part displays a nervously ornamented style (Ex. 10) while the other voices are relegated to a subordinate chordal role. The supporting function of the lower parts is clearly evident in another *Nunc dimittis* setting belonging to this late group, based on Lassus's own madrigal 'Io son si stanco' of six years before.[49] Here it is all the more remarkable

[46] 'Memor esto' appeared in print in 1585; 'Aurora' was not published in Lassus's lifetime, but can be assumed to belong to the same group of late motets.

[47] W. Boetticher, 'Ein spezieller Beitrag zur Frage geistlich-weltlicher Übertragungstechnik im 16. Jahrhundert', *International Musicological Society: Report of the Eighth Congress New York 1961*, i (Kassel & Basel, 1961), 214 ff.

[48] Collected together in Munich, Bayerische Staatsbibliothek, Codex 14, which was compiled (with clear corrections in the hand of the composer himself) in about 1592.

[49] For the sources see *Lasso und seine Zeit*, pp. 580, 689. The five-part madrigal was published in 1585.

Ex. 10

since Lassus avoids all trace of dance-like character, and adheres strictly
to the pictorially inspired theme of his late madrigal, with its wearily
(*stanco*) drooping figure (Ex. 11).

Ex. 11

Consideration of these monodic elements changes the conventional
assessment of Lassus's style considerably. The evidence is unmistakable:
the early 'Latin madrigals', as we have called them; the hexametric
motets; the wedding pieces (*Epithalamia*); the middle-period political
court motets subsequently adapted for ballet and their texts altered for
performance with scenery and dancing, as we know from documentary
evidence; the last chansons in the settings of Pibrac's *Quatrains*; the
growing use of canzonetta models. These influences are found predominantly in the realm of secular music, though the last group of
parody compositions involve sacred words. One final question remains:
can a similar change of purpose be observed in Lassus's last motet book,
a cycle of thirty six-part pieces dating from the year of his death?

First of all it must be said that the actual music of this *opus ultimum*
among the motets has been overshadowed by the preface to the printed
edition, in which Lassus only a few weeks before his death criticized
the younger generation for their 'over-production'.[50] This no doubt
referred to the mass of facile early Baroque domestic music and the
many species of *concertato* compositions which flooded the market
shortly before 1600. Even this last collection of motets, however, contains hidden pointers to a change of style. Naturally, one could not
expect to find early continuo practice. But this concept (*basso continuo,
bassus principalis, bassus seguente* and so on), as Friedrich Blume has
observed,[51] is in any event no more than a crude generalization and

[50] *Lasso und seine Zeit*, pp. 672 ff.
[51] *Das monodische Prinzip in der protestantischen Kirchenmusik*, Leipzig,
1925, p. 26.

represents only the final stage of a gradual evolution. As Max Schneider pointed out in connection with a manuscript of the 1580s,[52] individual aspects of the practice must go back a long way. The corpus of publications before Viadana's *Centi concerti ecclesiastici* (1602) is admittedly full of lacunae; nevertheless, examination of hitherto unknown part-books does reveal examples from around 1600 or earlier that clearly presuppose a *bassus principalis*.[53] In this connection, besides Venetian sonority and the development of a small-textured 'sacred concerto' for two upper parts and continuo, there is a third factor that has so far received little attention, namely the changing face of the classical five- and six-part motet texture, of which Lassus was a late representative. It cannot be overlooked that Lassus enjoyed unusual popularity in the early Baroque—though mainly with his few-voiced compositions. The process begins with Adam Gumpeltzhaimer (*Compendium musicae*, 1591) and Maternus Beringer (1610), who introduced numerous examples by Lassus for didactic purposes, although some of them are in corrupt versions typical of the early Baroque.[54] To satisfy the demand for *concerti a due voci* (high voices) a spurious Lassus publication appeared in 1601, which turns out to consist of the *Bicinia* of 1577 with a spurious 'Tertia vox' (added about 1600);[55] and the *concertato* technique resulted in 'corrections' to the two authentic parts where the new texture demanded it. The stylistic foundation of these 'corrections' corresponds closely to the new features encountered in Lassus's last six-part motets, which—no doubt for that reason—exerted a similar fascination on the early Baroque generation. For here too can be found, perhaps more clearly than in Viadana's radically simplified pieces, premonitions of the arioso and recitative styles which are associated with early opera and rather loosely classified as 'dramatic'.

In this respect Lassus in his later works was a prophet of the new

[52] *Die Anfänge des basso continuo*, Leipzig, 1918, and 'Die Aufführungs-praxis der Musik des 16. und 17. Jahrhunderts', *Archiv für Musikwissenschaft*, i (1918), 205 ff.

[53] W. Boetticher, 'Zum Problem der Übergangsperiode der Musik 1580–1620', *Kongressbericht Kassel 1962*, Kassel & Basel, 1963, pp. 141 ff. This includes a discussion of the newly discovered *Basso principale da sonare delli salmi a versetti* by the Milanese musician Serafino Cantone (dedication 1601), hitherto presumed lost, which makes possible a more accurate assessment of the technique as applied to five-part texture. The five-part *Salmi intieri* with instrumental bass by Orfeo Vecchi (1598) unfortunately survive only incomplete.

[54] See *Lasso und seine Zeit*, pp. 464 ff.

[55] W. Boetticher, 'Eine französische Bicinien-Ausgabe als frühmonodisches Dokument', *Festschrift K. G. Fellerer*, Regensburg, 1962, pp. 67 ff.

aesthetic which superseded the abstract polyphonic style and paved the way for a new affective language, the spiritual forerunner in Italy of the opera, and in central Germany of the *musica poetica* of Heinrich Schütz. The period in question is 1592–4, that is, only about two years before Viadana's *novo modo*.[56] Lassus's motets, scattered indiscriminately among volumes 11–19 of the old complete edition as a result of the posthumous *Magnum opus musicum* (1604) having been used as the source, require further investigation.[57] No unifying literary concept acts as a foundation for this last cycle, which embraces free neo-Latin verses (including a drinking song, a dedicatory motet for his ducal master, and pastoral idylls), followed by psalms, parts of the Requiem and of the Revelation of St. John, and so forth. This textual diversity provides a convenient basis for examination.

First of all it is striking how four-part chordal writing for various combinations of voices occurs within the six-part texture, producing striking dramatic effects and lending the expression of the words an impassioned character.[58] Curiously stiff series of repeated chords are also found,[59] and the bass line is treated apart from the rest of the texture, swinging between tonic and dominant.[60] Another unusual feature is the use of rapid decorative figuration in two or three parallel parts,[61] and this contrasts with ponderously moving bass lines.[62]

[56] In the preface to the *Cento concerti ecclesiastici* of 1602 Viadana mentions having encountered this practice in Rome some five or six years previously.

[57] For an earlier discussion, see *Lasso und seine Zeit*, pp. 672 ff.

[58] 'Heu quis armorum'. The text reads: 'Alas, what martial might the tyrant commands! He rages like an adder coiled to strike, and from his throne he desires to take the saints by the throat'. The *secunda pars* ('Jam satis') begins: 'For long enough has the fury of wicked men reigned over sea and land . . .'.

[59] 'Heu quis armorum', bars 18, 20, etc.; 'Luxuriosa', bars 7, 9, etc. (for descriptive purposes to the word 'tumultuosa'); 'Deus iniqui' at the word 'potentium'. Instances of note repetition at a slower speed occur in 'Si ergo', bars 26, 33–4.

[60] 'Jam satis', bars 2, 3, 19–22, etc.; 'Luxuriosa', bars 18–20; 'Diligam', bars 24–7. Triadically descending bass lines occur in 'Conserva me', bars 25–7, 30–31; 'Sancti qui', bars 16–17, 18–19. The tendency to treat the bass in such places almost in ostinato fashion is unmistakable.

[61] 'Luxuriosa', bars 21–4, 28–31; 'Respicit', pictorially on the word 'stultitiae'; 'Rursum', bars 8 ff. (treated polyphonically); 'Ad primum morsum', bars 45, 47–8, etc.

[62] 'Luxuriosa' to the word 'ebrietas'; 'Prolongati', bars 18–21; 'Inveterata', bars 9 ff. (pictorially at 'expectant dolores mortis'); 'Si ergo', bars 8–11 (pictorially at 'servum tuum in pace'); 'Si coelum', bars 26–8; 'Qui vincerit' (pictorially at 'a morte secunda'); at the beginning of 'Vidi calumnias'; 'In dedicatione' and 'Quis non timebit', to the words 'omnes gentes' in each case.

Opening phrases, for example in 'Nectar' (Ex. 12),[63] display the sort

Ex. 12

of melodic shape encountered before, which moves through the compass of a fifth and prompts a slow harmonic rhythm. The liking for octave leaps in the lowest voice is noteworthy.[64] Falling scale motives, such as were discussed in connection with the Vecchi parody, are also found.[65] In the top part prominent use is made of sequence, rarely exceeding a third and with dance-like melodic character, as in 'Si coelum' (Ex. 13) and many other instances.[66] In the middle voices

Ex. 13

-ne, Do - - mi-ne, Do - - mi-ne, Do - - mi-ne De - us

there is abundant ornamentation (*diminutio*) without real polyphonic significance,[67] while the top part, in contrast, with its succession of long phrases, is song-like.[68] There is increasing use of leaps of a fifth in the bass,[69] and opening phrases in the top part that begin with a leap of a fifth or octave—a similar symptom of chordal thinking—are likewise new.[70] Short-breathed motives betray a dramatic approach, even when they are also prompted by pictorial connotations.[71] The

[63] Also in 'Si coelum', bar 14; 'Deficiat', bars 1 ff.; 'Respicit', bars 2–3, etc.; 'Confitebor', bars 1 ff. In several cases a fanfare-like disjunct motif occurs at the beginning of a piece: e.g. 'Si coelum', bars 1–8; 'Beatus homo cui donatum est', bars 1 ff.

[64] 'Prolongati', bars 15, 31, 33–5; 'Inveterata', bars 34, 35; 'Si ergo', bars 25–6, 33, 36, 37; 'Si coelum', bars 8–9; 'Vere Dominus', in the closing 'Allelujah' section; 'Timor Domini', bars 1 ff.; 'Ad Dominum' at 'sagittae' (see below); 'Heu mihi quia' at 'qui oderunt pacem' (also for pictorial purposes); 'Cantabant', bars 29–31, 36–7; 'Quam bonus', bars 6, 13–14, etc.; 'Quia non est', bars 1–3, etc.; 'Recordare', bars 14, 16, 18, etc.

[65] See above, pp. 92 ff.

[66] 'Qui timet', bars 30–3; 'Lauda anima', bars 43–52.

[67] 'Deficiat', bar 24 (Sexta vox); 'Ad primum' at 'laetus', etc.

[68] 'Deficiat', bars 14–19 (Cantus I, 'et anni mei'); at the beginning of 'Vincenti', etc.

[69] 'Ego cognovi', bars 44–6; also, at a slower speed, in 'Qui timet', bars 1–5, 11–15, etc.

[70] 'Respicit' (repeatedly); 'Ad Dominum' at 'clamavi' (also having expressive connotations); 'Ad primum', bar 32, etc.

[71] 'Ad Dominum' (at 'sagittae').

notes that ornament skeletal degrees of the melody are restricted to narrow confines, usually the second below, and create melodic contours closely corresponding to the *diminutio* of early monody.[72] The triadic structure of many initial phrases is unmistakable, even in the case of successive entries in a polyphonic manner.[73] A noteworthy figure occurring in the bass betrays its harmonic function and instrumental origins in the pattern involving a lower semitone returning note followed by a downward octave leap: g–$f\sharp$–g–G or g–$f\sharp$–g–d–G.[74] There are several instances of triadic figures in the top voice, not only at the beginning of pieces but later too.[75] Particularly noteworthy is the ostinato-like chain of triads in the course of the piece, again in the upper parts[76]—witness what may be called the ostinato structure of the motet 'Musica Dei donum' (composed on a free text), whose anticipation of monody is unmistakable.[77]

If any conclusions can be drawn from these observations, then the astonishing fact emerges that even in Lassus's sacred works there are distinct foreshadowings of a *seconda prattica* such as soon afterwards became the bone of contention between Monteverdi and Artusi. Future considerations of the origins of the *nuove musiche* will have to take account of the motets of Lassus's old age, which like the well-known secular madrigal forms belong to the ancestors of the new style. Our discussion of Lassus's modern tendencies can add a new facet to the portrait of a composer whose conservative features have been excessively stressed in the past. The reservation must of course be made that any historical analysis can only deal with one stylistic aspect at a time: the modern historian, removed from his subject in time and space, faces the laborious task of reassembling the parts of the whole. It still remains true that musical comprehension can never be more than approximate and partial, as Sir Jack Westrup has reminded us[78]—an appropriate note on which to conclude this investigation.

---

[72] 'Rursum', bars 23–4 (pictorially at 'vanitas'); 'Sancti qui', bars 30–31.

[73] 'Multifariam'; 'Exaltabo'. In this type the top part normally leads.

[74] 'Quam bonus', bars 31–2 ('quia zelavi'); 'Quia non est', bars 1–5.

[75] 'Recordare', bars 15–22. Analogous cases in the treatment of the lowest part: 'Fratres nescitis', bars 35–7; 'Genuit puerpera', bars 33–5; at the end of 'Domine, eduxisti', etc.

[76] 'Recordare', bars 41–3 (at 'tantus labor').

[77] See *Lasso und seine Zeit*, pp. 677 f.; also W. Kirsch, '*Musica Dei donum optimi*: zu einigen weltlichen Motetten des 16. Jahrhunderts', *Frankfurter musikhistorische Studien: Helmuth Osthoff zu seinem siebzigsten Geburtstag*, Tutzing, 1969, pp. 105 ff.

[78] 'Music—its Past and Present', *Lectures on the History and Art of Music: The Louis Charles Elson Memorial Lectures at the Library of Congress, 1946–1963*, New York, 1968, pp. 241–64

iv. Alessandro Scarlatti, *Griselda:* title-page of the autograph score (British Museum, Add. MS 14168)

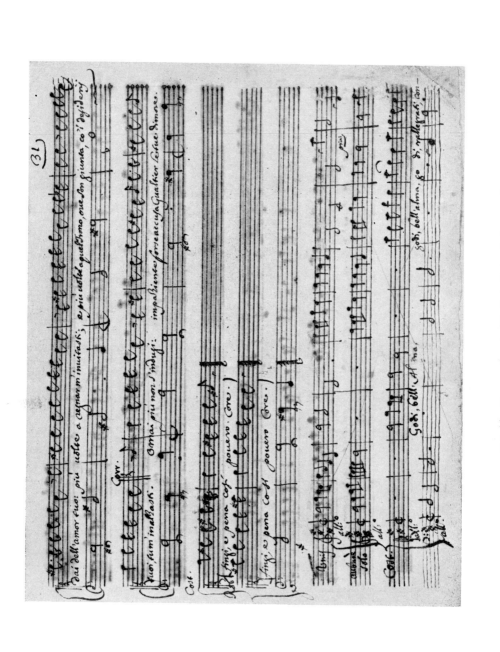

v. *Griselda*: Costanza's aria 'Godi, bell'alma', first version

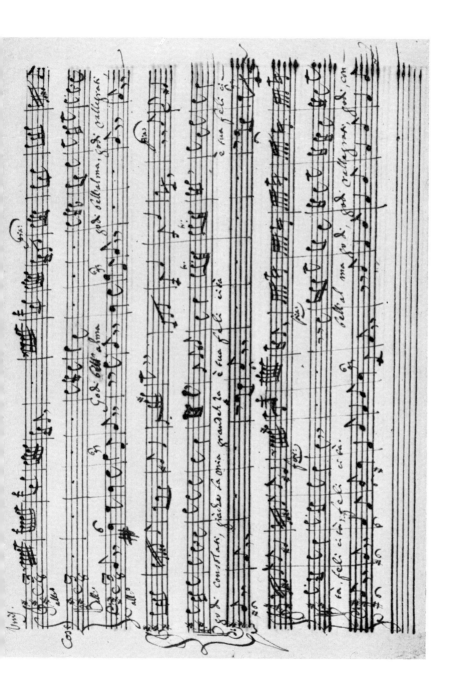

vi. *Griselda*: Costanza's aria 'Godi, bell'alma', second version

The Original Version of Alessandro Scarlatti's 'Griselda'

DONALD JAY GROUT

In the Scarlatti literature the first performance of *Griselda* is usually given as January or 'Carnival' 1721 in Rome. The title-page of the autograph score in the British Museum, Add. MS 14168 (see Pl. IV), reads:

ORIGINALE / GRISELDA / Opera 114 / Posta in Musica / Dal Cau[alier]ᵉ Alessandro Scarlatti / p[er] S[ua] Eccel[lenz]ᵃ Sig[nor] Prin[ci]pe Ruspoli / in Roma xbre [dicembre] *1720* e Genn[aio] *1721*

The specifying of two dates on the title-page is different from any Scarlatti opera autograph (or part or presumed autograph) known to me. The Brussels Conservatoire *Ciro* bears the date '8bre 1711'—presumably the date of composition, since the first performance took place in Rome in 1712; *Marco Attilio Regolo* (British Museum) is dated 'In Roma 1719', the year of the performance; *Telemaco* (Vienna, National-bibliothek) has 'Opera 109. in Roma / xbre 1717'—again, presumably the date of composition, the performance coming in the carnival season of 1718; the title-pages of *Massimo Puppieno* and *Tutto il male* (Monte-cassino), both written in a later hand, have no dates. The indication 'xbre *1720* e [!] Genn[aio] *1721*', evidently in the composer's own hand, on the title-page of *Griselda* thus suggests two separate performances, the earlier of which is not otherwise recorded, though it is suggested as a possibility in Giancarlo Rostirolla's recent catalogue.[1] There seems to be no outside evidence to show just when or in what order the numerous changes (all in Scarlatti's hand) in the autograph were made;

[1] In Roberto Pagano and Lino Bianchi, *Alessandro Scarlatti*, Turin, 1972, p. 357.

HEO

and of course it is not unusual to find alterations in performance scores of operas of this and other periods. Nevertheless, whether or not there was actually an earlier performance of *Griselda* in December 1720, there is ample evidence in the autograph and the libretto for the existence of an entity which I shall call the 'original' version differing in many respects from the one which the composer finally decided upon and which is faithfully transmitted in the only eighteenth-century copies of the complete score now known.[2]

The British Museum *Griselda*, which lacks Act II, consists of 129 folios, paper, 21 × 28 cm. That this was part of a performance score is evident from the worn lower right-hand corners of the pages, the markedly thicker note-heads in the continuo, and the *custos* marks in the continuo. There are no such marks in *B* or *S*; the device is purely practical and is used in the autograph with economy—only in the continuo part, and there as a rule only when the principal harpsichord is playing (not, usually, in the continuo passages marked 'Solo' and written in the tenor clef) and only at places where a quick page turn is necessary and the next following note cannot be inferred from the context (as it can in a cadence formula).

The manuscript was presented to the British Museum on 8 April 1843, together with a large collection of other music manuscripts, by Spencer Joshua Alwyne Compton, second Marquess of Northampton, who had lived in Italy from 1830 until the death of his wife in Rome in 1840. The collection, now catalogued as Add. MSS 14101–249, included six other Scarlatti opera scores. That of *Griselda* when I first saw it in January 1966 contained about 25 leaves or slips pasted by the edges over passages varying from a couple of bars to an entire page, the evident purpose being to guard against inadvertent playing of cancelled passages in a performance. The larger paste-over leaves were blank; their paper was of a different make from that in the body of the manuscript, though undoubtedly contemporary with it.[3] Several other pages or portions of pages in the score showed signs of having once been

---

[2] *S* = Münster, Santini MS 3894; *B* = Berlin, Staatsbibliothek Preussischer Kulturbesitz, Mus. MS 19640 (transcripts at Brussels Conservatoire, 1862, and Library of Congress, 1911; transcript formerly at Munich, Bayerischer Staatsbibliothek). Additional early sources are *P* = Paris Conservatoire D 11898 (twenty arias); and fragments, evidently copied from *P*, in Brussels Conservatoire MSS 4864–5.

[3] The watermarks are: for the manuscript, tip of a fleur-de-lys in a double circle; for the paste-over leaves, six-pointed star in a single circle surmounted by a cross, with inner circle enclosing an N (or IV connected). Neither appears n the standard indexes of watermarks (Briquet, Heawood, Eineder).

covered in the same way. The smaller paste-over slips were fragments of contemporary music-paper with staff lines and musical notation consisting for the most part of revisions in recitatives, some of them made to ensure a proper transition where a cut had been effected.[4] When the manuscript was rebound, preserving the existing gatherings, in March 1966, all the paste-overs were lifted off, the larger blank ones being discarded (except for two retained as samples) and the smaller ones being hinged-in at their original locations. The music thus uncovered, though usually crossed out, is still for the most part legible, as are passages and pages that had been merely crossed out without being pasted over. Altogether, nearly one third of the pages in the score show evidence of revision ranging from a couple of notes to entire numbers.

The autograph (hereafter designated *A*) has two foliations: one in pencil in a modern hand and the other, which goes through Act I only, in ink of the same colour as that of the manuscript and apparently contemporary with it. I shall call this the 'old' foliation and distinguish it from the modern one by means of italics. The following table shows the relationship of the two foliations of Act I:

Modern	Old
ff. 1–5	*1–5*
6–9	[*1*], *6–8*
10–13	*9–12*
14–17	*13–16*
18–21	*17–20*
22–25	*21* [+3]
26–29	[*4*]
30–33	*22–25*
34–40	*26* [+2], *27–31*
41–44	*32* [+2], *33*
45–47	*34–36*
48–51	*39–42*
52–55	*43–46*
56–59	*47–50*
60–63	*51–54*
64–69	*55* [+5]

Bracketed figures indicate leaves unnumbered in the old foliation. The gathering 34–40 includes one folio numbered 36*. On ff. *39* and *40*, the 9, 4 and 0 are heavily inked-on over some earlier figures; perhaps these two folios were first numbered *38* and *39* respectively, but it is impossible to be certain.

[4] The verso of the paste-over slips also usually contained fragments of music, apparently in Scarlatti's hand; I have not been able to match these fragments with any places in the score.

Gatherings in Act III begin with ff. 70, 79, 87, 95, 103, 110, 114 and 120. From f. 78^v on, the last page of each gathering (except 113^v) has a cue word to the first page of the next. F. 68–68^v has a 'Minuet' for voice and un-figured bass, in a different hand; the words are illegible and the music hardly decipherable, but it is certain that neither has any connection with the opera.

Evidence for the differences between the original and the revised versions of *Griselda* begins to appear as soon as we compare the auto-graph score with the printed libretto (hereafter called *L*).[5] In the latter, 118 lines of recitative are 'virgolated', that is marked with a double comma („) at the beginning to signify that the line would not be sung in the opera. All the 42 virgolated lines in Act I and ten of the eleven in Act III have been set to music in *A* and then cancelled by crossing out or pasting over or both. Likewise composed and cancelled are two non-virgolated lines in Act I, also four lines in Act I and five in Act III which do not appear at all in *L*. There are 65 virgolated lines in Act II of *L*. If these also, like those in Acts I and III, were composed and cancelled, the original version of the opera had 128 lines of recitative that do not appear in the revised version. Their deletion did not save much time, but it did have one advantage. None of the deleted lines is necessary for following the story; they dwell on situations already plain, or repeat something in different words, or inject superfluous *sententiae*. Omitting them had the good effect of speeding the action.

Three arias in *L* are marked with the sign *ₓ* in the margin, the usual indication for omission (like the „ in recitatives). Two of these were composed in *A* and crossed out; the third has no musical setting in any of the manuscripts. One other aria, not marked with asterisks in *L*, was also composed and crossed out; still another, the words of which are nowhere in *L*, was likewise composed and cancelled.

---

[5] GRISELDA / Dramma per musica / da recitarsi / Nella Sala dell'Ill.mo Sig. Federico / Capranica / Nel Carnevale dell'Anno 1721. / Dedicato / All'Ill.mo, & Ecc.mo Signore, il Signor / D. FRANCESCO M.A / Ruspoli / Principe di Cerveteri &c. / [Emblem] / Si vendono a Pasquino nella Libraria di Pietro Leone / all' Insegna di S. Giovanni di Dio. / IN ROMA, pe' Tinassi, MDCCXXI. / Con licenza de' Superiori. 89 pp. Pp. 3–4, dedicatory epistle, signed Federico Capranica; 5–7, Argomento; 7, Protesta, Imprimatur; 9, Mutazioni di Scene, with mention of 'Architetto delle Scene. Il Sig. Francesco Galli Bibiena'; 10, Attori, etc., with mention of 'Sig. Cavaliere Alessandro Scarlatti, Primo Maestro della Real Cappella di Napoli' as composer; also 'I Balli sono invenzione del Sig. Antonio Sarò'. No author named. Exemplar in Brussels Conservatoire, 20619.

On the libretto and its relation to Zeno's *Griselda* of 1701, see my essay 'La *Griselda* di Zeno e il libretto dell'opera di Scarlatti', *Nuova rivista musicale italiana*, ii (1968), 3–21.

In the 'appendix' (pp. 88–9) of *L* are found the words of two arias and a quartet, with directions as to where they are to be inserted in the opera. One of the arias, in Act II, is found set to music in all three eighteenth-century manuscript copies (*S, B, P*); but *B* also includes a setting of the text that this one was meant to replace. Apparently, then, both arias were composed and one of them cancelled; if this is so, the scribe of *B* ignored the cancellation—a most unusual procedure, seemingly, for in every instance where something has been cancelled in the autograph of Acts I and III the scribes of both *S* and *B* have simply omitted it without comment. The second aria in the appendix of *L*, also in Act II, has no musical setting in any of the copies; neither is there any music for the aria (on p. 51 of *L*) that this was meant to replace. Music for the quartet is found in *A* and in all copies.

In sum: there once existed music for (probably) 128 lines of recitative and five (perhaps six or more) arias, all of which was discarded or replaced in the final version of the opera. Now let us leave general statistics and see some of the specific changes that took place in the course of revision.

In only one instance did the changes result in lengthening a recitative. This occurs in I, 8, where the dialogue was expanded in an attempt to account for Gualtiero's apparently cruel and arbitrary repudiation of his faithful wife Griselda, or at least to present him in a somewhat more sympathetic light. The first part of the original recitative has been crossed out on f. 36*–36*ᵛ (*27–27ᵛ*) of *A*; the revised version begins on f. 35, continues on f. 36 (both added leaves, not numbered in the old foliation), resumes on the lower half of 36*ᵛ—the connection being shown by a pair of ╬ signs (equivalent to 'Vi-de')—and connects up with the original version at the top of f. 37 (*28*). Altogether seventeen bars were added. The text as revised corresponds to that of *L*, except that the latter, unlike *A*, numbers all this recitative after the first eight bars, together with the ensuing aria, as a new scene, 9.

The opera begins with a scene in which Gualtiero announces to his nobles and the assembled people his intention to repudiate Griselda, and summons her to appear before him. In the original version she enters to the accompaniment of two or three bars from the orchestra and begins at once her recitative 'Eccoti, o Sire, innanzi'. Both *L* and *A* show that here eight bars of chorus (acclamations of approval from the people) were inserted in place of the orchestral music for Griselda's entrance. The original brief entrance music and the first two bars of her recitative are at the bottom of f. 5ᵛ, heavily crossed out, with the rough figure of a hand with extended index finger and the word 'coro' (apparently not in Scarlatti's writing) pointing to the next page; the added chorus and the first two bars of Griselda's recitative then come on f. 6–6ᵛ (an added leaf), and the recitative continues on f. 7 (6).

The addition of this chorus was one of the many points of difference between Scarlatti's libretto and the one which Apostolo Zeno furnished for the first *Griselda* (Venice, 1701; music by Antonio Pollarolo) and which he later published with minor alterations in the collected edition of his dramatic works. There are a few other clues in Scarlatti's autograph which suggest that he may have been working initially from a libretto similar to Zeno's. At three different places in *A* we find cancelled passages of recitative taken directly from Zeno, but non-existent in *L*: in I, 16 (II, 1 in Zeno), on f. 59ᵛ (50ᵛ), three lines; in III, 11 (III, 8 in Zeno), on f. 106ᵛ, two lines;[6] and later in III, 11 (III, 9 in Zeno), on f. 109–109ᵛ, three lines. On the other hand, the autograph contains two cancelled passages of recitative (five bars in III, 3 on f. 76; three in III, 4 on f. 79) which are in neither *L* nor Zeno. I have not been able to find the source of these passages.[7]

There are a few other faint traces in *L* and *A* of an earlier version of the text. Among the personages in Zeno's libretto of 1701 was one Elpino, a 'servo faceto' who reappears, under various names, in several of the dozen or so *Griselda* librettos printed between 1701 and 1721 and who is retained in Zeno's own revisions of 1725 and 1744. A quite useless character, he is wisely dropped in *L*; but his ghost still hovers about, in

[6] In revising the libretto for Vienna in 1725 Zeno changed these lines—*Gual.* 'Se' custode / Del marital mio letto?'—to the more elegant 'Chi ti elesse / Del talamo custode?'

[7] The words are:

in III, 3:

Rob.	. . . cieco rigore stima fallo il dover, colpa l'Amore
Cost.	Qual dover ti costrinse a volere il tuo affanno e a farti mia non men che tuo tiranno?

in III, 4:

Gual.	Trai fantasmi del sonno mi vedesti giamai?
Cost.	Pur troppo io ti sognai
Gual.	Scaccio ogni tema . . .

the shape of two or three elusive personages who are not listed in the cast and who have nothing to say and little or nothing to do, but who are addressed or alluded to by the other characters: thus in I, 12 Griselda gives a command to one of the guards by name, 'Alceste'; in II, 4 there is a momentary appearance of a certain 'Araspe'; and in III, 10 one line is assigned in Zeno's libretto of 1701 to Elpino, in *L* to 'Are.' or 'Arc.' (Araspe? Alceste?), and in *A*, f. 105^v, to one of the principals—but crossed out (in pencil; hence probably not by the composer).

Keeping company, as it were, with these phantom personages is a phantom libretto and also, perhaps, a lost score. So far as anyone apparently knows, the only libretto ever printed for Scarlatti's *Griselda* was that of Rome, 1721 (*L*). But in the Brussels copy of the score (in I, 7; p. 28) the transcriber writes 'Hier sind 5 Wortzeilen ausgefallen, welche im Textbuch pg. 19 (Linie 2–6 von oben) stehen'. The 'Textbuch' in question is presumably not *L*, where the allegedly lacking words—

> *Cost.* Mal conosci il mio core,
> E pur tutto il possiedi,
> Andienne ora, se'l chiedi,
> Ov'è meno di rischio, e più di pace;
> Seguirò l'orme tue dove ti piace

—occur not near the top of page 19 but near the bottom of page 21. Furthermore, in *B*, from which this scribe was supposedly copying, these words are not missing and there is no evidence that they ever were. The transcriber of the Library of Congress copy, who presumably was also working from *B*, makes no special note at this point. Could the Brussels scribe have been copying from a different score and referring to a different libretto? Inquiries to both East and West Berlin have failed to unearth either. For the time being I can only call attention to this little puzzle without being able to solve it.

Scene 6 of Act I is one of those disembarkation scenes that are so plentiful in operas of this period. In the original version there was a 'Sinfonia per lo sbarco' in three short movements of which the last was a march-like Presto (ff. 21–22 = *20–21*), followed immediately by recitative (f. 22^v = *21^v*). This last movement and the first sixteen and a half bars of the recitative were cancelled and a big new aria inserted (ff. 23^v–28^v: added leaves), after which comes the recitative (f. 29–29^v), slightly altered from the first version. On f. 30 (*22*) may be seen the cancelled original three and a half closing bars of the recitative and the beginning of the next aria (not cancelled).

At one place in the inserted aria (on f. 25) Scarlatti has crossed out five bars in favour of a different continuation. It is noteworthy that here and in similar places elsewhere (second aria in I, 6, f. 31; aria in III, 12, f. 117ᵛ) the abandoned continuation consists of the voice line and words only: one might conjecture that in composing an aria Scarlatti habitually, or at any rate occasionally, made a plan (of the whole aria, or whole sections of it) by first writing the voice part, adding the accompaniment later.

Quite extensive changes were made towards the end of Act III. Beginning with scene 11 the original order of numbers was as follows:

1.	Recitative 'Griselda. (Ahimè)'	*L, A*: sc. 11
2.	Aria (Griselda) 'Se amori ascolterò'	
3.	Recitative 'Io, Signor, ti assicuro'	*L*: sc. 12
4.	Aria (Gualtiero) 'Non partir da chi t'adora'	
5.	Recitative 'Intesi, o m'ingannai?'	*L*: sc. 13
6.	Aria (Roberto) 'Non so che sia'	
7.	Recitative 'Numi: saria mai vero?'	*L*: sc. 14
8.	Aria (Costanza) 'Se vaga, se bella'	
9.	Aria (Corrado) 'Pargoletto che porti felice'	*L, A*: sc. 15
10.	Recitative 'Terminate, o Ministri'	
11.	Recitative 'Griselda. Altro non manca'	*Scena ultima*

In the course of revision the aria No. 2 in the above list was dropped. The text, slightly modified from Zeno's original, is marked with asterisks in *L*; the music in *A*, ff. 107ᵛ–109, is cancelled. The two recitatives Nos. 1 and 3 thus were made to run on without interruption, ending in *A* (at the end of a gathering) on f. 109ᵛ. At this point a new number, a 'set piece', was inserted, the quartet 'Non fu mai colpa Amor'. The text is in the appendix of *L* with instructions as to where it was to be sung; the music is in *A*, ff. 110–13, a complete gathering of four (probably inserted) leaves. The aria No. 4 (text also from Zeno) was deleted; it is marked with asterisks in *L*, and there is no music for it in *A*; if it was ever composed, the folios containing it must simply have been removed. The recitative No. 5 and the aria No. 6, constituting scene 13 in *L*, are in *A* beginning on f. 114 (a new gathering), both cancelled. Then follow the recitative and aria Nos. 7 and 8, with music in *A* on ff. 116ᵛ–19. The next aria (No. 9) was dropped: the text is lacking in *L*, and the music in *A*, ff. 119–20, is crossed out. Thus the new scene 15—at which point there is a *mutazione* or change of scenery—consists only of the short recitative No. 10, going then directly into the *scena ultima*. There may once have been an aria at the end of scene 15, but if so no trace of it remains. The entrance of all the characters for the final scene apparently takes place during the recitative No. 10.

As revised, then, this portion of Act III became:

1. Recitatives 'Griselda. (Ahimè)' and
   'Io, Signor, ti assicuro'   sc. 11
2. Quartet 'Non fu mai colpa Amor'

3. Recitative 'Numi: saria mai vero?'
4. Aria (Costanza) 'Se vaga, se bella'   sc. 12

5. Recitative 'Terminate, o Ministri'   sc. 13

6. Recitative 'Griselda. Altro non manca'   *Scena ultima*

Particularly interesting are the changes affecting the arias of Costanza, the role in which the famous castrato Carestini (*c.*1705–60) made his operatic début. He seems to have been rather specially favoured in the revisions—remarkably so, one would think, for a teenage débutant artist. (Did he have a powerful patron in Rome? Was Scarlatti so impressed with his talents?) To begin with, notice in the changes listed above that, whereas four of the other principals each lost an aria, Carestini-Costanza did not lose his: the new scene 12 (originally 14) is a solo scene for Costanza. Moreover the text of the aria is completely new, totally unlike the aria that Zeno had provided for this place. *B* has two complete versions of another of Costanza's solo scenes (II, 9) with almost identical opening recitatives but different arias. The second aria, a replacement (the text is in the appendix of *L*), is considerably more elaborate than the first, with a great deal of coloratura; one might surmise that Carestini—or his patron, or Scarlatti himself—at this point felt the need for something that would show off his vocal powers to better advantage. In the middle of II, 6 there is a quite superfluous aria, 'Ti voglio contentar', for Costanza-Carestini; the text is in its regular place in *L*, without asterisks, but no musical setting is found in any of the manuscripts. Since Act II is lacking in the autograph it is impossible to say with certainty whether Scarlatti ever composed this text; but the unusual presence in *B* of a double bar in the middle of the recitative, just at the place where the aria stands in *L*, suggests that an aria (cancelled?) once stood there. A similar situation occurs at the beginning of II, 11, where *L* has one text for an aria of Costanza at the proper place (not marked with asterisks) and another, a replacement, in the appendix; again one finds no musical setting in the manuscripts— but again this is not to say that none ever existed.

Costanza's first aria, 'Godi, bell'alma' (I, 9) was completely rewritten. The original setting (see Pl. V), in ₵ with unison violins and independent solo oboe, is on ff. 40–41ᵛ and 44 (*32–33ᵛ, 34*: five continuous pages in the old foliation) and has been cancelled; the new version (see Pl. VI), in ₵ $\frac{3}{8}$ without oboe, is on ff. 42ᵛ–43ᵛ (inserted leaves). It is a thorough *rifacimento* of the rather sober original, with livelier movement in the accompaniment, long passages of brilliant coloratura, and a whole silent bar near the end for a cadenza *ad libitum*. This is another case like that of the aria in II, 9; on the whole Carestini, for whatever cause, came out very well.

There is one other class of alteration in the autograph: in the ritornellos of certain arias (nine in Act I, five in Act III) passages from one to five bars in length have been cancelled. All such cancellations occur in the middle of the ritornello, never at the beginning or end. Many seem simply to be abandoned continuations, but others are apparently excisions for the purpose of tightening up a ritornello which Scarlatti felt to be too long, either for the particular dramatic situation or in proportion to the other ritornellos in the aria. There are, however, some puzzling features about these deletions which I hope to deal with in another article.

Now finally, and solely by way of hypothesis, I will try to outline the general order of events in the composition of *Griselda*. I assume: (*i*) that Scarlatti began the composition using a now lost version of the libretto, earlier than that which we have in *L* and closer than *L* to Zeno's original text; and (*ii*) that some though not all of the changes from this earlier libretto were decided upon before *L* was printed.

These earliest changes, therefore, will be seen only in *A*; they will leave no traces in *L*. Such were: (*i*) elimination of four non-virgolated lines of recitative in Act I, five in Act III and an unknown number in Act II; (*ii*) addition of the chorus in I, 1; (*iii*) substitution of an aria in place of the last movement of the 'Sinfonia per lo sbarco' in I, 6; (*iv*) elimination of Corrado's aria in the original scene 15 of Act III.

Doubtless also among the earliest revisions was the cancellation of those passages of recitative which are virgolated in *L*: 52 lines in Acts I and III and (probably) 65 more in Act II. Likewise an early decision, I believe, was the expansion of the recitative in I, 8. The text as it stands revised in *A* is exactly the same in *L*, but there it is divided into two scenes, 8 and 9; this apparently was done, however, only to respect the convention according to which any entrance or exit marked a change of 'scene'.

Further changes were made only after *L* had been printed, or at least set up in type. Scarlatti had composed an aria, 'Non lasciar', for Corrado in I, 17 which was cancelled too late to remove the words from the libretto but soon enough to set a triple asterisk against them in the margin. The radical changes in III, 11 onwards were also made after the libretto was printed. The recitatives and arias of the original version remain in *L* except for the one aria of Corrado which had already been eliminated. All that could be done now was to indicate with asterisks the arias of Griselda and Gualtiero and to direct in the appendix that scene 13 was to be omitted and the new quartet was to take its place. I imagine that this whole transformation started with someone, fairly well on in the preparations, conceiving the idea that since here are four good singers, why not give them a quartet somewhere? One thing led to another: this part of Act III was becoming rather too long, holding up the inevitable grand closing scene and the *lieto fine*, stringing out the almost unbroken alternation of recitatives and arias that had been going on all evening. Why not, then, introduce a little variety and put the quartet here? Make time for it by cutting out three arias and a recitative and so get ahead sooner to the finale.

It has already been pointed out that Carestini lost nothing in the course of this particular transaction. It may now be added generally that the changes involving his role of Costanza were among the last to be made. Costanza's arias in II, 6 and 11, both probably deleted, were in the middle and at the opening of their respective scenes—unfavourable spots, since they did not permit the full stop, the exit, and, if all went well, the applause that followed an aria when placed in its usual position at the end of a scene. That these two arias were removed only after the libretto had been printed is apparent from the fact that neither text is asterisked in *L* and the text of the intended substitute for one of them still remains in the appendix. As for Costanza's 'Godi, bell'alma' in I, 9, we know that it was completely recast and that the new version appears on two inserted folios in the autograph. The handwriting here, though it is certainly Scarlatti's, shows evidence of extreme haste; perhaps it is not too fanciful to suppose that this alteration was made at the very last minute.

It is common knowledge that Italian operas in the eighteenth century frequently underwent changes in both libretto and music. As a rule, however, such changes took place when an opera was revived at a later time, or in a different city, or with different singers; and they usually included, among other things, a fairly thorough revamping of the plot with changes in the cast of characters and the simple replacement of some or all of the original arias by new ones, usually by another composer. The changes in Scarlatti's *Griselda* are not of this kind. They were made by the composer himself, either before any public performance of the work or else immediately after a preliminary (?private) performance, in preparation for the official première. No changes were made in the plot, no characters shifted or renamed. Where arias were added, omitted or substituted, the evidence comes not from a different score or libretto; on the contrary, the very same documents that give us the final version of the opera enable us to reconstruct to a considerable extent the original version as well.

Handel's 'Sosarme', a Puzzle Opera

WINTON DEAN

In a sense nearly all Handel's operas are puzzle operas. In a surprising number of instances the source of the libretto has been identified wrongly or not at all, and we do not know who adapted it for Handel. No correspondence survives to throw light on the reasons for the choice, or the part played by Handel in the adaptation, though in some operas this must have been appreciable.[1] The music too raises many questions that have never been answered or fully investigated. Yet there is enough material to keep a posse of musicological detectives at work for years. By the study of autographs, sketches, performing scores, other manuscript copies, parts, printed librettos and early musical editions, evidence of the capacity of singers and various other sources, it is possible to plot in detail the history of almost every major work from the moment Handel put the first note on paper to the last revival during his life. Few great composers other than Beethoven have left so many clues to the inner working of their creative processes. The amount of unpublished music, whether rejected by Handel or omitted or not discovered by Chrysander, is enormous, and the conclusions to be drawn are nearly always illuminating and occasionally startling.

Sosarme is something of a problem child. No one would rank it among the greatest of Handel's operas, which are landmarks in the history of the art. It has had an indifferent press from historians and scholars. Burney, it is true, ranked it among Handel's 'most pleasing theatrical compositions', but he judged by standards that satisfy few critics today,

---

[1] No one else could have introduced words as well as music from works of the Italian period into operas written for London, a not infrequent occurrence from *Rinaldo* to *Alcina*. For further discussion of this point, see my *Handel and the Opera Seria*, London, 1970, pp. 41–2.

assessing each opera as a string of arias written for particular singers rather than a musical drama based on the conflict of character and emotion. To Streatfeild *Sosarme* was 'another of Handel's less important operas', to Dent 'another unsatisfactory opera'. Between Handel's only revival in 1734 and Alan Kitching's Abingdon production in September 1970 it was never performed in the theatre, despite the widespread enthusiasm that has resurrected more than thirty of Handel's thirty-nine surviving operas, many of them repeatedly, in the last half century. Yet it was one of the first to be broadcast by the BBC and made available on the gramophone (Oiseau Lyre, 1955, conducted by Anthony Lewis), and the first in which the voices (with one minor exception) were recorded at their original pitch. Most people who know the score or the recording would probably agree that it is full of magnificent music, whatever their reservations about the libretto.

It is this libretto that presents some, though not all, of the problems. Before reviewing them it is necessary to summarize the plot and the early history of the opera. There are discrepancies between Chrysander's edition, the 1732 printed libretto and the autograph as Handel left it, especially in the matter of stage directions. Those printed here in italics are from the libretto, except where stated; most of them are in the autograph too. Chrysander omits a fair number, among them the description of the duel in which two of the principal characters are wounded.

The background of the story is difficult to grasp without the aid of the Argument, given in Italian and English in the libretto on sale in the theatre but never reprinted:

Sosarmes King of Media falling in Love with Elmira, Daughter of Haliates King of Lydia, at the Report he heard of her Beauty, demanded her in Marriage of her Father, who readily assented: But about the Time that Elmira was preparing for her Departure to her Husband, a cruel Rebellion broke out in Lydia, which obliged the Princess to defer her Journey. The Author of this Rebellion was Argones, the eldest Son and Successor of Haliates, prompted to it by Jealousy he entertained, that his Father intended to advance his natural Son Melus, whom he tenderly lov'd, to the Throne. When Argones had openly declared himself a Rebel against his Father, the latter was obliged to take up Arms, and besiege the City of Sardis, where his Son and the Rebels had shut themselves up, and by Treachery made themselves Masters of the Palace itself. Both the Besiegers, and those they besieged were equally obstinate . . .

We learn in the course of the opera that Melo's mother was Anagilda, daughter of Haliate's trusted but treacherous old counsellor Altomaro. Elmira and her mother Erenice, Haliate's queen, are prisoners in the palace seized by Argone, whereas Sosarme and his forces are with Haliate's besieging army.

ACT I opens in *the great Square of Sardis, with Soldiers drawn up in Battalia*. The city has withstood every assault, but is in danger of succumbing to famine. Argone proposes a sortie to seize supplies from the enemy. He *draws his Sword, the Soldiers doing the same*, and after a brief military chorus all depart. Within the palace Erenice tells Elmira of a dream in which Hecate told her to cease weeping, since the war shall be ended this day by 'the Royal Blood thy Son shall shed'. Erenice fears the death of husband or son. Elmira tries to reassure her and leaves, but returns at once *with an afflicted Air*: Argone is preparing a sortie. Erenice's fears are reinforced, and Elmira goes off to try to dissuade her brother. Erenice follows: if Argone will not yield to her tears, he must kill her first. The scene changes to *an Incampment* outside the city. Altomaro compares his grandson's mental confusion to that of a moth when the light has gone out. Melo discusses the political situation with Sosarme, who finds him more worthy of the throne the more he scorns it. Melo supports Sosarme's mission to reconcile the warring parties, but this receives an immediate setback from Haliate, who swears to exact condign vengeance on Argone and his supporters without respect for sex, consanguinity, age or innocence. In that case, Sosarme replies, he will no longer be Haliate's son-in-law but his mortal enemy. Haliate's rage against Argone's insults and pride continues unabated. The next scene reverts to Sardis: *a Royal Court-yard. Argones armed with Soldiers and Officers*. He is still planning his sortie. *As he retires he meets with Erenice and Elmira*, who both beg him to abandon the enterprise. When Erenice bids him trample on the bosom that gave him life, *he continues in Suspense* until a repetition of the military chorus in the first scene recalls him to his resolution and he departs *in haste*. Erenice is desolate: whoever slays the other will rob her of half her happiness. Elmira asks Hecate how the shedding of royal blood can bring reconciliation: if that is the way the fates announce peace, how would they predict war?

ACT II. Elmira in the palace dreads the loss of father, brother or husband. She describes to Erenice the sortie from Sardis and the fight with Sosarme's soldiers, but dust and smoke prevent her seeing the result. *A warlike Symphony is heard*; Argone enters, his sword covered with blood. He says it is royal, and Sosarme's; *Elmira swoons*[2] *in the arms of*

[2] *'Viene'* (Chrysander's edition) should be *'sviene'*.

Erenice. Erenice charges Argone with three murders, 'one with thy cruel Sword, and two with Grief', and blushes 'to have a Monster for my Son'. *Elmira is carry'd away in a Swoon by her Ladies.*[3] Argone tries to explain, but Erenice dismisses him as a traitor to love and duty. In a *garden*[4] Haliate is unmanned by his defeat. Melo reports that Sosarme's Medes have mutinied and are demanding the rescue of their captured King. Altomaro accuses Melo of engineering the mutiny, and Haliate denounces both his sons: one is a rebel, the other wants to see him scorned and unavenged. Melo denies this; Altomaro emphasizes the duty of monarchs to quell the haughty. Haliate suddenly changes his mind and orders Altomaro to offer peace and pardon to Argone. Altomaro again chides Melo for abjuring his own greatness. Melo is convinced that providence punishes the guilty. Altomaro, all the more determined to place Melo on the throne, rejoices that his genius has discovered the means. The scene changes to *a Closet*[5] [in Sardis]. *Sosarme reposing on a Bed, and Elmira applying Remedies to his Wound.* He rejoices that so slight an injury should have brought him so great a reward. Both agree that the path to happiness passes through pain. Erenice reports the arrival of Haliate's peace offer and asks Sosarme to urge its acceptance on Argone. He says he came to Sardis and allowed himself to be captured for that very purpose; honour is the sole motive for military glory. In *a Room of Audience with a Throne* Sosarme persuades Argone to receive Haliate's envoy. *An Officer goes out to introduce Altomarus.* Argone promises to beg Haliate's pardon in return for the restoration of his right to the succession. Altomaro enters and says that Haliate will conclude peace if Argone first fights him in single combat. *Argones appears astonish'd*; Elmira, Erenice and Sosarme are outraged. Argone bitterly accepts the challenge. He and Altomaro depart in opposite directions.[6] Erenice, recommending Argone to Sosarme's care, sets off for Haliate's camp to soften his rage. Sosarme promises to appease Argone and then return to Elmira's arms for ever. Elmira hopes that Erenice and Sosarme will prevail and bring back Argone like a bird to its nest or a tigress to her young.

ACT III. *The Suburbs of Sardis, with Military Tents at a Distance.* Altomaro tells Haliate that Argone not only spurns his peace offer but challenges him to single combat, set on by Erenice 'with all the Art of Language'. Haliate once more hardens his heart. When Erenice enters

[3] 'Knights accompanying Argone' in Handel's autograph.
[4] 'A royal pavilion' in the autograph.
[5] The autograph has '*Fonderia Reale*'.
[6] This detail is in the autograph but not the libretto.

he has her arrested and put in Melo's charge: whether he himself or Argone is killed, the survivor will always be a source of remorse to her. Melo soon discovers Altomaro's perfidy from Erenice and sends her to his tent *attended by the Guards*. He means to expose Altomaro by taking his father's place in the duel, dropping his sword and embracing his brother. The scene changes to *a Royal Garden. Argones attended by an Officer, with two Swords. . . . As he is going out, he's stop'd by Elmira and Sosarmes*, who try vainly to detain him. He departs *in a Rage*. Sosarme follows, promising to quench Argone's fury with his own blood. Elmira, banishing tears, screws up her courage to confront Argone: pleasures are seasoned by the pain that precedes them. In *a Field appointed for the Duel* Haliate orders Altomaro to keep the lists clear and allow no one to obstruct his chastening wrath. Altomaro compares Haliate to Jove and bids him destroy his 'impious Offspring'. Haliate rejects Melo's plea to take his place. *Altomarus with two Swords, Haliates, Argones, with an Officer bearing two Swords*. After an exchange of insults Altomaro *presents a Sword to Argones whilst the Officer presents another to Haliates: They afterwards put themselves upon their Guard, and begin the Combat. The aforesaid, and Erenice, who advances to Argones and Melus, who goes to Haliates, and both of them are wounded [disgraziatamente feriti], the Mother by the Son, and Melus by the Father*. Altomaro declares that all is lost and *betakes himself to Flight, and Erenice goes to Haliates, whilst Melus advances to Argones. . . . They throw away their Swords and stand in Suspense*. Melo explains Altomaro's deception, presently confirmed by Sosarme and Elmira. Sosarme reports Altomaro's suicide, and all are reconciled.

Handel completed the score on 4 February 1732; there is no date at the beginning. The first performance took place at the King's Theatre on 15 February with the following cast:

Sosarme	Francesco Bernardi, known as Senesino	Alto castrato
Argone	Antonio Gualandi, known as Campioli	Alto castrato
Elmira	Anna Strada	Soprano
Erenice	Anna Bagnolesi	Contralto
Melo	Francesca Bertolli	Contralto
Haliate	Giovanni Battista Pinacci	Tenor
Altomaro	Antonio Montagnana	Bass

There were eleven performances during the season, and the reception was enthusiastic; Viscount Percival, Francis Colman, Burney and the anonymous author of a pamphlet, *See and Seem Blind*, are all in agreement on this. The two duets for Elmira and Sosarme were especially popular; 'Per le porte del tormento' was sung at least six times during the 1733–4 season, in the intervals of various plays at the King's Theatre and Drury Lane, by 'Miss Arne and Young Master Arne', the future Mrs. Cibber and the younger brother of the composer. Handel was to introduce it into *Imeneo* in Dublin in 1742. He revived *Sosarme* for three performances in 1734, the first on 27 April, at a time when his rivalry with the Opera of the Nobility was at its height and both companies were in low financial water. No printed libretto has been found. The future Mrs. Delany, who heard it twice, considered it 'a most delightful opera' and 'a charming one, and yet I dare say it will be almost empty! 'Tis vexatious to have *such music* neglected.' Her misgivings were well founded; *Sosarme* was not heard again for more than 200 years.

The autograph shows that two strange things befell the opera before the score was even finished. For the greater part of two acts the original scene of action was not Sardis but Coimbra in Portugal; the title was *Fernando, Rè di Castiglia*, and with the exception of Altomaro the characters all had different names. Sosarme was Fernando, Argone Alfonso, Melo Sancio, Haliate Dionisio, Elmira Elvida, and Erenice Isabella. Barclay Squire is not quite correct in saying that 'the first two acts were set to this book'.[7] When Handel transferred the scene from Iberia to Asia Minor, which he did by changing every name in the autograph up to the point he had reached,[8] Act I ended with Isabella's aria 'Due parti del core', the soprano aria 'Vola l'augello' (later the finale of Act II) occurred at Elvida's exit in I, 3, and 'Il mio valore' was probably not present, at least in the form we know.[9] Act II went as far as 'Vado al campo'; scenes 13 and 14 did not exist. The music had already undergone important revision, and the recitatives were much longer. This drastic abridgment of the recitatives, after they had been fully set, is the second strange fact. It did not tighten up the action; on the contrary, it obscured the motivation and rendered a none too convincing plot almost comically inconsequent. Chunks were removed from six scenes in Act I and five in Act II, and every character in the opera was affected. The cuts amounted in all to 134 bars, more than a hundred of them in Act I. Argone and especially Melo were more fully treated in the original version; Melo's resistance to Altomaro and sympathy with Sosarme were established with greater firmness. But

[7] *Catalogue of the King's Music Library*, i (London, 1927), 83.

[8] He made one or two other small changes; Isabella in her dream (I, 2) did not see 'Hecate . . . spuntar dal Cielo', but 'Irene . . . sorger dall'acqua'.

[9] It bears the name of Sosarme, not Fernando.

the character who suffered most was Haliate. His sudden change of mind towards Argone in II, 5 had been prepared by a much more extended treatment of his recitative in I, 8. Instead of the perfunctory eight bars that now stand in the score he had a prolonged soliloquy of 50 bars, in which he vacillated between thirst for revenge and the natural urge to spare and come to terms with his rebellious son; in the middle, when he has apparently decided on pardon, we find the direction *Stà un poco sospeso, poi infuriato*. This is a turning point in the action, and we might have expected Handel to give it a string accompaniment. He did not do so, but his setting is highly dramatic, and its suppression a serious loss.

Already at least seven questions present themselves. (*i*) What was the original source of the libretto? (*ii*) Who were the historical persons involved? (*iii*) Who adapted it for Handel? (*iv*) Why did Handel put himself to the trouble of altering nearly all the names half way through the composition? (*v*) Why did he injure the opera by decimating the recitatives? (*vi*) When did he carry out these two operations? (*vii*) What exactly happened in 1734, when his company included only one of the 1732 cast and several of the other voices were of different pitch? (It would be easy to pose further questions of an aesthetic nature: how did Handel come to accept such a wretched text in the first place, and how did it inspire him to so much marvellously inventive music? But the first is unfathomable, and the answer to the second is doubtless that Handel, though intensely susceptible to a dramatic story and the conflict of credible characters, was a musician of such exceptional fecundity that he could respond to a string of arias piecemeal and even conjure beauty out of a near-vacuum.)

Of the seven questions, only the first has ever received a firm answer —and it is wrong. It is also the only one to which I cannot offer a possible solution. According to Burney, Chrysander, Loewenberg and William C. Smith the source libretto was Matteo Noris's *Alfonso Primo*, set by Carlo Francesco Pollarolo for Venice in 1694. There is a copy of Noris's work in the Library of Congress, and it has no connection with *Sosarme* either in character or plot. Diligent search has so far failed to unearth the true source, whose probable title was that on the first page of Handel's autograph, *Fernando, Rè di Castiglia*.

Noris's title led Dent to propose Alfonso I, first King of Portugal, as the original of Argone. This is a red herring. Iberian history is so full of Fernandos, Alfonsos and Isabellas that it would be difficult to date the action from these names alone; but Dionisio gives the clue. He is Diniz, also known as Dionysius, King of Portugal from 1279 to 1325 and founder of the University of Coimbra. The other potentates are his son and successor Alfonso IV (The Fierce), chiefly remembered as the murderer of his son's mistress Ines da Castro, and Ferdinand IV, King of Castile from 1295 to 1312. This places the action closer to Handel's time than that of any of his other operas except *Tamerlano*. The point is academic; even the transmogrification of Portuguese into Lydians and Castilians into Medes makes very little difference in an *opera seria* of this period.[10]

There is a possible clue to the identity of Handel's collaborator in II, 5, where Altomaro fans the flame of Haliate's revenge with the words 'Debellar i superbi, è virtù regia'. This echo of Virgil's famous line in the *Aeneid*, 'Parcere subjectis et debellare superbos', is paralleled in two earlier Handel librettos, *Alessandro* and *Riccardo Primo*. Both are free adaptations of earlier material by Paolo Rolli. It seems likely that the same hand was at work on *Sosarme*, drawing on some libretto imported from Italy. The creaking mechanism of the plot is typical of Rolli, as the two operas cited and *Muzio Scevola* amply attest. If the original is ever found, it might prove to be a much more coherent piece of work than *Sosarme* as we have it.

The reason for the change of names was almost certainly political. King John V of Portugal, who reigned from 1706 to 1750, was the richest ruler in Europe, thanks to the mineral wealth of Brazil, and a man of excessive punctilio in matters of status, who in 1729 had arranged a dynastic marriage with the Spanish royal family.[11] The Portuguese were Britain's oldest traditional allies. A libretto that presented them in a most unflattering light, their king engaged in an undignified civil war with his son and requiring to be rescued by his neighbour of Castile, might well cause apprehension at the court of George II. Handel was not a political animal; it seems likely that his attention was drawn at a late stage to the risks of offending a friendly but touchy ruler and that this explains the abrupt translation of the story from the Iberian peninsula to a remote Sardis. The name Sosarme seems to have been invented for the occasion.

This does not account for the abridgment of the recitative. Here the decisive factor was beyond question the resounding failure of *Ezio*, produced exactly a month before *Sosarme* on 15 January 1732; it enjoyed

[10] Parts of *Siroe* (1728) and *Ezio* (late 1731), like *Sosarme*, were originally composed to different librettos.
[11] I am indebted to Professor Hugh Trevor-Roper for enlightenment on the historical background here.

fewer performances (five) than any of its predecessors—or indeed any of its successors before *Berenice* in 1737. London audiences were very critical of Italian *secco* recitative, which they found tedious if not positively absurd. Handel's natural reaction to failure would be a retrenchment in this direction. From about 1731 the proportion of recitative in his operas, whether new works or revivals, declined steadily and sometimes steeply from what it had been during the Royal Academy years. The point could be illustrated from almost any production of the period, especially after *Ezio*. The consequences are often baffling to anyone concerned to follow the development and motivation of the plots; but contemporary listeners were more interested in arias and singers, and they were helped by the explanatory Argument as well as the text (including some omitted passages) in the printed libretto.

The autograph makes it clear that the change of names and locale and the shortening of the recitatives were carried out at the same time. There are no recitative cuts in Act III other than four or five lines in the last scene that Handel wrote out but never set, a frequent occurrence in the autographs. At first glance it might be tempting to conjecture that the proto-*Sosarme* dates back to the Royal Academy period, before John V's Spanish marriage, but the compass and tessitura of the vocal writing make this untenable. The part of Altomaro was certainly composed for Montagnana, who did not arrive till the autumn of 1731; Boschi, a high baritone, could never have sung it. Although the autograph bears no initial date, it is likely that Handel began *Sosarme* in late December or early January and finished it after the production of *Ezio*, slashing the recitative in a desperate attempt to save it.

For the 1734 revival we must rely, in the absence of a libretto, on the two scores used by the continuo players in the theatre. Fortunately both survive, one among the collection of performance copies in the Staats- und Universitätsbibliothek, Hamburg, the other in Chrysander's private library, now deposited at the same place. With their aid it is possible to deduce not only what Handel performed, but a number of expedients that he considered and subsequently rejected. He now had a company comprising three sopranos, three altos and a bass, compared with one soprano, four altos, a tenor and a bass two years earlier. Strada was available to sing Elmira, but the second castrato was a soprano and there was no tenor. Several solutions were open to Handel; the one he adopted was almost certainly that given by Otto Erich Deutsch,[12] though where Deutsch found it is a mystery he was unable to elucidate in response to an enquiry some years ago. It is possible

[12] *Handel, a Documentary Biography*, London, 1955, p. 364.

that he discovered a libretto. This is his cast (the voices are the same as in 1732 except where stated):

Sosarme	Giovanni Carestini	Mezzo-soprano castrato
Argone	Carlo Scalzi	Soprano castrato
Elmira	Strada	
Erenice	Maria Caterina Negri	
Melo	Rosa Negri	
Haliate	Margherita Durastanti	Soprano
Altomaro	Gustavus Waltz	

Before settling on this it is clear from various transpositions scribbled on the first performing score (*H*) that Handel considered a different arrangement. (In the following pages the Hamburg score is designated *H*, Chrysander's library copy *C*, and his printed edition *HG*.) He marked Haliate's second aria up a sixth for contralto, probably Maria Negri, and several pieces in Erenice's part, including the duet with Argone, up a tone, which would take it outside the compass of either of the Negris. It seems to have been intended for Durastanti, whose voice had dropped nearly to mezzo-soprano; in the event she probably sang the tenor part of Haliate an octave above its written pitch, though the evidence is not absolutely conclusive. Several of these transpositions were marked by Smith on the other copy (*C*) but later cancelled.

Handel's difficulties were not yet solved. Carestini's voice, a coloratura mezzo-soprano similar in range to that of many Rossini heroines, was higher and wider in compass than Senesino's. Scalzi was not only a soprano but a far better singer than Campioli, an artist of such dubious attainments that Handel never composed an aria for him. Maria Negri was scarcely up to the standard of Bagnolesi, her sister Rosa well below that of Bertolli. Durastanti had been a fine singer (she was the original Agrippina in 1709, and Handel had composed many cantatas for her as early as 1707),[13] but her voice had declined in reliability as well as pitch, as all her parts at this period testify. Waltz was no Montagnana and in no position to tackle the tremendous span of 'Fra l'ombre'. Every one of these limitations was catered for by Handel with characteristic professional skill, though sometimes with more care for the voices than for the drama.

All Sosarme's music outside the recitative was modified for Carestini. In the two duets with Elmira Handel simply wrote (in pencil in *H*) higher alternatives for the low-lying passages; they appear in small notes in *HG*. 'Alle sfere' was put up a tone to G major (requiring the

[13] Ursula Kirkendale, 'The Ruspoli Documents on Handel', *Journal of the American Musicological Society*, xx (1967), 222.

use of brilliant horns in G, which Handel employed to such splendid effect in *Giulio Cesare*, *Alcina* and elsewhere), the very low-pitched 'In mille dolci modi' up a fourth,[14] also to G major. 'In mio valore' was replaced by 'Agitato da fiere tempeste', 'M'opporrò' by 'Nube che il sole adombra'. Both these arias had been written for Senesino in *Riccardo Primo*, and each was transposed up a major third, to D and G major respectively, with the words modified in places to fit the new context. The effect was to shift the balance and character of Sosarme's part, now confined to the major mode, in the direction of extrovert bravura and sharp keys. 'Agitato da fiere tempeste' can scarcely be considered a suitable introduction for a would-be peacemaker.

Scalzi as Argone received three arias: 'Corro per ubbidirvi' in I, 1 between his accompanied recitative and the *coro militare*; Sosarme's 'Il mio valore', transposed up a tone to A minor, in place of the duet with Erenice in II, 3; and 'Quell'orror delle procelle' in F major at the end of III, 6 (*HG*, p. 93, after Elmira's 'T'arresta'). The first and third of the inserted pieces are again from *Riccardo Primo*, an opera composed for a specific occasion that Handel never intended to revive and cannibalized freely in subsequent works. They had been sung by Faustina and Senesino respectively, the former at the same pitch (A major), the latter a fourth lower in C. The verbal changes disturbed the initial words, which in *Riccardo* are 'Vado per obedirti' and 'All'orror delle procelle'. In 'Corro per ubbidirvi' the music too was altered, the second half (before the return of the first line of text) being reduced from eighteen to seven bars. Handel's pencil annotations in *H* show that he took some time to make up his mind about the substituted arias. He allotted 'Agitato da fiere tempeste' to Argone in I, 1 and to Sosarme in I, 7, 'Il mio valore' to Argone in III, 6, and something now indecipherable to Sosarme in III, 7 before settling on the ultimate positions. When 'Il mio valore' was recopied in A minor for *H* the violin part was adjusted in the fourth bar and later to avoid the top E; Handel usually treated *d'''* as the violins' top note.

The other parts—except Elmira, which Strada sang unchanged except for a seemingly pointless cut of five bars in 'Padre, germano' (*HG*, pp. 42–3)—were all significantly shortened. Erenice lost the duet with Argone and 'Cuor di madre'. Melo lost 'Sò ch'il ciel' and the two passages in 'Sì, sì minaccia' bracketed in *HG*. Altomaro lost 'Fra l'ombre'. For Durastanti Handel made extensive cuts in the long and brilliant 'La turba adulatrice': not only the three indicated in *HG* but

---

[14] Handel changed his mind more than once about the interval, noting the new key first as G, then as F, then again as G.

two more, bars 28 and 29 (*HG*, p. 29) and no fewer than seventeen and a half bars in the second half, from the middle of bar 81 to the end of bar 98. This eased the veteran singer's task, incidentally removing the only top A in the aria—a note no longer accessible to Durastanti[15]—and involved alterations and rebarring at the end of the second half (of which more below). 'S'io cadrò' was probably also cut; Durastanti could not have sung it untransposed, and the note 'Segue l'aria' before it is crossed out in *H*. The words 'Haliate D' in the margin of *C* at the end of III, 10 (*HG*, p. 100, first bar), preceded by a modified cadence, suggest that Handel considered compensating her here; but there is nothing in *H*.

Handel's method of indicating cuts is worth comment. He did not remove or cancel whole arias, presumably because they might be reinstated, though he sometimes ran a pencil across the first or last page for the convenience of the continuo player. As a rule he made things doubly clear in *H* by marking an exit for the character (*Parte*) in the recitative, e.g. for Altomaro before 'Fra l'ombre', Melo before 'Sò ch'il ciel', and Erenice before 'Cuor di madre'. For recitatives and cuts within the set pieces the procedure was different. Handel crossed out what was to be omitted in pencil in one or both copies, and blank paper was then pasted over the music. Slight changes and modified cadences were sometimes necessary. Chrysander did not always record them. When Handel made the bracketed cut on *HG*, p. 12 he altered the notes to which the words 'il ciglio' were set from $a'-b'-b'$ to $b'-e-e$. Chrysander prints only the 1734 version.

The recitatives were treated even more ruthlessly in 1734 than they had been before the score was finished. Handel removed not only the eleven passages indicated in *HG* but several others (some 168 bars in all): the last five bars in II, 6 (after 'colla perfidia', *HG*, p. 52), the eight bars from 'ma di pietà' to 'quest'alma' in II, 8 (*HG*, p. 59), the first three words of II, 10 (*HG*, p. 72), the first six bars of III, 3 (*HG*, p. 86) and the last eight in III, 4 (after 'perfido Altomaro', *HG*, p. 90). Several of these cuts involved autograph changes in *H*, and the last of them evoked a new cadence in B major, written by Handel over the old recitative and copied by Smith on a fresh page in both copies.

By this time the reader may be wondering why Chrysander in *HG* chose to indicate some of the 1734 cuts and one of the transpositions ('In mille dolci modi'),[16] but ignored seven other internal cuts, two

---

[15] Handel had not written it for her since *Radamisto* in April 1720, though she reached it once in the 1722 revival of *Floridante*.

[16] In the 'A' version of the recitative before this aria the penultimate note in the bass should of course be C♯, not C♮ as printed.

transpositions, one aria transferred to another character and four inserted from another opera, all modified from their original form. To which there is no satisfactory answer, except that it is typical of his editorial method. There is no means of predicting how much he will print of what lies before him, whether in autographs, performing scores or other sources, and he offers no explanations. In some operas (*Ottone, Tamerlano, Scipione*) he prints music from the autographs that Handel rejected before performance; in others (*Flavio, Giulio Cesare*) he omits similar pieces of equal or superior quality as well as material in the performing score. Elsewhere (*Muzio Scevola*) he excludes music that was not only performed but printed in Handel's time, and gives one whole character to the wrong voice. Of two arias unperformed in *Ariodante* one is left and the other taken. Very seldom are we offered all the available material. The procedure seems totally haphazard.

This arbitrary method leads to an anomaly in 'La turba adulatrice', where Chrysander prints a conflation of two versions containing a floating half bar (bar 99, *HG*, p. 33). It is not inconceivable that Handel might have allowed this; in fact he took special care to avoid it. The autograph version (Ex. 1a), followed by the early copy (without recitatives) British Museum R.M.19.a.5 and the parts in the Newman Flower Collection, was altered in 1734: when he made the long cut mentioned above, Handel removed half a bar at the cadence and shifted the intervening bar-lines (Ex. 1b). This change is made by careful erasures and insertions in both performing copies, though there is a mistake in *C*, which has the equivalent of *HG*'s short bar 99 included in the cut.

Another type of error springs from Chrysander's exaggerated faith in the performing scores as against the autographs, based perhaps on a misapprehension of their purpose. Although one at least was always a full score,[17] they served in performance as continuo parts; there was of course no conductor wagging a stick and making sure the orchestra played what he had before him. If Smith made a mistake in copying the upper parts it might well remain unnoticed, or at least uncorrected;[18] the individual parts would naturally be put right. When Handel marked 'Alle sfere' for transposition up to G major, Smith, finding a convenient blank stave at the bottom of each page in *H*, copied the bass part a second time in the new key, leaving the rest of the aria in F. Where the reading

---

[17] The other often was not; *C*, originally a full score of the 1732 version copied by a hand other than Smith's, has only the voice part and bass of the inserted and most of the transposed arias.

[18] Chrysander himself quotes an instance of this in his preface to *Il Pastor Fido*, second version (1890).

Ex. 1

of the performing score differs from that of the autograph, unless a later change has been introduced in the former or Handel has made an obvious slip of the pen in the latter, there is an overwhelming presumption that the autograph will be correct: it is highly unlikely that Handel would have given Smith—who was a copyist, not an editor—verbal instructions to modify the text in detail. In taking the contrary view Chrysander sometimes perpetuated Smith's mistakes, even when they make no musical sense. There is an example in bar 26 of Erenice's aria 'Cuor di madre' (*HG*, p. 88), where the autograph, R.M.19.a.5 and the Flower parts all have obviously the correct reading (Ex. 2a), whereas in *HG*, following *H* and *C*,[19] the two lower violin parts are different (Ex. 2b). What must have happened is that Smith accidentally jumped a chord, and the other copyist transferred the mistake from *H* to *C*.

The first performing score (*H*) confirms the evidence of *Floridante* and *Giulio Cesare*, among other works, that Smith sometimes began to

[19] The Lennard and Coke copies and the Walsh and Arnold scores are also wrong.

Ex. 2

copy long before Handel had finished the labour of composition, perhaps when his ink was scarcely dry. In view of the exiguous interval of
time that often separated the completion of a score from its first performance this was no doubt a necessity, since the parts for singers and
instrumentalists had to be taken from Smith's copy. At least four
surviving pages in *H* carry sections of the recitatives suppressed when
Handel changed the names of the characters. Most of them were
blocked out later, but on one page (f. 30) the original names remain
uncancelled (the whole page was presumably covered up). Another
(f. 77) has the longer recitative without any names; perhaps Handel had
become alert to the danger of ruffling John V's feathers but not yet
received the new names from the librettist. In 'Dite pace' Smith
reproduced three single bars which are cancelled in the autograph; he
pasted them out later, but he must have copied the aria before Handel
had finalized it. By the time *C* was prepared these early variants had
disappeared and the text had settled into its 1732 form.[20] The turn-
over in both copies was always arranged at the same point, to facilitate
the transference or substitution of material. The scores were not bound
or foliated until after they had ceased to be used. A curious point in
connection with the names is that in Arnold's score (1788) Sosarme is
on one occasion (II, 12, *HG*, p. 74) addressed as 'Fermando' (*sic*) and
Haliate appears in the preliminary list of characters (though not in the
text) as 'Corrido'. Arnold printed only five of the operas, and his text
for *Sosarme* is peculiar. He gives the complete 1732 versions of the
arias, except 'La turba adulatrice' and 'Padre, germano', but (except at

[20] Chrysander used *C* for preparing his edition, but it was not the printer's
copy, since many of the 1734 cuts are still pasted out. It bears many annotations in his hand, as do a number of manuscript copies in the Royal Music
Library.

three points) the shortened recitatives of 1734. There are numerous mistakes, and the *coro militare* is omitted altogether; but Arnold must have collated at least two and possibly three sources, one of them reflecting material from before the first performance. That is the only explanation of 'Fermando', which is not in either of the performing scores at this point; 'Corrido' could be a mistake or a name temporarily allotted to Dionisio before he became Haliate.

Something needs to be said about the Flower parts, now in Manchester Public Library, which have only been open to inspection since 1965. They exist, sometimes accompanied by a score, for all the operas except *Almira* and for many other works, but have not yet been subjected to a thorough scrutiny. Conclusions must therefore remain in some respects tentative. The parts were supplied to Charles Jennens, the original owner of the Aylesford Collection, by Handel's copyists. They were not used in performance, and it is difficult to see what practical purpose they were intended to serve. There are no voice parts for the operas (though there are for most of the oratorios). The continuo never includes *secco* recitatives (which could, however, have been played from a score), and all the parts frequently omit other movements, including important arias; this is not due to incomplete survival, for each piece is numbered in sequence, and accompanied recitatives and sinfonias are often incongruously linked with arias in circumstances that make neither dramatic nor musical sense. The parts of different works reflect various stages of the text, sometimes before performance; they include rejected pieces, alternatives, versions otherwise unknown, arias added for revivals, and inconsistencies of pitch in the music of the same character.

It is tempting to suppose that they were copied from Handel's theatre parts (now all lost), which would give them considerable weight; but this seems unlikely. If they were, the theatre parts were startlingly inaccurate. In at least one opera (*Giulio Cesare*) it can be shown that the Flower parts were copied from a surviving manuscript score. This could be true of *Sosarme*, where they share many singularities with R.M.19.a.5, including repeat marks after the G major chord in bar 12 of the Act III sinfonia, found in no other source. On the other hand this copy includes the whole score except *secco* recitatives, whereas the parts omit the overture, Argone's accompanied recitative, the *coro militare* and a random group of five arias. The text is that of the 1732 performances. One of the most controversial features throughout the corpus is the treatment of the oboe parts, which often differ not only from *HG* but also from the autograph, performing scores and all other sources. The principal crux concerns their divergence from the violins where the staves carry a *tutti* mark; but sometimes they are given parts where other sources indicate violins only, and vice versa. The general, though not invariable, practice was for the oboes to hold their peace in *tutti* arias while the voice was singing, and more often than not the Flower parts conform to this. In *Sosarme* the oboes are silent in bars 14, 15, 25–8 and 36–41 of 'Forte in ciampo'; in 'Se discordia' they play only during the ritornellos, including bars 46–50; in 'Vorrei nè pur saprei' they play in the ritornello after the first half as well as at the beginning. On the other hand they are in continuous action throughout 'Tiene Giove', taking the higher octave in phrases where the *tutti* part goes below middle C. Here they contradict not only both performing scores but the autograph. (There are no parts for 'Il mio valore', 'Due parti del core' or 'M'opporrò'.) The most probable explanation, which seems to fit all the facts, is that the copyist was told to extract parts from a score and used his own judgment when he found no guidance in his source. It follows that the parts have no overriding authority. Nevertheless they are interesting as an indication of how a contemporary tackled an important matter of orchestration that bedevils many modern editors and performers. A parallel situation arises with the bassoon and cello parts, which regularly share the same stave, often with no indication as to when one or other instrument is to be silent; but the cello part of *Sosarme* makes no specific mention of the bassoon.

It remains to offer a critical estimate of the opera. The libretto as performed in 1732—and that is the version we must judge—presents little for admiration. The two principal limbs of the plot, Argone's rebellion against his father and Altomaro's attempt to use this to place Melo on the throne, are poorly articulated. We are given no reason for Argone's rebellion except the statement in the Argument that Haliate intended to make Melo his heir; but this is never made clear in the opera, and Melo's whole attitude undermines it as a dramatic motive. Argone is far too sketchily drawn, without a single aria. Altomaro has a motive of a kind, but it is not clear how such a rascal contrives to hold his job as Haliate's counsellor or how he expects to get away with his nefarious scheme, which a word from any of the other characters could expose at once. (The music further diminishes his credibility, but the libretto cannot be blamed for that.) Neither of the instigators of the action thus carries conviction. Moreover the role of the eponymous hero as potential peacemaker and lover of Elmira is largely passive. He comes tardily on the scene with an aria towards the end of Act I, and does not appear again until II, 8. Thenceforward he is more prominent, but much too late to justify his assumption of the title role. The librettist should have allowed him to take the lead early in the opera. Alternatively he could have expanded Melo into the true hero, a status his conduct certainly justifies. This, however, would have meant promoting a bastard above two kings, a consideration calculated to inspire Handel but a flouting of the conventions of dynastic *opera seria*. Elmira is a delightful heroine, and Melo and Haliate potentially interesting figures; but they remain stunted in the absence of an organic dramatic framework.

Handel's score is tantalizing. Dent calls it 'very unequal', too severe a judgment when almost every number exhibits some striking felicity of invention. Yet it scarcely fulfils the ideal of amounting to more than the sum of its parts. *Sosarme* does more honour to Handel as a musician than as a dramatist. The tension does not build up from scene to scene, because the behaviour of the characters inhibits presentation in depth. They sing exquisite music, but their conflicts seem contrived and artificial, like the manoeuvres of chessmen. This is presumably what Streatfeild meant in saying that the libretto contains 'no dramatic situations worthy of the name'. Burney's estimate, as we have seen, was higher; and time has not disturbed his conclusion that 'it seems impossible to name any dramatic composer who so constantly varied his songs in subject, style, and accompaniment'. The manifold resource in rhythm, melody, harmony and design is as striking as in any of Handel's operas. All three duets and the final *coro* are of exceptional merit. Yet *Sosarme* remains too close to the received idea of *opera seria* as a disjointed string of unmatched pearls.

The hero, already handicapped by the libretto, receives an uncertain start from Handel. His Act I aria, 'Il mio valore', is dramatically vital. It should establish him as a champion of human rights against cruelty and injustice; but despite expressive details, such as the upper violin pedals in the first half, it makes a somewhat negative impression. We gain no clear view of Sosarme until he lies wounded half way through Act II. From this point his music, all in major keys, is consistently first-rate. As in so many Senesino parts, it is that of a youthful and eager lover rather than a soldier; he is an attractive but not a dynamic figure. His three remaining arias are all sublimated dances. 'Alle sfere della gloria' resembles Trasimede's 'Se l'arco avessi' in *Admeto* in the great length of its initial ritornello and first half (36 and 162 bars respectively) and the delightfully rich yet open texture for horns, oboes and four-part strings variously contrasted and combined. The six-bar main theme with its springy rhythm, besides impelling the music forward in irregular periods, reinforces the impression that Sosarme regards the pursuit of glory as an extension of the hunting season. The second half lacks horns, but the oboes and violins toss the same material to and fro in insouciant fragments, and the da capo is neatly foreshortened.

'In mille dolci modi' has one of Handel's loveliest minuet melodies, exquisitely refined by art. The rare choice of rondo form, in which Handel always excelled, may have been suggested by the words: Sosarme pledges his love 'In a thousand sweet ways', and the music suggests some of them. The long phrases of the D major main theme (6 + 8 bars in the ritornello, 8 + 10 + 4 + 8 for the voice) build up to a rapturous paragraph of devotion, balanced by two shorter episodes in F sharp minor and B minor. The final return is enriched at the start by the earlier octave doubling of the voice and violins, and at the end by two subtle strokes: the entry of the ritornello on a high A before the vocal cadence and the arrival of the climactic D, the top note of the melody, four bars later. Both have been adumbrated at bar 22, but their novel spacing here sets the seal on a sublime inspiration. Handel did not hit the target first shot: the autograph contains a cancelled opening ritornello on the same material, but less expansively treated in ten bars instead of fourteen and with a conventional two-bar formula at the start (Ex. 3). The seeds go back earlier still, to a suppressed aria,

Ex. 3

'Questo core incatenato', in the original Act I of *Giulio Cesare* (1723), where the time, key, some of the rhythms and the upward octave leap are already established (Ex. 4). This in turn is based on the first phrase of an aria, 'Sei pur bella', in a continuo cantata (*HG*, No. 55) (Ex. 5).

Burney oddly allows 'great theatrical merit' to 'M'opporrò da generoso' on account of 'the agitation and fury of the character for

Ex. 4

Ex. 5

whom it was composed'. The catchy tune suggests rather the jaunty self-confidence of the sportsman as Sosarme sets out to intervene in the duel between father and son. It is in effect a gavotte with extra bar-lines changing the time to $\frac{2}{4}$; Handel first wrote a common-time signature against the top part. Again the ritornello is long, and the squareness of the melody is dissolved in long melismas for the voice.

Sosarme's two duets with Elmira are marvels of beauty; it is difficult to know which to rank the higher. 'Per le porte del tormento' is one of those touching scenes for lovers in misfortune in which Handel's operas abound; but unlike the great examples in *Tamerlano*, *Rodelinda* and *Tolomeo* it is in a major key (E), and one generally associated with confidence and serenity. The lovely lilting tune with its exquisite part-writing and characteristic melodic extensions (in particular the pro-longed cadence before the Adagio at the end of the first half) seems to hold time suspended, as if the lovers sought to preserve the moment for ever.[21] They do sustain it for a very long time, but we cannot wish it shortened, even if the twelve-bar second half seems little but an excuse to hear the first over again. 'Tu caro sei' expresses the lovers' relief after their trials are over with a light-heartedness that never descends to triviality. Perhaps no dramatic composer except Mozart rivals Handel's power to combine sublimity with good humour. As so often, the motive force is primarily rhythmic and structural. The ideas are clichés, but the impact is wholly fresh. Handel used several of them elsewhere, sometimes in very different contexts; the contour and syncopated rhythm of the first bar in the early psalm 'Laudate pueri' and the Second Harlot's air in *Solomon*, the rocking sequence in thirds that enters so unexpectedly at 'd'un alma amante' in *Rodelinda* ('Spietati')[22] and the chorus 'When his loud voice' in *Jephtha*. Even the time-worn cadential figure when Sosarme gives the expected answer to Elmira's question (last four bars of *HG*, p. 102) chimes in with a delicious aptness. The orchestra, though it occupies but three staves (for a time only two), reflects the touch of a master. Handel divides it into two groups, each with its own harpsichord: Elmira is supported by unison violins 'pianissimo' and 'Cembalo piano con i suoi Bassi, piano', Sosarme by four violas in unison and 'Cembalo secondo colla Teorba, e i suoi Bassi'. When at length the voices sing together the groups combine ('Tutti, mà pp' in the bass). The oboes double the violins in the fore and aft ritornellos, and at one point the bassoons leave the bass to join the violas.

Elmira's part is as rewarding as Sosarme's; like him she has a single aria in the minor (the last instead of the first), but her five solos, one an arioso, are well varied and all of the highest quality. 'Rendi'l sereno al ciglio', later to win wide popularity yoked to the unsuitable words 'Lord, remember David', is the only aria Handel ever wrote in B major. The tempo mark too, 'Largo assai', is very rare. It is brief and touchingly direct, as befits a daughter comforting her distraught mother: two bars of ritornello, ten bars in the first half, three in the second, no ritornello before the da capo. (Chrysander's omission of stage directions obscures the fact that this is an exit aria; Elmira goes out, but returns *with an afflicted Air* ('affannata') after Erenice's next line of recitative.) Such inspired simplicity, the prerogative of the greatest artists, defies analysis;

[21] At bar 33 there is a borrowing from the duet 'Una guerra' in the cantata 'Apollo e Dafne', where, however, the mood and (implied) tempo are very different.

[22] This also uses the syncopated rhythm in bars 4–6, and later in the voice, but the line is different.

but one notes the suppression of harpsichord and bassoons after the ritornello (at first Handel omitted them here too), the exquisite entry of the violins with a high B 'un poco forte' on an off-beat at the end of the first half, echoing at a higher pitch an earlier phrase of the voice, the allusion to this by both violins in thirds in the second half, and the beautifully judged return *dal segno*. This feature anticipates 'Angels, ever bright and fair' and 'Waft her, angels', of which 'Rendi'l sereno al ciglio' is a worthy forerunner. The similarity between the opening bars and a phrase in the duet 'Per le porte del tormento' is no doubt an accident, but a happy one. 'Dite pace' also looks forward to the late oratorios, especially *Theodora*, in its use of contrasted tempos and textures within the first half. This was of course suggested by the words ('Dite pace, e fulminate') and is a convention Handel had employed as early as *Teseo*; but there is greater depth and subtlety here. The first Adagio begins on a first inversion and returns later over a dominant pedal. The singer should be chary of ornaments, even in the da capo; to do otherwise would wreck the antithesis between this smooth legato and the lively violin figures and agile coloratura of the Allegro with its octave leaps and semiquaver runs. The modulations and chromatic restlessness of the second half have an almost Mozartian emotionalism. The return, though quite literal, achieves an effect of touching surprise through the juxtaposition of two Adagios.

The second act, like the first, is framed—so far as the set pieces are concerned—by two solos for Elmira. Handel wrote few lovelier ariosos than 'Padre, germano, e sposo'. Vocal line and accompaniment are perfectly balanced, internally and against each other. The ritornello presents the three main orchestral elements in concentrated form: a much ornamented violin line, sharply dotted figures and steady quaver movement. The last two alternate throughout between treble and bass while the voice pursues its independent way, moulding the initial broken phrases of grief into a sustained paragraph that mounts to a wonderful climax with the romantic aid of Neapolitan harmony. Behind Elmira's suffering we sense a sterling courage. 'Vola l'augello' is more relaxed. The transference of the aria from Act I has left a slight incongruity: while the simile is a valid symbol of hope, Elmira should surely be thinking of her wounded lover rather than her brother. Nevertheless, criticism collapses before the seductive charm of the music, which crowns a superlatively rich act. Handel's bird songs are not all as captivating as this. There is no risk of vapid chortles marring the design based on pedals, trills and the conjunct motion of voice and violins in unison, thirds, sixths and tenths. Handel varies this with such delicacy, placing the violins sometimes above and sometimes below the voice, as to convey an impression of sumptuous texture in the almost total absence of inner parts. The brief second half is more passionately engaged—just enough to circumvent the danger of facile uniformity.

Elmira's Act III aria, 'Vorrei, nè pur saprei', though Burney considered it of slight importance, once more raises the simple to the sublime with the predictable aid of rhythmic flexibility. The ritornello has two unequal limbs, of three and six bars; the latter, with its leaping fifths and sixths and sudden climb from the leading note to the subdominant a diminished twelfth above, is an unforgettable inspiration that might have sprung from Bach. It never occurs in the aria itself. After the same initial three-bar figure the voice introduces a new phrase, an unadorned rising sequence in the relative major ('che la speme del mio core'), that by some mysterious magic clutches at the heart. Like so many such details it was an afterthought. Although the phrase occurs once in the second half ('questi solo fanno avere'), its place here was at first occupied by a less memorable sequence used in slightly different form after the repeat (Ex. 6). This internal redistribu-

Ex. 6

tion of ideas was the making of the aria, which has no further resources. The first half is in binary form with repeats, the second uses the same material. Elmira is a heroine worthy of a greater opera.

Dent calls Erenice a managing matriarch, not a common type in Handel (despite Gismonda in *Ottone*, Matilde in *Lotario* and perhaps Storgè, who has cause enough for indignation). This is scarcely fair to a woman whose husband, son, daughter and prospective son-in-law are in constant danger of violent death. Her report of Hecate's words in her dream exhibits that unfailingly expressive choice of chords that is as characteristic of Handel's accompanied recitatives as of Bach's chorales; but neither of her arias in Act I transcends routine. The duet with Argone in II, 3 is a spirited piece of theatrical action, unorthodox in design despite the regular da capo. Argone begins without ritornello, but it is Erenice who takes command. She never allows him more than two or three words, and those at irregular intervals, interrupting on each occasion with angular phrases of scorching contempt and finally driving him out. As in most of Handel's ensembles where the characters are at odds, the orchestral parts are largely independent of the voices, the violins reinforcing Erenice's objurgations with fusillades of semiquavers. The modulations to flat minor keys (F major to C minor and F minor) strengthen the impact.

'Vado al campo' finds Erenice equally resolute. The 'presto' opening without ritornello, the first violins and bass in free imitation while the middle parts keep up a buzz of repeated quavers, propels the music with a vigour that the striding first violin figuration and rising vocal sequences never allow to slacken. The progression in bars 14–23, moving in a long crescendo from E flat to F, generates intense energy. The ritornello design assists the forward movement: nothing at the start (where Erenice's decision brooks no delay), but ten bars extending and developing the main theme after the first half, and five in G minor, the key in which the second half ends, before the brisk resumption of the da capo in E flat. This aria too was transformed during composition. The tempo was quickened from 'allegro' to 'presto', and the layout of the bass altered from a procession of even quavers unbroken throughout the first half except at the 'adagio' cadence. The new angular bass at each entry of the main theme was a multiple improvement: it strengthened the contrapuntal interest, let air into the texture at the vital words 'Vado al campo', deposed the regular symmetry (the dotted rhythm lasts for three, two and seven bars at its three incursions), and gave Erenice's bold purpose an extra urgency and rhythmic momentum. We can observe Handel's genius breaking up the settled routine of the new Neapolitan idiom. The upper notes for the voice in the first two bars, added in *H* in 1734, may be seen as a further improvement. Perhaps finer still is Erenice's last aria, 'Cuor di madre', in which the prospect of the duel between husband and son wrings from her a desolate F sharp minor lament. In each half Handel deploys an obbligato for solo violin (played by Castrucci), whose long curling phrases, contrasted with the ejaculations of the voice (twice extended in irregular periods of five and six bars), would not be out of place in a Bach sacred cantata. Handel originally included the voice at the start, as in bars 9 and 10, but crossed it out almost at once.

Of the other two altos, Argone remains a cipher. Even so Handel made capital out of Campioli's inadequacies, while confining him to the few abortive but cunningly placed phrases in his duet with Erenice and an accompanied recitative with the appropriate rhetorical gestures at the start of the opera. Melo is a much more individual figure, who would have repaid fuller treatment. He has two arias in minor keys that bear witness to Handel's interest in the bastard son who proves so much more sympathetic than his legitimate brother. In neither does the text imperatively demand the emotional treatment it receives. Both, like 'Cuor di madre', have a flavour of Bach, an accidental peculiarity that suffuses a number of Handel's works at different periods; *Tamerlano* and *Theodora* are notable examples. 'Sì, sì, minaccia' is built round another violin obbligato (unison, not solo), in which a short rhythmic pattern of graceful filigree work is repeated many times. The vocal divisions are very expressive, and the aria has an undercurrent of profound sadness, though Melo is merely urging Sosarme to take a strong line in reconciling Argone and Haliate. This assumes a colour of sombre, even tragic anguish in 'Sò ch'il ciel'. Here the autograph brings one of those major surprises that not infrequently make the Handelian scholar hold his breath in amazement. The words express confidence in heaven's power to frustrate the wrongdoer, and Handel originally set them, not to this music (Ex. 7a) but to that of Altomaro's following aria, 'Sento il cor' (Ex. 7b, c), which on a superficial reading they fit much better. This transference explains the similarity of the words, especially the rhymes, in the two arias; Handel must have asked the librettist to supply the second text for music already written. It also accounts for the appearance of downward scale figures, suggested by the line 'far cader l'indegna frode', at the same point in both. Only the first page (16 bars) of the version shown in Ex. 7b survives, apparently due to the accident that Handel used the other side for modifications to a recitative in another part of the opera. It differs from the bass setting in a number of minor but interesting particulars: the ritornello is one bar shorter, and the octave and unison doubling of the voice and the extension of its second phrase from four to five bars are not yet present. Handel may never have finished it. The circumstances suggest that other substituted drafts, not to mention sketches, could have vanished when he sorted out the autograph. There are more indications to this effect, such as the chance survival of part of Daniel's 'Chastity, thou cherub bright' in *Susanna* set to the music of his other aria, ''Tis not age's sullen face'. By no means every stage of Handel's composing process is open to our inspection.

Why did he undertake this extraordinary metamorphosis? He must

Ex. 7

(a)

Andante larghetto

Vns unis.

Melo

Sò ch'il ciel ben spes-so go – de fai ca-

Bass

– der l'in-de – – gna fro-de sù l'au

– tor che' l'in – ven – tò'

(b)

Allegro

Vns 1,2

Va

[Sancio]

Sò ch'il ciel ben spes – so go – de far ca – der l'in-

Bass

– de – gna fro – de sù l'au-tor che___ l'in – ven – tò

have changed his mind completely about Melo, converting him from an extrovert into an introvert; for no two settings could be more utterly opposed in mood. He is more than justified in the event. The counterpoint of words against music in the G minor 'Sò ch'il ciel' is profoundly moving; it suggests that Melo for all his faith has little confidence in the outcome. We are reminded of the *coro* at the end of *Tamerlano* and of Bajazet's 'A suoi piedi' in the same opera. In both arias the Bach parallels are striking. 'Sò ch'il ciel' has another violin obbligato of the type mentioned above, but still more eloquent. The broken figuration in the ritornello ranges over two octaves and a fifth,

with leaps of a twelfth and a tenth. The angular vocal intervals over a
chromatic bass, interrupted cadences and tense sequences might have
served for a meditation on the crucifixion (Ex. 8). The second half all

Ex. 8

but quotes the chorus at the end of Part I of the St. Matthew Passion,
which Handel cannot have known.[23] Much of the texture in the first
half has the sonorous economy one associates with Bach's solo violin
sonatas; that of the second, with the violins divided and constantly
crossing over a slow and irregular rising chromatic scale in the bass,
suggests a magical vista of clouds dissolving beneath the warmth of the
relative major key, only to re-form as the music droops towards D minor
before the da capo. The treatment of the violins in slurred semiquavers,
often in thirds, makes a wonderful contrast with the earlier anfractuosi-
ties. Melo's Act III aria, 'Sincero affetto', has a simple straightfor-
wardness (violins doubling the voice at the octave) that illustrates the

[23] The even more remarkable parallel in 'A suoi piedi' precedes the composition of Bach's work by several years.

words very prettily. But it is superficial in comparison with his earlier music; Melo is a character whose mettle shines brightest in adversity.

Haliate is one of several tenor potentates dating from the Second Academy period, when Handel enjoyed the services of Fabri and Pinacci. The plot forces him into wooden postures, but his three arias are all excellent. Two of them, as with Melo, are in minor keys. 'La turba adulatrice' is a C minor vengeance aria on the grand scale, an immensely powerful piece based on a typical series of contrasts. The ritornello has at least five ideas: a smooth half-sinister opening over a pedal, arpeggio and scale figures in rugged octaves, string tremolos over a marching bass, an angular gesture signing off with a trill, and a dotted cadential formula. They appear in the aria in a different order and all manner of transformations, the dotted figure supplying the seed of much of the second half. The first phrase is lengthened by imitation at the vocal entry and provided with a suave cadence in the relative major, making three and a half bars instead of one and a half. Later it appears in E flat throughout, lengthened by yet another bar, after a furious outburst of G minor semiquavers; the effect is of formidable reserves of strength. The voice has some lively coloratura of a type associated with tenor and bass tyrants. The second half is extensively developed, with much new material and further contrasts, the orchestra confined to sharp expostulations while Haliate works off his anger in phrases of every length from two beats to extended melismas of four and five bars. There are traces in this aria, and elsewhere in *Sosarme*, of the new homophonic style Handel had encountered in Italy, but he uses it with a resilient strength seldom if ever attained by Vinci or Pergolesi.

In Act II this explosive monarch relaxes in an aria of equal rhythmic and thematic resource but very different temper. 'Se discordia' has a gracious melody of the same family as the duet 'Cease thy anguish' in *Athalia* and the minuet in the overture to *Berenice*. The four-bar opening phrase of the ritornello is answered by one of no fewer than fourteen bars containing a remarkable proliferation of rhythmic patterns. This flexibility extends throughout the aria, whose voice part falls into phrases of approximately the following bar-lengths: 4, 3, 2, 6, 5, 5, 10 (with a beautiful hemiola extension), 9, 5, 6, 5 and 4. Yet the result is a seamless paragraph, the orchestra constantly overlapping the voice in a masterpiece of sustained articulation. The afterthought here, which extended the second limb of the ritornello by two bars and was grouted in two places later, was the three-bar sequence of slurred semiquavers in thirds (bars 13–15, 66–8, 95–7). The second half, with a particularly happy spacing of the string parts, is little inferior. 'S'io cadrò' finds Haliate in a mood of bitter reproach, conveyed by short phrases and a jagged violin obbligato extending over three octaves. Again one catches a glimpse of 'A suoi piedi' at the back of Handel's mind. The major key of the second half, on similar material, brings a moment of calm, but it is soon dissipated. The silent bar with fermata at the bottom of *HG*, p. 85 replaced three bars for voice and bass; Handel was never averse from allowing his singers a cadenza at appropriate moments.

It is difficult to know what to make of Altomaro. Here is a double-dyed villain, an unscrupulous bully, liar and potential murderer, who expresses himself in music of mellow gravity or bluff exuberance, always in major keys with no chromatic inflections. It is just possible that Handel meant to draw a superficially jolly old scoundrel, an honest Iago whom no one could suspect; but this seems unlikely, especially as two of his three arias originated in other mouths. Probably Handel gave him up as a character and allowed himself to exploit the sonorous voice of his new singer, Montagnana, a true *basso cantante*, not a bluster-ing baritone like Boschi. It was to Montagnana's singing in this part, his first aria in particular, that Burney applied the words 'depth, power, mellowness, and peculiar accuracy of intonation in hitting distant intervals'. 'Fra l'ombre' is certainly a challenge in these respects (Ex. 9).

Ex. 9

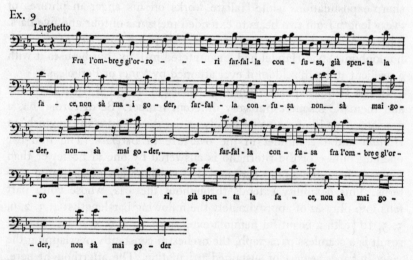

Handel adapted this from an aria for Polifemo in the 1708 Naples sere-nata *Aci, Galatea e Polifemo*, where the words and the musical material are almost the same but the vocal line, characterizing the clumsy vastness of the giant, is still more ungainly and a fifth wider in compass.[24] The cadences at the end of each half must be among the most eccentric ever written (Ex. 10). A comparison between the two versions offers a

Ex. 10

non sà —— mai go - der.———   pa - - - ce ne spe - ra pia -cer.

fascinating insight into Handel's methods in recomposition. The 1708 aria is strangely scored for two muted violins, viola and 'Violono grosso senza Cembalo'; the violins' semiquaver figures are not present; and the initial imitations, begun by the voice, are successive instead of overlapping. In 1732 Handel made the texture smoother, tauter, more contrapuntal and more sensuous. The grotesquerie has disappeared. The opening, where the falling arpeggio of the instrumental bass is freely imitated in turn by voice, first violin, viola and second violin, has a concentration preserved throughout with the aid of intricately crossing string parts (once the viola finds itself at the top and the first violin nearest the bass) and deep pedals. The second half is equally fine and returns to the da capo by way of fresh development. Most of these features were new in 1732. It is a superb piece of music, but Streatfeild's opinion that it 'seems to be enveloped in a weird atmosphere of guilt and horror' is difficult to sustain. The mood is rather of timeless serenity, as of some aged philosopher contemplating the remote past. So might Handel himself have looked back to his youth in Italy.

'Sento il cor' would have made an admirable drinking song. It is a very odd response to Melo's defiance, but as we have seen it was conceived for Melo. The descending scale figures in the bass and the leaping octaves associated with them are apt enough, though the image of falling that inspired them has gone. Handel used both ideas with characteristic resource, especially in the ritornello after the first half, where the scale tumbles down more than two octaves instead of an eleventh. Rollicking rhythms, which often take an unexpected turn, lively sequences and coloratura, and a second half that neatly combines the old with the new distinguish an aria more suited in its bass form to a bibulous clown, some Polyphemus guiltless of his fellow shepherds' blood, than to a crafty conspirator. The same is true of 'Tiene Giove', a genial gavotte with a ritornello melody of six bars that the voice promptly extends to sixteen. This gay dance is the last piece before the

[24] The part was probably written for Antonio Francesco Carli, who later sang Claudio in *Agrippina*.

duel and Altomaro's suicide. If Handel meant it for dramatic irony, he missed the target by a mile.

Sosarme has a fine and carefully composed overture. The preamble is not the usual dotted introduction but a stately sarabande in $\frac{3}{2}$. This may be a link with the original Iberian venue; one recalls the sarabandes in Handel's earlier Spanish opera *Almira*. The Allegro, more genuinely fugal than usual, has a springy subject related to the familiar melody used in the D major violin sonata and the symphony for the Angel's appearance in *Jephtha*. The minuet plays off a short-breathed tune with a rhythmic resemblance to 'God save the Queen', divided between woodwind and full orchestra, against a flowing counterpoint in slurred quavers for the first violins. The opening of Act I is theatrically effective, with two accompanied recitatives (the only examples in the opera) and a *coro militare* full of fanfares and flourishes before the first aria. The *coro* was sung by the soloists, presumably offstage, and it is repeated later in the act (I, 10), where it dramatically buttresses the hesitant Argone's resolve to lead the sortie. There was an interesting minor change here in 1734. In 1732 the D major *coro* followed a cadence in the dominant[25] (*HG* version 'A'); when Handel shortened the recitative to *HG* 'B' he cadenced in E, after which the entry of the *coro* comes as a sharper surprise. This reflects the stage direction in libretto and autograph *Mentre stà sospeso si senta il coro militare ad invitarlo*, which Chrysander omits. The final *coro*, like many others at this period, is a substantial movement, though in regular da capo form. The deceased Altomaro supplies the bass from the wings. It is a delightful pastoral in rare $\frac{9}{8}$ metre, with a strong foretaste of the duet 'O lovely peace' in *Judas Maccabaeus*. The texture is very rich, with copious double thirds for violins and oboes and the mellow reinforcement of horns. The second half, as so often in this opera, is developed at length, moving from the relative (D) minor to E major as the dominant of A minor. A ritornello in the latter key replaces the opening and drops straight back to the reprise in F major, supplying with the same stroke fulfilment, continuity and surprise.

The orchestra has no flutes or recorders, but the presence of trumpets and horns (each in two movements), the divided forces with theorbo in the duet 'Tu caro sei' and the full four-part accompaniment in the great majority of the arias leave an impression of exceptional amplitude. The unusual balance of voices in Handel's company during the years 1729–32, when he had several altos with a single soprano, tenor and bass, makes for further variety. *Sosarme* is the only opera he wrote

[25] In the first draft of the autograph it was in the mediant, F sharp minor.

for the particular combination SAAAATB. It is also the only one in which nine different major keys occur in set pieces; he never used D flat and F sharp outside recitatives, and A flat only in *L'Allegro*. The minor mode is less prominent than usual in the last two acts (five times in twenty numbers); Act II, the finest of the three, ends with six consecutive movements in major keys. No overall key pattern is discernible; in this, as in other respects, *Sosarme* is something of a sport among Handel's mature works.

POSTSCRIPT (to pp. 133–4): Handel also used the material of Exx. 3–5, in E flat and with further variants, in the first of the nine German arias on texts by B. H. Brockes, 'Künft'ger Zeiten eitler Kummer'. There is some doubt about their date, but it was certainly before 1727.

The Early Development of Opera in Poland

GERALD ABRAHAM

In different political conditions Polish opera might well have got away to a very early start. In February 1625 the future Władysław IV, an Italophile and music-lover like his father, was regaled by the Tuscan Court with an opera-ballet, *La Liberazione di Ruggiero*. The libretto was by Ferdinando Saracinelli, the music by Francesca Caccini, and both libretto and score were published in Florence the same year; the title-page of the score reads:

La Liberazione / Di Ruggiero / Dall' Isola d'Alcina / Balletto / Composto in Musica dalla Francesca / Caccini ne Signorini / Malaspina / Rappresentata nel Poggio Imp.le / Villa della Sereniss.ma Arcid.sa d'Austria / Gran Ducessa di Toscana / Al Sereniss.mo / Ladislao Sigismondo / Principe di Polonia / e di Suezia / In Firenze . . . 1625

The work is—unflatteringly—described by Hugo Goldschmidt,[1] who also prints six excerpts in his musical appendix.[2] But the prince seems to have been duly impressed, for one of his retinue, Stanisław Serafin Jagodyński, made a Polish translation of the libretto which was published at Cracow in 1628, a fact which suggests that a Polish production was contemplated. There is no record that any such performance took place, but Jagodyński's version, *Wybawienie Ruggiera z Wyspy Alcyny . . . Komedia tańcem z muzyką*, is considered to have some literary merit. It was reprinted in 1884, and an excerpt published by Zdzisław Jachimecki[3] in parallel with Saracinelli's original shows that it could have been fitted without much trouble to the music.

[1] *Studien zur Geschichte der italienischen Oper im 17. Jahrhundert*, i (Leipzig, 1901), 29–32.

[2] Ibid., i.174–9. Published complete, ed. Doris Silbert (Smith College Music Archives, vii), Northampton, Mass., 1945.

[3] *Muzyka polska w rozwoju historycznym*, Cracow, 1948–51, i.189–90.

While in Florence, Władysław was also present at a performance of Marco da Gagliano's *sacra rappresentazione, La Regina Sant'Orsola* (1624), and after his return to Poland he lost little time in introducing this novel form of art; in 1628 the court at Warsaw were given a *Galatea*, of which neither the poet nor the composer is known. It was a 'fisher idyll, diversified by numerous intermedi, with brilliant machine effects devised by a leading theatrical engineer brought from Mantua'.[4] Immediately on his accession to the throne in 1632 Władysław had a theatre constructed on the first floor of the royal palace, which was opened the following year with a *dramma per musica, La Fama reale, ovvero Il Principe trionfante Ladislao IV, monarca della Polonia, re di Suezia* (this branch of the Vasas still clung to the fiction that they were the rightful kings of Sweden). Either the words or the music, perhaps both, were by a Pole, Piotr Elert (d. 1653), a violinist or violist in the Royal Chapel and a man of considerable learning and substance, but it was clearly an Italian opera, not a Polish one. So were its successors. The new king's enthusiasm for opera was probably encouraged by his younger brother, Aleksander Karol, for whose benefit Landi's *Sant' Alessio* (1632) was revived in Rome in 1634, and during the next thirteen years the royal brothers commanded a whole series of new operas, mostly for Warsaw but also for special occasions at Gdańsk, Wilna and Cracow. First came a *Dafne* (1635, repeated 1638), possibly Gagliano's, and in the same year a *Giuditta* that, judging from the Polish synopsis which is all that survives, was a scenic oratorio rather than an opera; it was performed as part of the festivities marking the conclusion of a peace treaty with Russia, in the presence of the Papal nuncio and the Muscovite ambassador. The libretto was by Virgilio Puccitelli, the king's secretary and also a singer in the Royal Chapel, who supplied the texts of all but one of the later works of the reign. Władysław's marriage to his first wife, Cecilia Renata, was commemorated on 23 September 1637 by an 'Italian comedy, called *recitativa*, about St. Cecilia, which pleased everyone vastly; it cost 15,000 gold pieces'. The ballet of gladiators which followed, with 'dances of soldiers and silver-covered chariots', cost 35,000. This time we know the composer of the opera, if not of the ballet: Marco Scacchi, master of the Royal Chapel from 1628 to 1648. Then came *Il Ratto d'Elena* (1638), *Narciso trasformato* (1638), also composed by Scacchi, *Armida abbandonata* (1641) and *Andromeda* (1641). Scacchi's last opera, *Le Nozze d'Amore e di Psyche* (1646), greeted Władysław's second queen, Maria Gonzaga, when she landed

[4] Hieronim Feicht, 'Muzyka w okresie polskiego baroku', *Z Dziejów polskiej kultury muzycznej*, i (ed. Zygmunt M. Szweykowski, Cracow, 1958), 175.

at Gdańsk, and was subsequently performed at Warsaw and at Cracow for her coronation. A Frenchman in the queen's train, Jan le Laboureur, has left us in his *Histoire et relation du voyage de la Royne de Pologne* (Paris, 1648) his impression of the Royal Chapel:

La musique du Roy . . . est estimée la première de l'Europe, et composée particulièrement des meilleures voix de l'Italie, et couste extrèmement, tant en pension qu'en récompenses et en liberalitez au Roy, à qui la passion qu'il a pour ce plaisir véritablement Royal, ne fait rien espargner pour attirer à son service tous ceux qui excellent.[5]

There was one more *dramma per musica*, a *Mars ed Amore* by Michelangelo Brunerio, 'basso del Rege cappellano della Regina', but then the curtain fell. Władysław's reign ended in the middle of the terrible rebellion of Bohdan Chmielnicki; his successors had to cope with Swedish invasion, Russian invasion, Turkish invasion; and the first great flowering of Italian opera outside Italy was cut off before it could strike native roots. It actually disappeared without leaving traces, for not a note of these operas survives. All we have is a handful of librettos by Puccitelli, which, as Jachimecki says,[6] were 'entirely based on Florentine models':

there were passages in madrigal style and free forms in the solo parts, ariosos and recitatives, dialogues between soloists and between soloists and chorus, and then favourite echo effects introducing word-play involving anacolutha, antonyms and puns.

As for the instrumentation, we gather from the librettos at least that in *Il Ratto d'Elena* Paris sang to the *lira da braccio* and that the shepherds in *Narciso* were accompanied by the bagpipe (*zampogna*) (or perhaps instruments imitating it).

It is not obvious why Polish composers did not try their hands at opera composition; the Royal Chapel included at least two gifted men familiar with contemporary Italian music, Marcin Mielczewski and Adam Jarzębski, but they displayed their gifts only in instrumental music and *concertato* church music. Ironically, Jarzębski—who also had literary talent—has left an account of the 'comedies with singing', ballets and so on at court[7] in his narrative poem *Gościniec albo Krótkie opisanie Warszawy* ('The Highway, or A Short Description of Warsaw') (1643). Operas were occasionally given at court under Jan Kazimierz and Jan Sobieski to enhance special festivities, but to the end of the century they were written and composed by Italians: for instance, *Per*

---

[5] Quoted from Jachimecki, *Historja muzyki polskiej*, Cracow, 1920, p. 87.
[6] *Muzyka polska*, i.198.   [7] Quoted by Jachimecki, ibid., i.195.

goder in amor ci vuol constanza, written by Giovanni Battista Lampugnoni, secretary to the Papal nuncio, composed by Augustino Viviani, a member of the Royal Chapel, and performed by the Italian members of the Chapel at Warsaw on 28 March 1691 to celebrate the marriage of the king's son Jakub.

The accession of Augustus II, Elector of Saxony, to the Polish throne in 1697 certainly gave a fresh impetus to opera performance in Poland but did nothing to nationalize it. The Dresden Court Opera was distinguished long before the appointment of Hasse in 1731 and commanded much greater resources than Władysław IV's almost domestic performances can have done; it visited Waraw and Cracow, but naturally spent most of its time in Saxony; in any case, its repertory was still Italian. However, in 1725 the first public theatre in Warsaw was opened with the performance of a ballet, *Proserpina*, conducted—and presumably composed—by Augustus's Dresden *Kapellmeister*, Johann Christoph Schmidt. And in the same year the nobility began to take a hand; a *Venceslao* (probably Carlo Francesco Pollarolo's setting of Zeno's libretto) and *La Fede ne' tradimenti* (perhaps also with Pollarolo's music) were performed in the Lubomirski Palace in Cracow, and two years later a *Griselda* was given there (possibly by Domenico Sarri, who also composed a *La Fede ne' tradimenti*). Some of the nobility actually had Italian opera composers in their service, as the Rzewuskis had the Bolognese Giuseppe Maria Nelvi (1698–1756), who composed four operas while he was in Poland. The heyday of the public opera in Warsaw came later, in the reign of Augustus III, a greater lover of opera than his father: he not only ordered in 1748 the construction of a bigger and better theatre, but, when expelled from Saxony by the misfortunes of the Seven Years War and obliged to settle in his Polish capital for five whole years, consoled himself and entertained his subjects with a splendid series of Hasse productions, ten in all, of which at least two, *Il Sogno di Scipione* (1758) and *Zenobia* (1761), were first performances.[8]

All this came to an end soon after Augustus's death in 1763, and the company dispersed. But the next reign, that of Stanisław August (Poniatowski), which suffered the Partitions and ended in 1795 with the Third Partition, was to see the belated beginning of genuinely Polish opera. (A five-act comedy translated from the French and produced in 1749 at a country palace of the Radziwiłłs had included a 'pastoral

[8] For a complete list, and further particulars of the Warsaw opera under the Saxon kings, see Jan Prosnak, *Kultura muzyczna Warszawy XVIII wieku*, Cracow, 1955, pp. 28 ff.

LEO

opera' intermezzo consisting of 'arias, dialogues and choruses' sung in Polish and composed by an anonymous musician; but this was hardly a beginning.) Native opera was by no means the consequence of the election of a native king or even of an immediate eruption of patriotic feeling produced by the First Partition of 1772. During the first thirteen years of Stanisław Poniatowski's reign, Italian opera was challenged only (as elsewhere) by *opéra comique*, beginning in 1765 with an *Annette et Lubin* (to Favart's libretto) by Gaetano Pugnani, which thus antedates his Italian version, *Nanetta e Lubino* to Carlo Francesco Badini's text, by four years. But of course *opera seria* had mostly given way to *opera buffa*, and there was a new generation of Italian composers—Piccinni, Sacchini, Galuppi, Salieri. Besides them and the composers of *opéra comique*—Duni, Monsigny, Philidor and, later, Grétry—Germans and Austrians were performed: Haydn's *Der krumme Teufel* (1774), Gluck's *Orfeo* (1776), Gassmann and Johann Adam Hiller.[9] It was against this background that the earliest opera composed to a Polish text made its appearance in 1778: *Nędza uszczęśliwiona* ('Misery Made Happy'), a text by Franciszek Bohomolec originally intended for a cantata but now expanded into a two-act opera libretto by Wojciech Bogusławski (1757–1829) and set to music by a composer of Slovak origin, Maciej Kamieński (1734–1821). It was dedicated to the king, who had interested himself in the work, and it was produced in the theatre of the Radziwiłł Palace in Warsaw on 11 July 1778.[10]

The plot of *Nędza uszczęśliwiona* could hardly be more simple. A poor countrywoman, a widow, Anna, has a daughter, Kasia, with two suitors. One, Antek, is poor; the other, Jan, is well off—and, needless to say, Kasia loves the poor one. 'Misery' is 'made happy' by the intervention of a kindly and generous landlord.[11] The music—eleven solo songs, a duet for Kasia and Antek to end Act I, a quintet for all the soloists to end Act II, with an overture to each act—is equally artless, though Kamieński expected his soloists to tackle showy coloratura, and there is some fire in the two overtures,[12] for instance the opening of that to Act II (Ex. 1).

[9] For a chronological list of operas produced in Warsaw during the reign of Stanisław August, see Prosnak, op. cit., pp. 103–13 (based on Ludwik Bernacki's monumental *Teatr, dramat i muzyka za Stanisława Augusta*, Lwów, 1925).

[10] The date 11 May, given by Aleksander Poliński (*Dzieje muzyki polskiej w zarysie*, Lwów, 1907, p. 170), who has been followed in *Grove's Dictionary* (5th edn.), art. 'Kamieński', and other authorities, is incorrect.

[11] Full details of the plot, the genesis of the work, and musical incipits are given in Prosnak, op. cit., pp. 145 ff.

[12] The first movement of the overture of Act I is given in the musical appendix volume of Prosnak, p. 103.

Ex. 1

Kamieński's orchestra consists of two violins, viola and bass, pairs of flutes, oboes and horns and a bassoon. There is little local colour, even in Kasia's 'Tempo di Polacco' in the second act, or the krakowiak-type songs of Anna and Jan in the first. The general flavour is mildly Italianate. Nevertheless some of the songs enjoyed considerable popularity for a time, and Kamieński strengthened his Polish accent in his later works: *Prostota cnotliwa* ('Virtuous Simplicity'), in three acts with libretto by Bohomolec (1779); *Zośka czyli Wiejskie zaloty* ('Zośka, or Rustic Courtship'), a one-act vaudeville, libretto by Stanisław Szymański (1779); *Balik gospodarski*, a three-act vaudeville on Franciszek Zabłocki's translation of Favart's *Le Bal bourgeois* (1780); *Tradycja dowcipem załatwiona* ('Tradition Settled by Ingenuity'), one-act libretto by Zabłocki (1789); and *Słowik czyli Kasia z Hanką na wydaniu* ('The Nightingale, or Kasia Persuaded by Hanusia'), two-act libretto by S. Witkowski (1790).[13] In these there are hints of the Lydian mode and much more flavour of popular song. Jan's first song in Act I of *Tradycja*, 'Listen, Barbara!', is a quite respectable polonaise (Ex. 2),[14] and a little later in the same act Szczepanowa begins her song 'Sługa, sługa' with two bars which present the kernel of the opening of Chopin's A major Polonaise, Op. 40, No. 1, identical even in key.[15] Like *Nędza uszczęśliwiona*, both *Tradycja* and *Słowik* are *Singspiele* with the slenderest of plots.

Kamieński was not left alone in the new field. Foreign operas,

---

[13] Details and incipits of *Tradycja* and *Słowik* in Prosnak, op. cit., pp. 153 ff.; the others are lost, except for a few fragments. The manuscript materials of all three of Kamieński's surviving operas are now in the possession of the Warszewskie Towarzystwo Muzyczne.

[14] Quoted from Tadeusz Strumiłło, *Żródła i początki romantyzmu w muzyce polskiej*, Cracow, 1956, p. 39.

[15] Two other numbers, the quintet and the quartet-finale, are printed in the musical appendix to Prosnak, pp. 115 and 126.

including *Die Entführung* in 1783, began to be performed in Polish, and foreign-born composers produced new works: Gaetani (sometimes spelled Kajetani and possibly not an Italian), conductor of the Royal Opera from 1780 to 1793; the Hanoverian Johann David Holland

Ex. 2

(1746–*c*.1825), who conducted the Radziwiłłs' opera at Nieświez; Gioacchino Albertini (1751–1811), who served first the Radziwiłłs and then the king and composed a *Don Juan czyli Libertyn ukarany* to a libretto which Bogusławski translated 'from the Italian',[16] produced in Warsaw in 1783; and Antoni Weinert (1751–1850), of Czech origin, flautist in the Royal and other opera orchestras in Warsaw for more than 60 years (1778–1839). Weinert married Kamieński's daughter and composed the overture to his father-in-law's *Tradycja*.[17] But all their works have been destroyed in the wars that have devastated the unhappy capital—with one exception. This is a setting of *Żółta szlafmyca albo Kolęda na Novy Rok* ('The Yellow Nightcap, or A Present for New Year'), a three-act libretto which Bogusławski—who as playwright, director, actor and bass singer long played such an important part in the Polish theatre that he has been called its 'father'—had translated from a French comedy, *Les Etrennes de Mercure* by Pierre Barré and A. de Pils. It was produced in 1788, and the music has been variously attributed to Kamieński, Gaetani and one Ertini,[18] who was master of the court chapel of the Chancellor, Stanisław Małachowski. Prosnak seems to accept that two settings of the same libretto were performed in 1788, Gaetani's and Ertini's.[19] Kamieński's claim appears to rest solely on

[16] Mozart's *Don Giovanni* was given at Warsaw in Italian in 1789, but Albertini's survived this competition at least until 1805. Other librettos translated by Bogusławski include *Die Zauberflöte*, *Der Freischütz*, *Lodoïska*, *La Dame blanche* and *L'Italiana in Algeri*.

[17] Printed in Prosnak, musical appendix, p. 108.

[18] It is tempting to identify this shadowy figure with Albertini, master of the Royal Chapel from 1784 to 1795, but the dates are inconsistent.

[19] Op. cit., p. 114. In a note on p. 287 he says it was 'unquestionably' Ertini's opera that was produced at the National Theatre in November 1788.

an entry in Andrzej Zalewski's *Krótka kronika teatru polskiego 1764–1807* (Warsaw, 1814). But the fragmentary manuscript copy, luckily made in 1938 from the since destroyed original in the library of the Warsaw Opera, and now in private possession, firmly ascribes the music to Gaetani. Possibly the score was a collective work; it would not be the only Polish opera of the period with 'musique de plusieurs auteurs, principalement de Mr. Gaetano'.

The music of the *Żółta szlafmyca*, whoever wrote it, is notable for its links with popular music. Prosnak has no difficulty in demonstrating the relationship between the trio in Act I and a popular song of the day, that the *kolęda* at the end of Act I has a genuine oberek accompaniment (the word *kolęda* has two meanings: Christmas or New Year present, as in the sub-title, or carol), that the first two bars of the duet for Zofia and Żona in Act II[20] are practically identical with the corresponding bars of 'Dąbrowski's Mazurka' (later adopted as the Polish national anthem) and that the $\frac{3}{4}$ section of the duet for Fircyk and Czesław at the beginning of Act III, with its rhythmic patterns and melodic motives and sharpened fourths, is very close to more than one folk mazurka—though he is perhaps straining a point when he claims that a phrase in Czesław's song in Act II is based on the old Christmas lullaby 'Lulajże, Jezuniu', where the partial identity seems to be fortuitous. And it is hazardous to suggest that the composer always borrowed from 'the people'; judging from dates, it seems more likely that 'Dąbrowski's Mazurka' was suggested by the opera melody rather than vice versa—though, naturally, both may have had a common prototype.

The national element is even more prominent in another work to a Bogusławski libretto, with music by the Czech-born Jan Stefani (1748 or 1746–1829), member of the royal orchestra[21] and conductor at the National Theatre: *Cud mniemany czyli Krakowiacy i Górale* ('The Supposed Miracle, or Cracovians and Mountaineers'), which like Mozart's *Il dissoluto punito* is known solely by its alternative title. Although the plot is only an elaboration of the almost inevitable one of divided lovers brought together or reconciled by or through a third person—the kindly landlord in *Nędza uszczęśliwiona*, Szczepanowa in *Tradycja*, Hanusia in *Słowik*, Mercury in *Szlafmyca*—the elaboration

[20] Musical appendix, p. 143.

[21] A list 'des Personnes qui composent l'Orchestre de Sa Majesté', dated 22 February 1784, headed by 'Mr. Albertini' as *Maître de Chapelle* and 'Mr. Gaetano', *Directeur de la Musique*, shows 'Steffan de Prague' as one of the three first violins. The string complement was small: four seconds, one viola, three cellos and two basses. But the rest of the orchestra was 'Classical', with a third flute and a pair of clarinets.

includes one feature so unexpected that it deserves to be described. Nor is the end altogether without significance.

The action takes place in a village in the Cracow district, not far from the Tatra mountains. A village lad, Stach, loves Basia, daughter of the miller Bartłomiej by his first wife; the miller has no objection to the match but Basia's stepmother, Dorota, has—she is attracted by Stach herself and would like to get the girl out of the way by marrying her instead to a mountaineer, Bryndas. The lovers are in despair, for Bartłomiej is a weak character unable to stand up to Dorota, but their conversation is overheard by a wandering student, Bardos, who happens to be passing through the village carrying on his back his books and an 'electrical machine'. Moved by their distress, he promises his help. When Bryndas and his friends come down from the mountains for the betrothal festivities, Bartłomiej—egged on by Bardos and emboldened by his presence—retracts his long-promised consent and says he leaves the choice to Basia. Bryndas is furious and swears he will be avenged for the injury, and Bardos fails to appease him; with his friends he seizes the Cracovians' cattle and makes off for the mountains. Once more it is Bardos's intervention that is decisive. Taking a short cut through the forests, he gets ahead of the mountaineers with his electrical machine and stretches an electrified wire across their path; before they have recovered from their surprise and shock the pursuing Cracovians come up and set about them with sticks. Bardos stops the fight, however, and the mountaineers, still bewildered and frightened by the 'supposed miracle' of the electrified wire, not only surrender the stolen cattle but even agree to go back to the village and take part in celebrating the betrothal of Basia and Stach. Dorota is likewise persuaded by the benevolent young scientist to abandon her designs on Stach and reconcile herself to the marriage. Finally, amid the general rejoicing, he announces that having 'corrected Dorota, prevented bloodshed and reconciled the obstinate', he has no wish to return to Warsaw, where 'perverse fashion' reigns and people like himself who 'live from the ink-stand' often have to go hungry, but intends to stay there in the village among the simple, decent countryfolk.

Krakowiacy i Górale was first performed on 1 March 1794, barely a month before the national uprising led by Kościuszko, provoked by the outrages of the Second Partition. In this atmosphere of intense patriotic excitement the music in itself, closer to the national idiom than any earlier opera,[22] with krakowiaks such as the one sung by the male

---

[22] See Prosnak's parallel quotations from folk music and Stefani's score, op. cit., pp. 140–2.

villagers in Act I (Ex. 3) and at least one genuine song from the Tatras, was bound to make a particularly strong effect. But the libretto must have made an even stronger one. The figure of Bardos, the very up-to-date intellectual, embodied many current ideals; his appeal for the renunciation of internecine conflicts, which had been the curse of Poland, had direct and urgent meaning. Indeed many passages in the text allude unmistakably to the political situation. It was not solely for its artistic merits, which are modest, but because it was 'the opera of the Kościuszko rising'[23] that *Krakowiacy i Górale* won and long kept its place in the hearts of the Polish people.[24]

Ex. 3

Nie u-wa-zaj, mi-ła Zo-siu, lep-sy chło-pak świe-zy

There was no more royal opera. Freedom shrieked and Kościuszko fell—though he survived the fall for nearly a quarter of a century. In the Third Partition Warsaw came under Prussian rule and remained under it until in 1807 Napoleon set up his 'Grand Duchy of Warsaw' (with his cat's-paw Friedrich August, King of Saxony, as duke), which in turn became in 1815 the so-called 'Congress Kingdom', with Alexander I of Russia as king and his brother, the Grand Duke Constantine, as viceroy. Bogusławski, the key figure in the National Theatre, left Warsaw for some years, and most of his colleagues dispersed. However, temporary companies were got together to perform comedies and operas. The first of these companies revived an old opera of Gaetani's in 1795, and the following year another company put on two new works by Stefani, *Drzewo zaczarowane* ('The Enchanted Tree') and *Wdzię-czni poddani panu* ('The Master's Grateful Slaves'), neither of which was successful and both of which are lost. He continued to compose unsuccessful operas, one of the last of which, *Rotmistrz Gorecki czyli Oswobodzenie* ('Captain Gorecki, or Liberation'), produced on 3 April 1807, appears from its title to have been concerned with recent events: French troops had entered Warsaw four months before.

These political events naturally resulted in a certain amount of emigration, and Poland lost two very gifted amateur composers, both

[23] Strumiłło, *Źródła i początki romantyzmu*, p. 45.

[24] The statement in *Grove's Dictionary* (art. 'Stefani') that it was 'performed in Warsaw over 200 times within a couple of years' seems hardly credible. Alfred Loewenberg (*Annals of Opera*, 2nd, rev. edn., Geneva, 1955, i.513) says 'given at Warsaw 144 times until 1859' but mentions no authority.

artistocrats: Michal Kleofas Ogiński (1765–1833) and Prince Antoni Radziwiłł (1775–1833). Having taken a prominent part in the Kościuszko rising, Ogiński, who has an honoured place in Polish musical history as a composer of instrumental polonaises, fled to the West and spent most of his life there; like so many Poles, he built great hopes on French Republican help and to that end wrote in 1799 the words and music of a one-act opera, *Zélis et Valcour, ou Bonaparte au Caïre*, in which the lovers—harem-favourite and French prisoner—are saved by Napoleon himself. Bonaparte sings an aria in praise of liberty, which he calls the 'seul but de mes travaux', and then in a recitative invites Valcour:

> Sous mes drapeaux, servez votre patrie!
> Combattre les méchants, les rois, la tyrannie
> De tout Français, c'est le devoir![25]

But Ogiński's opera was not produced in Paris, as he expected, or anywhere else. Radziwiłł, on the other hand, opted for Prussia in 1795 and the following year married the sister of a still more distinguished amateur, Prince Louis Ferdinand; all the same, as governor-general of the Grand Duchy of Posen after 1815, he opposed Prussianization. Radziwiłł composed no operas, but the music for *Faust*, on which he worked for many years, shows great dramatic power.[26]

The principal composer of Polish opera during the first decades of the nineteenth century was not a Teutonized Pole but a Polonized German, not an aristocratic amateur but the son of a Silesian carpenter and a thoroughly professional composer, violinist, conductor and teacher: Joseph Xaver Elsner (1769–1854), of whom older editions of *Grove's Dictionary* say that 'his surest claim to remembrance is the fact that he was the master of Chopin'. He has other claims. He founded various schools and societies, including a Society for the Cultivation of Religious and National Music (1815) and the Warsaw Conservatoire of Music, of which he was the first director (1821). He was a prolific

[25] Quoted from Jachimecki, *Historja muzyki polskiej*, p. 115. The score is preserved in the Bibljoteka Jagiellońskia, Cracow.

[26] *Compositionen zu Goethes 'Faust'*, Berlin, 1835; the overture, based on Mozart's C minor Adagio and Fugue, K.546, was published separately in piano arrangement, Berlin, c.1840; the very fine cathedral scene is given complete in the appendix volume to Strumiłło, op. cit., 71–95—but Strumiłło (p. 145) takes Mozart's Adagio to be a composition by Radziwiłł. Chopin was greatly impressed by the *Faust* music (cf. *Selected Correspondence*, tr. and ed. Arthur Hedley, London, 1962, p. 37), Schumann less so (cf. *Gesammelte Schriften*, ed. Heinrich Simon, Leipzig, 1888–9, ii.103)—but he also took the opportunity to say of Mozart's fugue that 'no one can call it a masterpiece, if one knows Bach and Handel'.

composer of music of almost every kind, editor of Polish popular songs, author of numerous theoretical and didactic writings. But above all he was a composer of operas. While theatre *Kapellmeister* at Lemberg (Lwów) in Austrian Poland (1792–9) he had already composed two German operas—one to his own libretto—when he met Bogusławski, who was now directing the theatre there, and provided incidental music for a French tragedy which Bogusławski had translated. Then came three other works in collaboration with Bogusławski: two three-act melodramas and a two-act 'heroic-comic opera', *Amazonki czyli Herminia* (1797).[27] When in 1799 Bogusławski returned to Warsaw as director of the National Theatre, he invited Elsner to accompany him as principal conductor, a post he held for 25 years, becoming a patriotic citizen of his adopted country and even publishing in 1818 a treatise on the rhythms and metres of the Polish language 'with special reference to Polish verse from the point of view of music'. In 1810 Bogusławski appointed a native Pole, Karol Kurpiński (1785–1857), as second conductor; he succeeded Elsner in 1824 and held the post till 1840. Like his colleague, Kurpiński was highly literate; he was the founder and editor of the first Polish musical periodical, *Tygodnik Muzyczny* (1820–21), and wrote not only on musical but on non-musical subjects (such as 'the moral state of humanity'). It was these two, Elsner and Kurpiński, who developed Polish opera most fully before the advent of Stanisław Moniuszko (1819–72), with whose *Halka* (first version, in two acts, 1847), *Straszny dwór* ('The Haunted Mansion', 1865) and other works it may be said to have reached maturity.

Some of the 'operatic works' listed in the article on Elsner in the fifth edition of *Grove's Dictionary* are really melodramas,[28] others are trivial or of slight interest. His first Warsaw opera was the two-act *Sultan Wampum* (1800), based on an adaptation by Bogusławski and Augustyn Gliński of Kotzebue's *Sultan Wampum, oder Die Wünsche* (for which, in its original form, Kamieński had composed music six years earlier). This is a comic-fantastic piece set in Persia, though Elsner's local colour does not go much deeper than conventional janissary music, and the overture actually has a mazurka-like opening theme and a *Ländler* second subject, while the second-act finale begins 'alla polacca'. Hussein's

[27] Autograph full score in Warsaw, Bibljoteka Narodowa, MS 6319 (vocal score MS 6320). Alina Nowak-Romanowicz gives copious musical examples, some in full score, in her definitive work, *Józef Elsner*, Cracow, 1957, pp. 60–68, and Irena's aria in Act II complete in full score in the supplementary volume of musical examples, p. 14.

[28] An excerpt from a four-act melodrama, *Ofiara Abrahama* ('Abraham's Sacrifice', 1821), is given in Nowak-Romanowicz, supplementary vol., p. 58.

'Ach! ten Królow król prawdziwy, Pan' in Act I[29] is a good Italianate patter aria, as Irena's 'Niech ręka najsroższych wrogów' in *The Amazons* is a fine Italianate rage aria. In both, as in his music generally, Elsner shows a command of technical resource decidedly superior to that of his predecessors; but they lack marked individuality. In 1804 came two one-act operas to librettos by Ludwik Dmuszewski: *Mieszkańcy Wyspy Kamkatal* (on a French original, *Les Sauvages de Kamkatal*, which had provided the subject for a ballet in Warsaw in the early 1790s) and *Siedem razy jeden* ('Seven times one'), a skit on the Parisian dress and manners then fashionable in Warsaw, with a sparkling overture and one of Elsner's best vocal polonaises sung by a character who is 'a friend of old ways'.[30] A third two-acter followed the next year: *Stary Trzpiot i Młody Mędrzec*, on a translation of *Le Jeune Sage et le vieux fou* by François Hoffman (pardonably confused by Alina Nowak-Romanowicz with Elsner's friend E. T. A. Hoffmann, who was then living in Warsaw).[31] The three-act *Wieszczka Urzella* (1806) was a new setting of the Polish translation of Favart's *La Fée Urgèle* which had been made for the Warsaw production of Duni's opera in 1783.

In the course of 1807 Elsner produced—in addition to two three-act melodramas—three operas in connection with the French 'liberation' and the setting up of the Grand Duchy. First came a one-act *Andromeda*, later named *Perseusz i Andromeda*, to a libretto by Ludwik Osiński which left no doubt that Napoleon was the Perseus who had freed the Polish Andromeda; it was produced on 14 January 1807 and repeated four days later, with a cantata also composed by Elsner, in the presence of the emperor himself, who followed with the help of a French libretto. History does not record what he thought of it. Then on 1 May, a month after Stefani's *Rotmistrz Gorecki*, came *Pospolite Ruszenie, czyli Bitwa z Kozakami* ('The *Levée en masse*, or The Battle with the Cossacks') in two acts, with a libretto by Dmuszewski demonstrating the charity of the Poles towards the now distressed Prussians in their country—Hoffmann was among the distressed Prussians—and showing the young hero enlisting in Napoleon's Polish Legion. And on 5 December the new Grand Duke, Friedrich August, attended the first performance of a two-act historical work, *Karol Wielki i Witykind* ('Charlemagne and Witikind', text by Tekla Łubieńska)—also with cantata—

---

[29] Complete full score, ibid., p. 22. Locations of Elsner's operatic autographs etc. are given in the main volume, pp. 288–95.

[30] Complete vocal score, ibid., supplementary vol., p. 34.

[31] E. T. A. Hoffmann sang the tenor solo in Elsner's cantata *Muzyka* on 3 July 1806. They had been friends since the Posen days.

which drew a parallel between Charlemagne's relationship to the Saxon Prince Witikind II and Napoleon's to Friedrich August.

These works give a general idea of Elsner's output, which continued on the same lines as long as the Grand Duchy lasted, though the only important work was the two-act *Leszek Biały czyli Czarownica z Łysej Góry* ('Leszek the White, or The Witch from the Bare Mountain', 1809), text by Dmuszewski. After the withdrawal of the French, Elsner abandoned the theatre for five years, partly because of disagreements with Bogusławski, partly because of Kurpiński's successes, partly because of other preoccupations. But on 3 April 1818 he reappeared with the best of all his operas, *Król Łokietek czyli Wiśliczanki* ('King Dwarf, or The Girls of the Vistula', two acts: Dmuszewski). His last opera, *Jagiello w Tenczynie* ('King Jagiełło in Tenczyn', 1820), was a complete failure. All three of these works are quasi-historical. Leszek 'the White' was an early thirteenth-century prince whose love for a Galician princess gave Elsner a pretext for introducing that national element which always lights up his otherwise rather colourless scores: in fact two national elements, for the Poles, characterized by polonaises —the overture is a really symphonic treatment of the polonaise—and a mazurka, are contrasted with the Ukrainians, who are characterized by a dumka (Ex. 4) which proved so successful that he introduced similar ones in both *Król Łokietek* and *Jagiello*.[32]

Ex. 4

Cdzie sze - ro - kim   nur - tem pły - nie Dniepr jak mó - wią   mio - dem mle - kiem   na (szczęśliwej Ukrainie)

The little patriot king, Władysław I, affectionately nicknamed 'King Dwarf', spent much of his early life as a fugitive and exile before in 1306, with peasant help, he freed his country from the Bohemian over-lordship invited by the nobles, and the 'adagio' opening of the *Król Łokietek* overture[33] reflects the tragic gloom of Poland under the Bohemian yoke. Then comes a quasi-symphonic treatment of krako-wiak themes comparable with that of the polonaise in the overture to *Leszek*, suggesting the popular element which was to carry Władysław to victory. Indeed krakowiak melodies and rhythms recur throughout the opera from the first chorus to the last; one in Act II is characterized

[32] The dumka in *Król Łokietek* is given in vocal score in Nowak-Romano-wicz, supplementary vol., p. 56.
[33] Complete full score, ibid., p. 38.

by the sharpened fourth and drone-fifth accompaniment so characteristic of Polish folk music. Elsner caught both letter and spirit of folk music so well that one of the mazurkas from this opera, sung by two of the 'girls of the Vistula', became adopted as a folksong and was included by Kolberg, with different words, in the first series of his great collection of 'Songs of the Polish people';[34] this was the mazurka on which Paganini composed variations[35] which he performed at his last concert in Warsaw, on 14 July 1829. The figure of the king himself is musically lost amid the wealth of popular melodies; except for one song, his part is entirely in recitative.

There is one curious episode in *Król Łokietek* foreshadowing Libuše's vision in Smetana's opera: one of the Czech characters, Hinkon, falls asleep and in his dream beholds a series of scenes from Polish history, from the time of the Dwarf King's reign to the then contemporary. For this Elsner selected a series of musical quotations—from popular music (such as the so-called 'Dąbrowski's Mazurka'), from his own works (including a polonaise from *Karol Wielki* and a march from *Leszek*) and from other composers—which, even without words, would be strongly evocative to a Polish audience. In an article on musical expression, Kurpiński referred to Hinkon's dream as an outstanding example of the expressive power of instrumental music:

You hear only two bars and already you understand everything; the heart throbs, you are involuntarily enthralled; and if you can for a moment regain your senses and turn your attention to the whole audience, you will be astonished that all at the same time are possessed by only one emotion.[36]

Kurpiński himself had begun his operatic career in 1808 with a setting of a translation of Rousseau's *Pygmalion*, probably for one of the private theatres; but, like the handful of operas by Franciszek Lessel, Karol Lipiński (the violinist) and Józef Deszczyński composed for provincial or private theatres, it has disappeared. His substantial activity began after his appointment as *Konzertmeister* and second conductor at the National Theatre in July 1810. And quite substantial it was. Although some of the '24 operas' listed in the fifth edition of *Grove's Dictionary*[37] consist of no more than an overture and half a dozen vocal

[34] *Pieśni ludu polskiego*, series 1, Warsaw, 1857, No. 461.

[35] Presumably this is the unpublished *Sonata Varsavia*, 'seven variations on a Polish theme', which Geraldine de Courcy (*Paganini the Genoese*, Norman, Oklahoma, 1957, ii.382) tentatively dates 1838 and says 'there is no record of his ever having played this work'.

[36] 'O ekspresji muzycznej i naśladowaniu', *Tygodnik Muzyczny i Dramatyczny* (1821), Nos. 1–6.

[37] One of them, *Kazimierz Wielki*, is probably not by Kurpiński.

numbers, like *Dwie chatki* ('Two Huts', 1811), or are melodramas, like *Ruiny Babilonu* ('The Ruins of Babylon', 1812), he did write no fewer than fifteen genuine operas and operettas during the period 1811–21. After that date he wrote only one opera, the two-act *Cecylia Piasecczyńska* (libretto by Dmuszewski) produced in 1829.

Like Elsner's idiom, Kurpiński's was essentially cosmopolitan but with an even stronger admixture of Polish elements. One of his last operas, the two-act *Kalmora czyli Prawo ojcowskie Amerykanów* ('Kalmora, or The Paternal Law of the Americans', libretto by K. Brodziński, 1820), is said to show the strong influence of Rossini, but the main Western influences were Viennese and French. Indeed from his earliest successful opera onwards—the four-act *Pałac Lucypera* ('Lucifer's Palace', libretto by A. Żółkowski, 1811)—he showed a marked predilection for librettos translated from the French; one, *Łaska Imperatora* ('The Emperor's Favour', one act, by Dmuszewski, 1814), is based on Kotzebue (*Fedora*). Nevertheless nationalism keeps breaking in. The one-act melodrama *Marcinowa w seraju* ('Marcinowa in the Seraglio', from the French, by Pękalski, 1812), has an overture in sonata form 'sur le thème de Mazurek',[38] the development section of which consists of a 50-bar fugato on the mazurka theme (Ex. 5). And

Ex. 5

the mayor in *Szarlatan czyli Wskrzeszenie umarłych* ('The Charlatan, or The Resurrection of the Dead', two acts, Żółkowski, 1814) has a lively 'tempo di polacca' aria.

Kurpiński's most enduring operas are *Jadwiga, królowa Polski*

[38] Complete full score in Strumiłło, appendix vol., p. 30. A considerable amount of Kurpiński's opera music—overtures and separate numbers in piano arrangements—was published during his lifetime.

('Jadwiga, Queen of Poland', three acts, J. U. Niemcewicz, 1814), *Zabobon czyli Krakowiacy i Górale albo Nowe Krakowiaki* ('Superstition, or Cracovians and Mountaineers, or The New Cracovians', three acts, J. N. Kamiński, 1816), *Jan Kochanowski w Czarnym Lesie* ('Jan Kochanowski in the Black Forest', two acts, Niemcewicz, 1817) and *Zamek na Czorstynie czyli Bojomir i Wanda* ('The Castle of Czorstyn, or Bojomir and Wanda', two acts, J. W. Krasiński, 1819). The title which at once catches one's attention is of course *Nowe Krakowiaki*; it is in fact a complete reworking of the old Bogusławski libretto with the same characters but entirely new music. The very opening of the overture (Ex. 6), on an open-fifth pedal, strikes the authentic note, and the

Ex. 6

score as a whole is the most thoroughly Polish that Kurpiński ever wrote. The opera is still revived occasionally, kept alive by its pretty mazurka songs (Ex. 7).

Ex. 7

The two operas to texts by Niemcewicz, a distinguished man of letters, are on historical subjects. The character and sacrifice of Jadwiga, the queen who renounced her Austrian lover and married the Lithuanian prince Władysław Jagiełło for the sake of her country, offer obvious opportunities, and Kurpiński seized them in the best musical character-drawing he ever achieved; Jadwiga's first aria in itself earns him an honourable place among the Mozart-epigones. There is a fine choral conclusion to the first act, and the second is preceded by a striking imitative entr'acte suggesting dramatic tension.[39] That *Jan Kochanowski* is less successful was not altogether Kurpiński's fault. Kochanowski was the greatest poet of the Polish Renaissance—and

[39] Facsimile of the first page of the autograph score in *Z dziejów polskie kultury muzycznej*, ii (Cracow, 1966), facing p. 113.

more than a poet—but the lives of great men do not necessarily provide good operatic material (as Spontini found with Milton), and Niemcewicz did not gain much by giving his hero a daughter torn between two lovers. Nor was Kurpiński's idea of evoking a long-past age by suggestions of eighteenth-century idioms altogether happy. *Zamek na Czorstynie* is also set in the past; the year is 1683 and the hero is on his way home from the Turkish wars. But he belongs not to history but to the Gothick novel. The haunted castle in which he insists on spending the night is—unknown to him—the prison of his beloved Wanda, shut up there by a cruel father, out of her mind for love, and from whose nocturnal wanderings has originated belief in a ghost. Bojomir has a mournful dumka, Wanda a pretty but not at all tragic *romance*, which provide the first and second subjects of the Allegro of the overture. But the most interesting figure, musically, is Bojomir's peasant guide, who is characterized by a striking folk melody, 'Za horami, za lasami' ('Beyond the hills and forests'), which he sings in Act II and on which is based the 'lento' introduction to the overture (Ex. 8).

Ex. 8

Compared with Weber and Spohr, Boieldieu and the young Rossini, Elsner and Kurpiński seem insignificant. Compared more fairly with Weigl and Paer, Morlacchi and Cavos, they seem much less so. Considered simply in the context of their place and time, they are seen to be important. It was not for nothing that Bogusławski wrote in his 'History of the Polish theatre'[40] of his pride that 'the foundation of Polish opera, the attraction of Mr. Elsner to the service of the nation and the development of Mr. Kurpiński's talent, which has brought honour to the Poles, belong to that period when I directed the National Theatre'. Their interest in subjects from Polish history is highly significant; it really began after the establishment of the 'Congress Kingdom', when Warsaw first came under the Russian heel—however gently it pressed at first. But, as we have seen, opera in Poland always had been conditioned by political history. The early stops and starts—quasi-Florentine opera under the Vasa kings, *opera seria* under the Saxons, *opera buffa* and *opéra comique* and the beginnings of genuinely Polish opera under Stanisław Poniatowski—would be inexplicable apart from the political background.

[40] *Dzieje teatru narodowego w Polsce*, Przemyśl, 1884; modern edn., Cracow, 1951, p. 119.

Beethoven's 'Fidelio' and the 'Leonore' Overture No. 3

EGON WELLESZ

The Beethoven bicentenary revived discussion about the staging of his opera *Fidelio*; it also provided an opportunity of seeing performances of *Leonore*, the first version of the opera, and of admiring its wealth of *Singspiel* music, which was cut down in the final version. The awkwardness of the heroine's preserving her incognito in the long-drawn-out scenes with the enamoured Marcellina was the real cause of the failure of the performance in 1805; the occupation of Vienna by the French army and the absence of Beethoven's patrons (mentioned by Wegeler and Ries) were not the only reasons.

Fidelio, however, has remained on the operatic stage ever since the performance of its final version in 1814, though its dramatic construction has always been criticized. Even in the final version the introductory scenes were found to be too long and too slight. This criticism was intensified when it became customary to replace the E major overture by *Leonore* No. 3. Written for Vienna, *Fidelio* achieved its greatest number of performances there, but the interest in this rescue opera diminished markedly with the reaction after the crushing of the 1848 Revolution, though it was held in high esteem by the adherents of Wagner.

However, the main reason for the fact that *Fidelio* has not attracted big audiences may be found in the static last scene of the opera, which merely confirms what we have seen at the end of the dungeon scene, the victory of justice over tyranny. This last scene is musically of extreme beauty. It breathes the same elated spirit of brotherly love as the last movement of the Ninth Symphony and the Choral Fantasia.

Dramatically, however, the opera comes to an end with the ecstatic duet of Florestan and Leonora.

When the curtain falls after the dungeon scene the enthusiastic audience regularly applauds and the singers take a bow; the lights are turned on, chatter begins and the tension is broken. When after six to ten minutes the curtain rises again, the last scene is a beautiful tableau but has lost its dramatic effect. The audience enjoys the speech of the minister and approves the punishment of the tyrant; but, as I know from my own experience and that of many others, the continuity of the action cannot be restored. Even a quick change of scene on a revolving stage takes too long. However, even with the undisciplined audiences of today the tension can be maintained if Mahler's ingenious arrangement is followed.

Speaking about tragedy, Beethoven confirmed Aristotle's view that in the beginning tragic heroes must be shown living in happiness; he considered as merely tedious a tragedy 'which begins sadly and continues sadly'. For that reason *Fidelio* begins in Rocco's house with the scene between Jaquino and Marcellina and gradually introduces the tragic element. Therefore the E major overture is the right introduction for the first scene, not the third *Leonore* overture.

At the end of the duet in the dungeon scene Mahler kept the house in darkness, omitted the few spoken words of scene 6, and led with the last chord of G major directly into the third *Leonore* overture, thus avoiding the slightest break in the tension. On the contrary, linking together the dungeon scene and the hymn-like finale, the overture recalls to our memory what we have seen and heard during the performance, so that the last scene achieves the same mood of exultation as the choral section of the Ninth Symphony and at the same time is felt as the dramatic climax of the opera.

Mahler's innovation raised, of course, similar outbursts of opposition to that after the performance of *Leonore* No. 2 in an Augarten Concert in 1806, when the 'posthorn solo' was condemned by a critic as 'far from any idea of sublimity'. If in the future some projection technique, for instance, could allow the last scene to follow the duet without a break, then *Leonore* No. 3 would not be necessary, but one may doubt whether the quick transition from darkness to light would be as effective as the insertion of this overture. It is, after all, remarkable that in this age of changing productions Mahler's version is still given at the Vienna Opera and still exerts its dramatic effect on the audience.

MEO

A Note on Opera at Oxford

ERIC WALTER WHITE

When I went up to Balliol in the mid-1920s, I felt that at that moment music in Oxford was subject to two different tendencies. The first was the need to revive the old academic traditions which had inevitably been disrupted by the war years; the second was the wish of the post-war generation of students, whose university careers had been interrupted or postponed because of the war, to catch up with the contemporary scene and find out what had been happening to music in Europe during the first quarter of the twentieth century. Established organizations like the Oxford Bach Choir and the Holywell Music Club were able to resume their programmes of choral and chamber music. Occasionally, visiting virtuosos gave recitals in the Town Hall—in particular I remember a recital by Paderewski one winter afternoon, when he used the Chopin works printed on the programme merely to play himself in and then followed up with a series of encores played with increasingly sensitive musicianship in an unlit hall that was getting progressively darker and darker. But there was a dearth of good orchestral music whether performed in the concert hall or theatre. Gramophone records went some way towards making up this deficiency, but radio was discouraged in college, and in any case the quality of reception was so execrable that only a travesty of the true original sound came through the earphones or loudspeaker.

In these conditions, the intensive quest for new music occasionally led to practical joking. I remember a science student at Balliol baffling a number of keen musical friends by playing them the record of a cantata by a new unknown Magyar composer, reported to be much more advanced than Bartók, which on subsequent examination turned out to be the 'Hallelujah Chorus' played backwards on a specially

Richard Kent in a booklet published in 1950 to celebrate the 25th anniversary of the club's foundation, from information provided largely by Robert L. Stuart:[4]

One afternoon during Torpids Week in the Hilary Term of 1925 R. L. Stuart, a graduate of Corpus Christi, fell into conversation with Gervase Hughes, an undergraduate of the same college, who was working for a B.Mus. Between races Hughes described to Stuart a comic opera [*Castle Creevey*] he had written and Stuart suggested it would be amusing to form an Operatic Society and to perform it. Hughes agreed, and the two approached a third Corpus man, Lionel Barnaby, in whose rooms a meeting shortly afterwards took place. Among a number of friends invited to the meeting was J. A. Westrup, of Balliol, then reading for Greats and a B.Mus. The Group named itself the Oxford University Operatic Society and, pending the consent of the University authorities, elected a Committee.

After a time the proposal to produce *Castle Creevey* was dropped in favour of Mozart's *Die Entführung aus dem Serail*, which got as far as a musical rehearsal before it was realized that it was beyond the new society's capacity. At this point Arundel del Re of Balliol, then lecturer in Italian, drew attention to Monteverdi's *Orfeo*.

Copies of Malipiero's edition were immediately obtained and del Re wrote to Edward J. Dent, at that time a musical journalist living in London, telling him that it was proposed to perform *Orfeo* in Italian during the Trinity Term, and inviting his comments. Dent's reply was discouraging. He plainly considered the undertaking far too ambitious for what he imagined, not unjustifiably, to be a handful of Oxford amateurs. In fact, it was difficult to persuade anyone, outside a handful of the more enlightened and enterprising senior members of the University, to take the project seriously. . . . However Stuart visited Dent in person and convinced him that he was genuinely determined to undertake *Orfeo*. When he realised Stuart was in earnest Dent advised him not only to have an English translation of the libretto made, but also to have the score re-edited, since he considered Malipiero's edition unsuitable. Encouraged by Dent's advice Stuart carried out the translation, and Westrup, who had heard meanwhile of the decision to perform *Orfeo*, made a complete transcription of the 1615 edition of the score in the Bodleian Library.[5]

Nugent Monck was engaged as producer. Michael Martin-Harvey, formerly of Christ Church, designed the costumes and scenery and arranged the dances. Westrup worked closely with William Harris, organist of New College, who as conductor made a new realization of the *basso continuo*; and the performing edition of the score was brought

[4] *The Oxford University Opera Club: a Short History (1925–1950)*, Oxford, 1950, p. 5.
[5] Ibid., p. 6.

as near as then seemed possible to Monteverdi's original intentions. The first performance was given on 7 December 1925 in the old Playhouse and created quite a stir. In recent years there had been stage performances in Paris (1911), Breslau (1913) and Mannheim (1925); but this was the first to be given in Britain, and the enterprise of the group was highly commended.

Two years later the club consolidated its pioneering work on behalf of Monteverdi by producing *The Coronation of Poppea* at the New Theatre (6 December 1927). In this case the only previous twentieth-century stage productions had been in Paris (1913), Northampton, Mass. (1926) and Buenos Aires (1927). As with *Orfeo*, a special translation of the libretto was made by Stuart, and Westrup edited the score, making a realization (for strings and continuo) of the figured bass. In his explanatory introduction to the libretto, Stuart wrote:

In translating the opera I have striven above all things to render the literal meaning of the author [Giovanni Francesco Busenello] into English except where the result would have proved ludicrous. . . . I offer no apology for the stilted arrangement of many of the lines. It must be remembered that these lines are written to be sung principally to broken recitative, and if they can be sung without creating a forced and artificial impression in the minds of the audience I shall have achieved my object.

As an example of Stuart's idiom, it may be of interest to quote Virtue's words from her contest with Fortune in the allegorical prologue:

Shame; aroint thee, vile abortion, evil nightmare of the nations, made a god by shameless mortals.
I am the only ladder by which man's nature to Highest Good ascendeth,
I am the Tramontana, alone which teacheth the intellect of the mortal
How he may steer his bark towards High Olympus.
Of me it may be said without any flattery whatever
'My Pure and Incorruptible essence terminateth and mergeth in the Godhead',
And that cannot be said of you, Fortuna.

These live performances of *Orfeo* and *The Coronation of Poppea* were of considerable importance in Britain. Until then the frontiers of opera had only on exceptional occasions been pushed back as far as the seventeenth century—in 1895, for instance, Purcell's *Dido and Aeneas* had been revived on the stage by the Royal College of Music for the first time in nearly 200 years, and in 1920 Rutland Boughton mounted at the Glastonbury Festival the first production of Blow's *Venus and Adonis* since it was originally performed before Charles II. The Oxford revivals led to the focusing of interest on Monteverdi's music and prepared the way for the revival in the 1960s of some of Cavalli's numerous operas and for a general reassessment of Italian theatrical music of the seventeenth century.

As will be seen from the list of productions at the end of this article, however, the Opera Club has not confined itself to the revival of forgotten or neglected works by composers like Monteverdi, Alessandro Scarlatti and Berlioz, or even the reproduction of works that are in the current operatic repertories of other countries but are unfamiliar here. There have been moments when it has gone out of its way to bring forward new and maybe controversial contemporary operas. For instance, Egon Wellesz's *Incognita* received its first performance in 1951. A few years later English audiences were given a rare chance of hearing one of Alan Bush's operas, which have been produced in various opera-houses in Eastern Europe, but few of which, apart from the Oxford production of *Men of Blackmoor*, have received stage performances here. In 1969 an unusual record was achieved with the production of *Agamemnon*, an opera written when both the composer (Richard Morris) and librettist (Anthony Holden) were still undergraduates at the University.

The club is by no means the sole purveyor of opera in Oxford. There are still visits from the regular touring companies; and sometimes a special occasion occurs, such as the pious commemoration of Delius in 1953 through the first performance of his opera *Irmelin* sixty years after its composition. This was mounted for a short run at the New Theatre—a quixotic gesture characteristic of Delius's friend Sir Thomas Beecham, who conducted the performances. But the existence of the club provides a permanent incentive to the true opera amateurs in the University to put to the test their belief that opera is still an important art form. It is a stamping-ground where many young men and women, who have later become professional singers, conductors, producers, designers and so on, have had an early chance to try out their skill. It is this workshop aspect that proves so rewarding in the long run. The devotees who helped to found the club and those who have helped direct its varying fortunes during the last half century or so deserve praise and thanks from those who have the true cause of opera at heart: none deserves them more than J. A. Westrup, who not only assisted at the club's foundation but from 1947, when he became Heather Professor of Music in the University, directed the performances (and often translated the operas) for sixteen consecutive years.

PRODUCTIONS OF THE OXFORD UNIVERSITY OPERA CLUB
from its foundation to Sir Jack Westrup's retirement as Heather Professor of Music

Academic Year*	Composer	Opera	Conductor
1925–6	Monteverdi	Orfeo (ed. J. A. Westrup)	W. H. Harris
1926–7	Gluck	Alceste	{ W. H. Harris / S. T. M. Newman
1927–8	Monteverdi	The Coronation of Poppea (ed. J. A. Westrup)	J. A. Westrup
1928–9	Weber	Der Freischütz	Reginald Jacques
1929–30	Smetana	The Bartered Bride	{ Sir Hugh Allen / Bernard Naylor
1930–31	Lortzing	Zar und Zimmermann	Bernard Naylor
1931–2	Rimsky-Korsakov	A Night in May	Bernard Naylor
1932–3	Dvořák	Kate and the Devil	{ Reginald Jacques / Trevor Harvey
(February 1933)	Vaughan Williams / Purcell	{ The Shepherds of the Delectable Mountains / Dido and Aeneas }	Trevor Harvey
1933–4	Gluck	Iphigenia in Aulis	Trevor Harvey
1934–5	Rameau	Castor and Pollux	{ Trevor Harvey / Robert Irving
1936–7 (March 1937)	{ Blow / Holst	Venus and Adonis / Savitri	Denis Mulgan / Sydney Watson

* Productions have normally been in Michaelmas Term.

1959–60	Mussorgsky	Khovanshchina (tr. J. A. Westrup)	J. A. Westrup
1960–61	Alan Bush	Men of Blackmore (first British performance)	J. A. Westrup
1961–2	Alessandro Scarlatti	Mitridate Eupatore (tr. Sir Jack Westrup)	Sir Jack Westrup
1962–3	Glinka	Russlan and Ludmilla (tr. Sir Jack Westrup)	Sir Jack Westrup
1963–4	Verdi	The Sicilian Vespers	John Byrt
1964–5	Nicolai	The Merry Wives of Windsor	John Byrt
1965–6 (February 1966)	Mozart	The Magic Flute	{ David Lumsden / David Pettit
1966–7	Weill	The Rise and Fall of the City of Mahagonny	Henry Ward
1967–8	Stravinsky	The Rake's Progress	Henry Ward
1968–9	{ Blow / Roussel	Venus and Adonis / Le Testament de Tante Caroline }	Henry Ward
1969–70	Richard Morris	Agamemnon (first performance)	Peter Robinson
1970–71	Gluck	Armide	Richard True

A Bibliography of the Published Writings and Music of Sir Jack Westrup

PETER WARD JONES

In this bibliography items have been listed chronologically within each section. Though it is impossible to guarantee the completeness of such a list, it is hoped that all significant published works have been covered. A few minor articles in the nature of concert or book reviews have been deliberately omitted. Many important products of Westrup's literary and musical activities, however, have remained in manuscript, including his editions of Monteverdi's *Orfeo* and *L'incoronazione di Poppea*, Matthew Locke and Christopher Gibbons's *Cupid and Death*, translations of opera texts, and incidental music for plays. Thanks are due to Sir Jack Westrup himself, who read through the final draft and provided a number of additions.

BOOKS (including published lectures)

1 *Purcell* (The Master Musicians), London, Dent, 1937 (revised editions 1960, 1965, 1968, 1975; French translation, Paris, Janin, 1947)
2 *Handel* (Novello's Biographies of Great Musicians), London, Novello, [1938]
3 *Liszt* (Novello's Biographies of Great Musicians), London, Novello, [1940]
4 *Sharps and Flats*, London, Oxford University Press, 1940 (articles originally published in the *Daily Telegraph*, *Monthly Musical Record* and *Musical Opinion*)
5 *British Music* (British Life and Thought, xviii), London published

for the British Council by Longmans Green & Co., 1943 (revised editions 1946, 1949; Dutch and Polish translations, London, British Council, 1945)

6 *The Meaning of Musical History. The Philip Maurice Deneke Lecture delivered at Lady Margaret Hall, Oxford on 21 November 1945*, London, Oxford University Press, 1946

7 *An Introduction to Musical History* (Hutchinson University Library), London, Hutchinson, 1955

8 *The Nature of Recitative. Aspects of Art Lecture* (Proceedings of British Academy, 1956, xlii), London, published for the British Academy by the Oxford University Press, 1957 (also issued separately)

9 *Music—its Past and its Present. A lecture delivered by Sir Jack Westrup in the Whittall Pavilion of the Library of Congress, September 3, 1963* (The Library of Congress: The Louis Charles Elson Memorial Fund), Washington, The Library of Congress, 1964

10 *Bach Cantatas* (BBC Music Guides), London, BBC, 1966

11 *Schubert Chamber Music* (BBC Music Guides), London, BBC, 1969

12 *Musical Interpretation*, London, BBC, 1971

WORKS EDITED OR REVISED

13 Ernest Walker, *A History of Music in England*, third edition, revised and enlarged by J. A. Westrup, Oxford, Clarendon Press, 1952

14 *Everyman's Dictionary of Music*, compiled by Eric Blom, revised by J. Westrup, London, Dent, 1962 (fifth edition, revised by Sir Jack Westrup, with the collaboration of John Caldwell, Edward Olleson and R. T. Beck), London, Dent, 1971

15 Alfred Einstein, *Gluck*, translated by Eric Blom, revised edition [by J. A. Westrup] (The Master Musicians), London, Dent, 1964

16 *Essays presented to Egon Wellesz*, edited by J. Westrup, Oxford, Clarendon Press, 1966

17 Edmund H. Fellowes, *English Cathedral Music*, new [fifth] edition revised by J. A. Westrup, London, Methuen, 1969

18 *Hutchinson University Library*, London, Hutchinson; music series edited by J. A. Westrup

19 *The Master Musicians*, London, Dent; series edited by J. A. Westrup

WORKS OF JOINT AUTHORSHIP AND CONTRIBUTIONS TO COMPOSITE WORKS

20 *The Oxford History of Music, ii, The Polyphonic Period: part ii, Method of Musical Art 1400–c.1600*, by H. E. Wooldridge, second edition revised by P. C. Buck, London, Oxford University Press, 1932: chapter V, 'Song', pp. 256–374

21 *Grove's Dictionary of Music and Musicians*, fourth edition, edited by H. C. Colles, supplementary volume, London, Macmillan, 1940: 'Edric Cundell'; 'Howard Ferguson'; 'Gerald Finzi'; 'Walter Leigh'; 'Herbert (Henry John) Murrill'; 'Edmund Rubbra'

22 *Schubert: a Symposium*, edited by Gerald Abraham (Music of the Masters), London, Drummond, 1946: 'The Chamber Music', pp. 88–110

23 *British Music of Our Time*, edited by A. L. Bacharach (Pelican Books), Harmondsworth, Penguin Books, 1946 (second revised edition, 1951): chapters V, 'Frank Bridge'; XII, 'Lord Berners'; XIV, 'E. J. Moeran'

24 *Musical Education: a Symposium*, edited by H. W. Shaw, London, Hinrichsen, 1946: 'University Musical Education', pp. 52–60

25 *The Character of England*, edited by Ernest Barker, Oxford, Clarendon Press, 1947: chapter XIX, 'Music', pp. 397–407

26 *The Wadham Miscellany*, edited by C. M. Bowra and Derek Jewell, Oxford, Wadham College, 1948: 'Music and Symbolism', pp. 68–73 [name incorrectly printed as 'John Westrup']

27 *Die Musik in Geschichte und Gegenwart*, Kassel, Bärenreiter, 1949 ff.: 'Anthem'; 'Arne'; 'Frederic Austin'; 'Ballad Opera'; 'Banister'; 'Burney'; 'Dibdin'; 'England' (sections A, D, F and bibliography); 'John Farmer'; 'Thomas Farmer'; 'Fox Strangways'; 'Galliard'; 'Gay'; 'Giles'; 'Glee'; 'Grabu'; 'Greber'; 'Heather'; 'Oratorium' (section G); 'Oxford'; 'Purcell'; 'Rezitativ'; 'Nahum Tate'; 'Silas and Sylvanus Taylor'; 'Westrup'; 'Anthony à Wood'

28 *Bach-Gedenkschrift 1950*: im Auftrag der Internationalen Bach-Gesellschaft herausgegeben von K. Matthaei, Zürich, Altlantis, 1950: 'The Continuo in the *St. Matthew Passion*', pp. 103–17

29 *The Heritage of Music*, iii, collected and edited by Hubert Foss, London, Oxford University Press, 1951: chapter I, 'Claudio Monteverdi 1567–1643', pp. 1–14

30 *The History of Music in Sound*, general editor Gerald Abraham:

J. A. Westrup edited the accompanying books for volumes iv, *The Age of Humanism (1540–1630)*; v, *Opera and Church Music (1630–1750)*; vi, *The Growth of Instrumental Music (1630–1750)*, London, Oxford University Press, 1953–4

31 *Grove's Dictionary of Music and Musicians*, fifth edition, edited by Eric Blom, London, Macmillan, 1954: 'Howard Ferguson'; 'Song (beginnings)'

32 *Musique et poésie au XVIᵉ siècle* (Colloques internationaux du Centre National de la Recherche Scientifique; Sciences humaines, v), Paris, Editions du Centre National de la Recherche Scientifique, 1954: 'L'Influence de la musique italienne sur le madrigal anglais', pp. 129–38

33 *The New Oxford History of Music, ii, Early Medieval Music up to 1300*, edited by Anselm Hughes, London, Oxford University Press, 1954: chapter VII, 'Medieval Song', pp. 220–69

34 *Fanfare for Ernest Newman*, edited by Herbert Van Thal, London, Arthur Barker, 1955: 'Cherubino and the G minor Symphony', pp. 181–91

35 *English Music: Guide to an Exhibition* [compiled by J. A. Westrup, F. Ll. Harrison and A. Rosenthal], Oxford, Bodleian Library, 1955

36 *Collins Music Encyclopedia*, by J. A. Westrup and F. Ll. Harrison, London, Collins, 1959 (published in the U.S.A. as *The New College Encyclopedia of Music*, New York, Norton, 1960)

37 *Riemann Musik Lexikon*, twelfth edition edited by Wilibald Gurlitt and Hans Heinrich Eggebrecht, Mainz, Schott, 1959–67: 'Britten'; 'Purcell'; 'Britische Musik'

38 *Natalicia Musicologica Knud Jeppesen Septuagenario Collegis Oblata*, ed. B. Hjelmborg and Søren Sørensen, Copenhagen, Wilhelm Hansen, 1962: 'The Cadence in Baroque Recitative', pp. 243–52

39 *Festschrift Karl Gustav Fellerer zum sechzigsten Geburtstag am 7. Juli 1962 überreicht von Freunden und Schülern*, edited by Heinrich Hüschen, Regensburg, Gustav Bosse, 1962: 'Purcell's Music for Timon of Athens', pp. 573–8

40 *Choral Music*, edited by Arthur Jacobs (Pelican Books), Harmondsworth, Penguin Books, 1963: chapter VI, 'Church and State in England c.1625–c.1715', pp. 108–21

41 *Festschrift Friedrich Blume zum 70. Geburtstag*, edited by Anna Amalie Abert and Wilhelm Pfannkuch, Kassel & Basel, Bärenreiter, 1963: 'Cathedral Music in Seventeenth-Century England', pp. 375–80

42 *Enciclopedia della musica*, Milan, Ricordi, 1963–4: 'Bax'; 'Bliss'; 'Blow'

43 *Essays presented to Egon Wellesz*, edited by J. Westrup, Oxford, Clarendon Press, 1966: 'Bizet's *La Jolie Fille de Perth*', pp. 157–70

44 *La Musica*, sotto la direzione di Guido M. Gatti, a cura di Alberto Basso, Turin, Unione Tipografico-Editrice Torinese, 1966–71: 'Purcell'

45 *Encyclopaedia Britannica*, Chicago, Encyclopaedia Britannica Inc. (1967 and subsequent editions): 'Libretto'; 'Claudio Monteverdi'; 'Music'; 'Henry Purcell'; 'Song'; 'Variations'

46 *New Looks at Italian Opera: Essays in Honor of Donald J. Grout*, edited by William W. Austin, Ithaca, N.Y., Cornell University Press, 1968: 'Alessandro Scarlatti's *Il Mitridate Eupatore* (1707)', pp. 133–50

47 *Studies in Musicology: Essays in the History, Style and Bibliography of Music in Memory of Glen Haydon*, edited by James W. Pruett, Chapel Hill, N.C., University of North Carolina Press, 1969: 'The Paradox of Eighteenth-century Music', pp. 118–32

48 *Congresso internazionale sul tema Claudio Monteverdi e il suo tempo: Relazioni e comunicazioni*, edited by Raffaele Monterosso, [printed in] Verona, 1969: 'The Continuo in Monteverdi', pp. 497–502

49 *Renaissance-Muziek 1400–1600: Donum Natalicium René Bernard Lenaerts*, edited by J. Robijns and R. Lagas, Louvain, Katholieke Universiteit, Seminarie voor Muziekwetenschap, 1969: 'The Significance of Melody in Medieval and Renaissance Music', pp. 317–22

ARTICLES IN PERIODICALS AND NEWSPAPERS

Acta Musicologica

50 'Edward Joseph Dent, 16 July 1876–22 August 1957', xxix (1957), 109–10

Arte Musical

51 'No. 300 Aniversario de Henry Purcell', xxviii (1959), 105–6

The Chesterian

52 'Seeing and Hearing', xxi (1940), 67–72

53 *Daily Telegraph*
Westrup was on the staff of the *Daily Telegraph* as music critic

from 1934 to 1940, during which period a continuous series of reviews and articles appeared under his name or initials. Eleven of the articles were reprinted in *Sharps and Flats* (No. 4 above).

The Durham University Journal
54 'Elgar and Programme Music', xxxv (1943), 90–97
Great Thoughts
55 'Italian Influence in Music', June 1938, 21–6
Hinrichsen's Musical Year Book
56 'Musical Research 1942–43', [i] (1944), 23–6
57 'Musical Research 1943–44', [ii–iii] (1945–6), 285–7
58 'Musical Research 1945–46', iv–v (1947–8), 407–12
59 'Musical Research [January 1947–June 1948]', vi (1949–50), 143–6
60 'Practical Musicology' (*Hinrichsen's Eleventh Music Book*, entitled *Music Libraries and Instruments. Papers read at the Joint Congress, Cambridge, 1959, of the International Association of Music Libraries and the Galpin Society*, edited by Unity Sherrington and Guy Oldham), London, Hinrichsen, 1961, 25–30

The Listener
61 'A Lost English Madrigal Composer [Peter Philips]', 23 October 1935
62 'Music for String Orchestra [by Arthur Bliss]', 20 November 1935
63 'The Viennese School', 11 December 1935
64 'Mozart's String Quintets', 27 May 1936
65 'Handel's Flute Sonatas', 17 June 1936
66 'The Travelling Companion [by Stanford]', 8 July 1936
67 'Quatuor—Germaine Tailleferre', 15 July 1936
68 'Domenico Scarlatti', 12 August 1936
69 'William Hurlstone', 9 September 1936
70 'The Early Days of Comic Opera', 25 November 1936
71 'The Heyday of the Lute', 6 January 1937
72 'Handel's Cantatas', 10 March 1937
73 'The Development of Genius', 31 March 1937
74 'Spanish Church Music', 19 May 1937
75 'J. J. Quantz', 18 August 1937
76 'The Bach Dynasty', 1 September 1937
77 'Haydn the Untried', 1 December 1937
78 'C. P. E. Bach—a Touchstone to Taste', 2 March 1938
79 'English Music at the Commonwealth', 27 April 1938
80 'Haydn's *The Seasons*', 16 June 1938
81 'Beethoven's Violin Sonatas', 6 October 1938

82 'Bach's Passion Music', 30 March 1939
83 'The English Masque', 27 April 1939
84 'Mendelssohn's *Songs Without Words*', 3 August 1939
85 'In Praise of St. Cecilia [Purcell's St. Cecilia's Day Odes]', 7 September 1939
86 'Some Aspects of Handel's Genius', 14 September 1939
87 'Early Polish Music', 28 September 1939
88 'Categories and Individuality', 2 November 1939
89 'Schumann and the Metronome', 9 November 1939
90 'A Sullivan Gem [*Trial by Jury*]', 16 November 1939
91 'Out-of-the-way Music', 23 November 1939
92 'Lyrical Elements in the Symphony', 21 December 1939
93 'Bach's Violin Concertos', 1 February 1940
94 'The Craft of Orchestral Transcription', 7 March 1940
95 'Schubert and the Sonata', 4 April 1940
96 'Brahms' Second Thoughts', 30 May 1940
97 'A Minor English Master [Boyce]', 18 July 1940
98 'Purcell and his Operatic Style', 22 August 1940
99 'Mozart and the Violin Concerto', 10 October 1940
100 'The Art of Improvisation', 31 October 1940
101 'A Great Irish Musician [John Field]', 23 January 1941
102 'An Eminent Victorian [Sullivan]', 13 March 1941
103 'Mendelssohn and Beethoven', 19 June 1941
104 'Haydn's Perennial Youth', 21 August 1941
105 'Tchaikovsky's Best Opera [*Eugene Onegin*]', 16 October 1941
106 'The Greatest Pleasure of any Music', 22 January 1942
107 'The Creation', 12 March 1942
108 'The Virtuosity of Benjamin Britten', 16 July 1942
109 'Rubbra and the Symphony', 13 August 1942
110 '*Elijah* Reconsidered', 19 November 1942
111 'A Weberian Comedy [*Abu Hassan*]', 28 January 1943
112 'Schubert and the Sonata', 18 March 1943
113 'Purcell and Dryden', 29 April 1943
114 'A Great English Song-writer [Purcell]', 22 July 1943
115 'The *Christmas Oratorio*', 23 December 1943
116 'Problems of *Messiah*', 6 April 1944
117 'Early English Instrumental Music', 6 July 1944
118 'Dryden and Handel', 16 November 1944
119 'The Schubert Octet', 8 February 1945
120 'Henry Purcell: 1659–1695', 15 November 1945
121 'The Range and Variety of Broadcast Music', 20 November 1947

122 'Songs of the Twelfth and Thirteenth Centuries', 20 December 1951
123 'Edmund Rubbra and the Symphony', 6 October 1955
124 'The Monteverdi Vespers', 23 October 1958
125 'Berlioz at Peace', 19 January 1961
126 'From Carissimi to Mendelssohn', 2 November 1961
127 '*Iolanthe* Reconsidered', 28 December 1961
128 'Purcell's Instrumental Music', 27 September 1962
129 'Writing about Music', 11 October 1962

Monthly Musical Record

Westrup was editor of this periodical from 1933 to 1945 and was responsible for the unsigned articles, often in the form of book reviews, which appeared under the title 'Notes for the Day'. Eighteen of these were included in *Sharps and Flats* (No. 4 above). In addition the following signed articles appeared:

130 'Monteverde's *Il Ritorno d'Ulisse in Patria*', lviii (1928), 106–7
131 'What is Opera?', lix (1929), 137–8
132 'Debussy as Critic', lix (1929), 163–4
133 'Mr. Newman's "Physiology" ', lix (1929), 259–60
134 'Music under the Microscope', lix (1929), 297–9 (reprinted in *Sharps and Flats*)
135 'Medieval Music', lxii (1932), 202–4 (reprinted in *Sharps and Flats*)
136 'Bach's Orchestra', lxiii (1933), 51
137 'Ebenezer Prout (1835–1909)', lxv (1935), 53–4
138 'A Fantasy on John Bull', lxvii (1937), 217–20
139 'Amateurs in Seventeenth-century England', lxix (1939), 257–63
140 'The Dry Bones of History', lxix (1939), 299–302
141 'The Continuo in the *St. Matthew Passion*', lxx (1940), 52–6
142 'Sonata Form and the Teacher', lxx (1940), 171–4
143 'The Chapel Royal under James II', lxx (1940), 219–22
144 'Stradella's *Forza d'Amor Paterno*', lxxi (1941), 52–9
145 'Church Music at the Restoration', lxxi (1941), 131–5
146 'Parish Church Music in the Seventeenth Century', lxxii (1942), 227–31
147 'What is Counterpoint?', lxxiv (1944), 108–12
148 'The Survival of Music', lxxiv (1944), 203–7
149 'The Future of the Orchestra', lxxv (1945), 35–9

Music and Letters

Westrup has been editor of *Music and Letters* since 1959. In addition to editorials, he has contributed the following articles:

150 'Nicolas Saboly and his *Noëls Provençaux*', xxi (1940), 34–49
151 'Monteverdi and the Orchestra', xxi (1940), 230–45
152 'William Byrd (1543–1623)', xxiv (1943), 125–30
153 'Sir Hugh Allen (1869–1946)', xxvii (1946), 65
154 'Stanley Robert Marchant (1883–1949); Ernest Walker (1870–1949)', xxx (1949), 201–3
155 'Two First Performances: Monteverdi's "Orfeo" and Mozart's "La Clemenza di Tito"', xxxix (1958), pp. 327–35 (a paper read at the Midwest Chapter of the American Musicological Society, East Lansing, 18 May 1957, slightly revised)
156 'Purcell and Handel', xl (1959), 103–8

Music Review
157 'Monteverdi's *Lamento d'Arianna*', i (1940), 144–54
158 'Dent as Translator', vii (1946), 198–204
159 'Purcell's Parentage', xxv (1964), 100–103

Musica
160 'Das Englische in Henry Purcells Musik', xiii (1959), 170–73

Musical America
161 'Henry Purcell', lxxix (August 1959), 20

Musical Opinion
162 'An Amateur Musician', li (1928), 1176–8 (reprinted in *Sharps and Flats*)
163 'Interpretation in *Messiah*', lxiii (1940), 247–8, 294–5
164 '*Alexander Balus*: a Neglected Oratorio', lxiv (1940), 5–6

Musical Quarterly
165 'Foreign Musicians in Stuart England', xxvii (1941), 70–89

Musical Times
166 'Mysticism in Music', lxv (1924), 804–5
167 'The Misuse of the Trombone', lxvi (1925), 524–5 (see also the correspondence, pp. 634–5, 735–6, 833)
168 'Monteverde's *Orfeo*', lxvi (1925), 1096–1100
169 'On Playing Wrong Notes', lxvii (1926), 403–4
170 'Sidelights on the Serpent', lxviii (1927), 635–7
171 'Monteverde's *Poppaea*', lxviii (1927), 982–7
172 'French Tunes in *The Beggar's Opera* and *Polly*', lxix (1928), 320–23
173 'Stages in the History of Opera, i: Claudio Monteverde', lxx (1929), 706–8

174 'Stages in the History of Opera, ii: Early English Opera', lxx (1929), 797–9 (see also the letter, p. 928)

175 'Annibal Gantez: a Merry Musician', lxx (1929), 937–9

176 'Tchaikovsky and the Symphony', lxxxi (1940), 249–52

177 'Edmund Rubbra's Fourth Symphony', lxxxiii (1942), 204

178 'The British Council and Music', lxxxv (1944), 236–7

179 Contribution to 'Elgar Today: a Symposium . . . ', xcviii (1957), 302–7

180 'Jean Sibelius', xcviii (1957), 601–3

181 'Purcell's Reputation', c (1959), 318–20

182 'Words for Music', ci (1960), 693–4

183 'Berlioz and Common Sense', ci (1960), 755–6

184 'Noise', cii (1961), 20–21

185 'New Light on Haydn', cii (1961), 85–6

186 'Bandsmen's Huts and Suburban Vestries', cii (1961), 228–9

187 'Bach, the Bible, and Byrd', cii (1961), 288–9

188 'A Still Small Voice: the RCO Presidential Address', cvii (1966), 243 (also printed in *The Royal College of Organists' Year Book 1966–7*: see 199 below)

Die Musikforschung

189 'Kritische Anmerkungen zu "Die Musik in Geschichte und Gegenwart", Band 9 bis 14', xxii (1969), 217–27

Musikrevy

190 'Bach in England' (January 1950)

Nordisk Tidskrift foer Musik on Grammofon

191 'Bach i England', v/1 (January–February 1950)

Oxford Magazine

192 'Gluck's *Iphigenia in Tauris*', lxviii (1949), 168–70

Pan: Rassegna di lettere, arte e musica

193 'Monteverdi in Inghilterra', iii (1935), 442–6

Proceedings of the Musical Association (later *Royal Musical Association*)

194 'The Originality of Monteverde', lx (1933–4), 1–25

195 'Fact and Fiction about Purcell', lxii (1935–6), 93–115

196 'Domestic Music under the Stuarts', lxviii (1941–2), 19–53

197 'Elgar's "Enigma" ', lxxxvi (1959–60), 79–97

Revue Internationale de Musique (Brussels)
198 'Le Mouvement pianistique en Angleterre', i (1939), 863–70

Royal College of Organists' Year Book
199 Presidential addresses at presentations of diplomas, January 1965, July 1965, January 1966; printed in the RCO Year Books, 1965–6, 1966–7 (the January 1966 address also printed in *Musical Times*: see 188 above)

The Score
200 'Monteverdi and the Madrigal', i (1949), 33–40

Studia Musicologica Academiae Scientiarum Hungaricae
201 'Bach's Adaptations', xi (1969), 517–31

Universities Quarterly
202 'University Music-making', x (1956), 143–7

GRAMOPHONE RECORD NOTES (see also No. 30 above)

203 Handel, Suites for Harpsichord, played by Wanda Landowska, London, HMV, 1936
204 Monteverdi, Selected Works, performed under the direction of Nadia Boulanger, London, HMV, 1937, reissued 1957

REVIEWS

205 Reviews of books and music have always played a large part in Westrup's literary output, and their quantity has precluded a listing of individual reviews here. Most have naturally appeared in those journals of which he has been, or is, editor, *The Monthly Musical Record* and *Music and Letters*, but other journals to which he has contributed reviews include *The Chesterian*, *The Music Review*, *The Musical Quarterly*, *The Musical Times* and *The Oxford Magazine*.

PUBLISHED MUSICAL COMPOSITIONS

206 God is our Hope and Strength: Anthem for SATB and Organ (York Series, 892), York, 1925
207 Prelude: Unison Song, words by R. L. Stevenson (The Year Book Press Series of Unison and Part-Songs, 299), London, 1927

208 Come, Here is Adieu to the City: Unison Song, words by R. L. Stevenson (The Year Book Press Series of Unison and Part-Songs, 315), London, 1928

209 When Israel came out of Egypt: Motet for double choir unaccompanied, London, 1940

210 Weathers: Part-song for SATB, words by Thomas Hardy (The Winthrop Rogers Edition of Choral Music for Festivals), London, 1941

211 Divertimento for bassoon, cello and piano (or tenor saxophone, cello and piano, or viola, cello and piano), London, 1948

212 Three Shakespeare Songs with piano accompaniment ('Come away, death'; 'Take, O take those lips away'; 'Orpheus with his lute'), London, 1948

213 Five Chorale Preludes for organ, London, 1949

214 Crossing the Bar, for soprano solo, chorus and organ, words by Tennyson (York Series, 919), York, 1949

215 Nearer, my God, to Thee: Anthem for SATB and organ, words by S. F. Adams (*The Musical Times*, 1347), London, 1955

216 God be merciful unto us: Anthem for SATB and organ (Novello Anthems, 1427), London, 1962

MUSIC EDITED

217 Songs and Duets from the Works of Claudio Monteverde, arranged and edited by J. A. Westrup, new English translations by R. L. Stuart (8 Nos.), London, 1929

218 Poland's Soul has not departed (Jeszcze Polska nie zginela): the Polish national hymn, piano accompaniment by J. A. Westrup, English translation by W. J. Rose from the Polish of J. Wybicki, London, 1939

219 J. S. Bach, Bist du bei mir, arranged by J. A. Westrup, London, 1940 (new edition, with English translation by J. A. Westrup, London, 1967)

220 J. S. Bach, Flocks and herds may graze contented (Schafe können sicher weiden), arranged, edited and with an English version by J. A. Westrup, London, 1941 (published in the keys of F and B flat)

221 Henry Purcell, Lord, how long wilt thou be angry, edited by J. A. Westrup (Henry Purcell Popular Edition of Selected Works, 13, Novello's Octavo Anthems, 1262), London, 1944

222 Joseph Haydn, Adagio from a keyboard sonata in A flat, arranged for wind or strings by J. A. Westrup (Oxford Orchestral Series, 131), London, 1944

223 Domenico Scarlatti, Tempo di ballo from a harpsichord sonata in D major, arranged for wind or strings by J. A. Westrup (Oxford Orchestral Series, 130), London, 1944

224 J. S. Bach, Chorale Preludes, arranged by J. A. Westrup for 2 pianos, 4 hands, London, 1948, reissued 1957